CASENOTE LEGAL BRIEFS

CRIMINAL LAW

Adaptable to courses utilizing Kadish and Schulhofer's casebook on Criminal Law and Its Processes

NORMAN S. GOLDENBERG, SENIOR EDITOR

PETER TENEN, MANAGING EDITOR

ROBERT J. SWITZER, EDITORIAL DIRECTOR

STAFF WRITERS

KEMP RICHARDSON

RICHARD A. LOVICH

PUBLISHED BY

CASENOTES PUBLISHING CO. INC.   P.O. BOX 3946   BEVERLY HILLS, CA 90212

89NE

ISBN 0-87457-056-5

FORMAT
FOR
THE CASENOTE LEGAL BRIEF

The following outline indicates the organization of a Casenote Legal Brief:

*THE CASENOTE CASE CAPSULE: This **bold face section** highlights the procedural nature of the case, a short summary of the facts, and the rule of law. This is an **invaluable quick-review device** designed to **refresh the student's memory** for **classroom discussion and exam preparation.***

NATURE OF CASE: This section indicates the *form of action* (i.e., breach of contract, negligence, battery, etc.), the *type of proceeding* (i.e., demurrer, appeal from trial court's jury instructions, etc.) and the *relief sought* (i.e., damages, injunction, criminal sanctions, etc.).

FACT SUMMARY: The fact summary is included merely to *refresh the student's memory*. It is assumed that the student has already read the complete discussion of the facts and is familiar with them. This section is therefore not a complete and thorough presentation of the facts. It can be used to quickly recall the facts of the opinion when the student is chosen by an instructor to brief a case.

CONCISE RULE OF LAW: This portion of the brief, like the fact summary, is included to *refresh the student's memory*. This section is not intended to provide a full presentation of the rule and rationale in this case. Rather it should be used for instant recall of the court's holding and for classroom discussion or home review.

FACTS: Here the editors present a precise expression of all *relevant facts* of the case including the contentions of the parties and lower court holdings. It is written in a logical order to enable the student to have a clear understanding of the case. The plaintiff and defendant are indicated by their proper names throughout and are always labeled with a (P) or (D).

ISSUE: The issue is a *concise question which brings out the essence of the opinion* as it relates to the section of the book in which it appears. Both substantive and procedural issues are included if relevant to the decision.

ZAHN v. TRANSAMERICA CORPORATION
U.S. Cir. Ct. of Apls., 3d Cir. (1947) 162 F.2d 36.

NATURE OF CASE: Derivative action alleging breach of fiduciary duty.

FACT SUMMARY: Zahn (P), a holder of Axton-Fisher Class A stock, asserted that Transamerica (D), as majority stockholder in Axton-Fisher, breached a fiduciary duty owed the minority when it got Axton-Fisher's board to engage in a pre-liquidation redemption of Class A stock so as to benefit Transamerica (D).

CONCISE RULE OF LAW: In exercising their right to control a corporation, the majority shareholders owe a fiduciary duty to the minority as well as the corporation.

FACTS: Transamerica (D) was the majority stockholder when Axton-Fisher's board of directors voted to engage in a redemption of Class A stock. Zahn (P), a Class A stockholder, insisted that Transamerica (D) violated its fiduciary duty by using its control over the board to bring about the redemption plan for its own benefit (based on the non-public knowledge it had that tobacco held in storage by Axton-Fisher had risen sharply in value). The plan, he charged, was to bring about a redemption of Class A shares, then liquidate Axton-Fisher so that Transamerica (D) (as the holder of most of the remaining non-preferred stock) would gain for itself most of the value of the warehoused tobacco. His suit was dismissed for failure to state a cause of action.

ISSUE: Do majority stockholders owe a fiduciary duty to the minority?

HOLDING AND DECISION: Yes. As a fiduciary relationship is imposed by law on the directors of a corporation in respect to the corporation and its stockholders, a similar relationship governs those who are in charge of the corporation's affairs by virtue of majority stock ownership or otherwise. The majority has the right to control, but in exercising that right it owes a fiduciary duty to the minority as well as to the corporation itself or its officers and directors. Although the act of the board of directors in calling the Class A stock could be legally consummated by a disinterested board, if the allegations made are true, it was effected at the direction of the majority stockholder in order to profit it. In such a case, an action would definitely lie, and Transamerica (D) would be liable for breach of its fiduciary duty to the minority. Reversed.

EDITOR'S ANALYSIS: This case points up one situation (liquidations) in which the law prohibits controlling shareholders from exploiting their position to the detriment of the minority. While the fiduciary duties of controlling shareholders (breach of which can give rise to liability) are not quite coextensive with the fiduciary duties of directors, at least in cases of self-dealing, the issuance of stock, interference with voting rights, dissolutions, and the sale of assets, most courts will hold the majority to a duty of good faith, care, and diligence in the protection of minority rights and interests. Note also that most courts today give special scrutiny to situations in which a sale of control is effected by a controlling shareholder. See *Perlman v. Feldman*, 219 F.2d 173.

HOLDING AND DECISION: This section offers a clear and in-depth discussion of the *rule of the case and the court's rationale*. It is written in easy-to-understand language. When relevant, the student is provided with a thorough discussion of the exceptions listed by the court, the concurring and dissenting opinions, and the names of the judges.

EDITOR'S ANALYSIS: This addition to the brief is a new innovation. It is a hornbook style discussion of how the case is relevant to the section of the book and to the entire course. It indicates whether the case is a majority or minority opinion. It compares the principal case with other cases in the casebook. It also provides analysis from restatements, uniform codes, legal encyclopedias and treatises. This section points out the history of the case, the type of transaction involved and ways to avoid problems the case presents for the lawyer. In other words, it gives the student a broad understanding of *where the case "fits in" with other cases in the section of the book and with the entire course*. The editor's analysis will prove to be invaluable to classroom discussion.

NOTE TO THE STUDENT

It is the goal of Casenotes Publishing Company, Inc. to create and distribute the finest, clearest and most accurate legal briefs available. To this end, we are constantly seeking new ideas, comments and constructive criticism. As a user of Casenote Legal Briefs, your suggestions will be highly valued. With all correspondence, please include your complete name, address, and telephone number, including area code and zip code.

Casenote Legal Briefs are printed on perforated, three-hole punched sheets for easy inclusion in ringed binders. To remove a page, first fold the page at the perforations and then tear the sheet using care not to rip the punched holes.

EDITOR'S NOTE: Casenote Legal Briefs *are intended to supplement the student's casebook, not replace it. The student must master the skill of briefing if he/she expects to succeed in the study of law. There is no substitute for the student's own mastery of this important learning and study technique. If used properly, Casenote Legal Briefs are an effective law study aid which serve to reinforce the student's understanding of the cases.*

SUPPLEMENT REQUEST FORM

REF. # 1021-89-890

At the time this book was printed, a brief was included for every major case in the casebook and for every existing supplement to the casebook. However, if a new supplement to the casebook (or a new edition of the casebook) has been published since this publication was printed and if that casebook supplement (or new edition of the casebook) was available for sale at the time you purchased this Casenote Legal Briefs book, we will be pleased to provide you the new cases contained therein AT NO CHARGE when you send us a stamped, self-addressed envelope.

TO OBTAIN YOUR FREE SUPPLEMENT MATERIAL, **YOU MUST FOLLOW THE INSTRUCTIONS BELOW PRECISELY** OR REQUEST WILL NOT BE ACKNOWLEDGED!

1. Please check if there is in fact an existing supplement and, if so, that the cases are not already included in your Casenote Legal Briefs. Check the main table of cases as well as the supplement table of cases, if any.

2. *REMOVE THIS ENTIRE PAGE FROM THE BOOK.* You MUST send this ORIGINAL page to receive your supplement. This page acts as your proof of purchase and contains the reference number necessary to fill your supplement request properly. No photocopy of this page or written request will be honored or answered. Any request from which the reference number has been removed, altered or obliterated will not be honored.

3. Prepare a STAMPED self-addressed envelope for return mailing. Be sure to use a FULL SIZE (9 × 12) ENVELOPE (MANILA TYPE) so that the supplement will fit, and AFFIX ENOUGH POSTAGE TO COVER 3 OZ. ANY SUPPLEMENT REQUEST NOT ACCOMPANIED BY A STAMPED SELF-ADDRESSED ENVELOPE WILL ABSOLUTELY NOT BE FILLED OR ACKNOWLEDGED.

4. MULTIPLE SUPPLEMENT REQUESTS: If you are ordering more than one supplement, we suggest that you enclose a stamped, self-addressed envelope for each supplement requested. If you enclose only one envelope for a multiple request, your order may not be filled immediately should any supplement which you requested still be in production. In other words, your order will be held by us until it can be filled completely.

5. CASENOTES prints two kinds of supplements. A *"New Edition"* supplement is issued when a new edition of your casebook is published. A *"New Edition"* supplement gives you all major cases found in the new edition of the casebook which did not appear in the previous edition. A regular *"supplement"* is issued when a paperback supplement to your casebook is published. If the box at the lower right is stamped, then the *"New Edition"* supplement was provided to your bookstore and is *not* available from CASENOTES, however CASENOTES will still send you any regular *"supplements"* which have been printed either before or after the new edition of your casebook appeared and which, according to the reference number at the top of this page, have not been included in this book. If the box is not stamped, CASENOTES will send you any supplements, *"New Edition"* and/or regular, needed to completely update your Casenote Legal Briefs.

6. Fill in the following information:
    A. Full title of CASEBOOK ___CRIMINAL LAW___

    B. CASEBOOK author's name ___KADISH___

    C. Date of new supplement which you are requesting _____

    D. Name and location of bookstore where this *Casenote Legal Briefs* was purchased

    E. Name and location of law school you attend _____

    F. Any comments regarding *Casenote Legal Briefs* _____

    NOTE: IF THIS BOX IS STAMPED, NO *NEW EDITION* SUPPLEMENT CAN BE OBTAINED BY MAIL.

CASENOTES PUBLISHING, CO., INC.   P.O. Box 3946   Beverly Hills, CA 90212-0946

PLEASE PRINT

NAME _____ PHONE _____

ADDRESS/CITY/STATE/ZIP _____

CASENOTE LEGAL BRIEFS

PRICE LIST — EFFECTIVE JULY 1, 1990 ● PRICES SUBJECT TO CHANGE WITHOUT NOTICE

Ref. No.	Course	Adaptable to Courses Utilizing	Retail Price
1380	ACCOUNTING	FIFLIS, KRIPKE & FOSTER	7.50
1265	ADMINISTRATIVE LAW	BONFIELD & ASIMOW	11.00
1263	ADMINISTRATIVE LAW	BREYER & STEWART	14.00
1261	ADMINISTRATIVE LAW	DAVIS	10.00
1260	ADMINISTRATIVE LAW	GELHORN, B., S., R. & S.	13.00
1264	ADMINISTRATIVE LAW	MASHAW & MERRILL	12.50
1262	ADMINISTRATIVE LAW	SCHWARTZ	13.00
1290	ADMIRALTY	HEALY & SHARPE	15.50
1291	ADMIRALTY	LUCAS	13.50
1350	AGENCY & PARTNER. (ENT. ORG.)	CONARD, KNAUSS & SIEGEL	15.00
1280	ANTITRUST	AREEDA & KAPLOW	14.50
1281	ANTITRUST (TRADE REG.)	HANDLER, B., P. & G.	11.50
1282	ANTITRUST	OPPENHEIM, W. & M.	12.50
1610	BANKING LAW	SYMONS & WHITE	9.00
1303	BANKRUPTCY (DEBT.-CRED.)	EISENBERG	12.00
1440	BUSINESS PLANNING	HERWITZ	9.50
1040	CIVIL PROCEDURE	COUND, F., M. & S.	15.00
1043	CIVIL PROCEDURE	FIELD, K. & C.	14.00
1046	CIVIL PROCEDURE	LANDERS, MARTIN & YEAZELL	13.00
1041	CIVIL PROCEDURE	LOUISELL, HAZARD & TAIT	14.00
1047	CIVIL PROCEDURE	MARCUS, REDISH & SHERMAN	15.00
1044	CIVIL PROCEDURE	ROSENBERG, S. & K.	15.00
1311	COMMERCIAL LAW	FARNSWORTH & HONNOLD	14.00
1312	COMMERCIAL LAW	JORDAN & WARREN	14.00
1310	COMMERCIAL LAW	SPEIDEL, SUMMERS & WHITE	14.00
1312	COMMERCIAL PAPER (COMM. LAW)	JORDAN & WARREN	14.00
1320	COMMUNITY PROPERTY	VERRALL & BIRD	13.50
1071	CONFLICTS	CRAMTON, CURRIE & KAY	13.00
1070	CONFLICTS	REESE, ROSENBERG & HAY	15.00
1082	CONSTITUTIONAL LAW	BARRETT, COHEN & VARAT	17.00
1086	CONSTITUTIONAL LAW	BREST & LEVINSON	12.00
1080	CONSTITUTIONAL LAW	GUNTHER	15.00
1084	CONSTITUTIONAL LAW	KAUPER & BEYTAGH	14.00
1081	CONSTITUTIONAL LAW	LOCKHART, K., C. & S.	14.00
1085	CONSTITUTIONAL LAW	ROTUNDA	16.00
1087	CONSTITUTIONAL LAW	STONE, S., S. & T.	15.00
1017	CONTRACTS	CALAMARI, PERILLO & BENDER	17.00
1014	CONTRACTS	DAWSON, H. & H.	14.00
1010	CONTRACTS	FARNSWORTH & YOUNG	14.00
1011	CONTRACTS	FULLER & EISENBERG	15.00
1100	CONTRACTS	HAMILTON, R. & W.	13.50
1013	CONTRACTS	KESSLER, GILMORE & KRONMAN	17.50
1016	CONTRACTS	KNAPP & CRYSTAL	15.00
1012	CONTRACTS	MURPHY & SPEIDEL	16.00
1018	CONTRACTS	MURRAY	16.00
1015	CONTRACTS	ROSETT	14.00
1019	CONTRACTS	VERNON	14.00
1501	COPYRIGHT	NIMMER	14.50
1218	CORPORATE TAXATION	LIND, S., L. & R.	9.00
1050	CORPORATIONS	CARY & EISENBERG (ABR. & UNABR.)	14.00
1054	CORPORATIONS	CHOPER, MORRIS & COFFEE	16.50
1350	CORPORATIONS (ENT. ORG.)	CONARD, KNAUSS & SIEGEL	15.00
1053	CORPORATIONS	HAMILTON	13.00
1051	CORPORATIONS	HENN	15.00
1055	CORPORATIONS	JENNINGS & BUXBAUM	13.50
1056	CORPORATIONS	SOLOMON, SCHWARTZ & BOWMAN	15.00
1052	CORPORATIONS	VAGTS	12.00
1300	CREDITOR'S RIGHTS (DEBT.-CRED.)	RIESENFELD	15.00
1550	CRIMINAL JUSTICE	WEINREB	12.50
1020	CRIMINAL LAW	BOYCE & PERKINS	17.00
1024	CRIMINAL LAW	DIX & SHARLOT	12.00
1025	CRIMINAL LAW	FOOTE & LEVY	12.00
1027	CRIMINAL LAW	JOHNSON	17.00
1021	CRIMINAL LAW	KADISH & SCHULHOFER	14.00
1026	CRIMINAL LAW	KAPLAN & WEISBERG	12.50
1023	CRIMINAL LAW	LaFAVE	13.00
1022	CRIMINAL LAW	WEINREB	10.00
1200	CRIMINAL PROCEDURE	KAMISAR, LaFAVE & ISRAEL	14.00
1204	CRIMINAL PROCEDURE	SALTZBURG	12.00
1203	CRIMINAL PROCEDURE (PROCESS)	WEINREB	13.50
1303	DEBTOR-CREDITOR	EISENBERG	13.00
1302	DEBTOR-CREDITOR	EPSTEIN, LANDERS & NICKLES	13.00
1300	DEBTOR-CREDITOR (CRED. RTS.)	RIESENFELD	15.00
1301	DEBTOR-CREDITOR	WARREN & HOGAN	13.00
1304	DEBTOR-CREDITOR	WARREN & WESTBROOK	13.00
1223	DECEDENTS EST. (WILLS, T. & E.)	DUKEMINIER & JOHANSON	14.50
1224	DECEDENTS ESTATES	RITCHIE, ALFORD & EFFLAND	15.50
1222	DECEDENTS ESTATES	SCOLES & HALBACH	14.50
1231	DECEDENTS ESTATES (TRUSTS)	WELLMAN, W. & B.	13.00
1244	DOMESTIC RELATIONS (FAM. LAW)	AREEN	16.00
1242	DOMESTIC RELATIONS (FAM. LAW)	CLARK	13.00
1241	DOMESTIC RELATIONS (FAM. LAW)	FOOTE, LEVY & SANDER	12.00
1243	DOMESTIC RELATIONS (FAM. LAW)	KRAUSE	17.00
1240	DOMESTIC RELATIONS (FAM. LAW)	WADLINGTON	14.00
1350	ENTERPRISE ORGANIZATIONS	CONARD, KNAUSS & SIEGEL	15.00
1341	ENVIRONMENTAL LAW	FINDLEY & FARBER	14.00
1340	ENVIRONMENTAL LAW	HANKS, TARLOCK & HANKS	8.50
1254	EQUITY (REMEDIES)	LAYCOCK	14.50
1253	EQUITY (REMEDIES)	LEAVELL, LOVE & NELSON	15.00
1252	EQUITY (REMEDIES)	RE	18.50
1255	EQUITY (REMEDIES)	SHOBEN & TABB	16.50
1250	EQUITY (REMEDIES)	YORK, BAUMAN & RENDLEMAN	18.00
1217	ESTATE & GIFT TAXATION	BITTKER & CLARK	10.00
1214	ESTATE & GIFT TAXATION	KAHN & WAGGONER	12.00
1213	ESTATE & GIFT TAXATION (FED. WEALTH TRANS.)	SURREY, McDANIEL & GUTMAN	11.00
1090	ETHICS (PROF. RESPONSIBILITY)	PIRSIG & KIRWIN	10.00
1064	EVIDENCE	CLEARY, STRONG, BROUN & MOSTELLER	15.50
1065	EVIDENCE	GREEN & NESSON	13.00
1061	EVIDENCE	KAPLAN & WALTZ	13.00
1063	EVIDENCE	LEMPERT & SALTZBURG	7.00
1062	EVIDENCE	McCORMICK, SUTTON & WELLBORN	17.00
1066	EVIDENCE	MUELLER & KIRKPATRICK	14.00
1060	EVIDENCE	WEINSTEIN, M., A. & B.	15.50
1244	FAMILY LAW (DOMESTIC REL.)	AREEN	16.00
1242	FAMILY LAW (DOMESTIC REL.)	CLARK	13.00
1241	FAMILY LAW (DOMESTIC REL.)	FOOTE, LEVY & SANDER	12.00
1243	FAMILY LAW (DOMESTIC REL.)	KRAUSE	17.00
1240	FAMILY LAW (DOMESTIC REL.)	WADLINGTON	14.00
1360	FEDERAL COURTS	BATOR, M., S. & W.	15.00
1362	FEDERAL COURTS	CURRIE	12.00
1363	FEDERAL COURTS	LOW & JEFFRIES	11.00
1361	FEDERAL COURTS	McCORMICK, C. & W.	15.00
1510	GRATUITOUS TRANSFERS	CLARK, LUSKY & MURPHY	13.00
1371	INSURANCE LAW	KEETON	15.00
1370	INSURANCE LAW	YOUNG & HOLMES	11.00
1392	INTERNATIONAL LAW	HENKIN, P., S. & S.	15.00
1390	INTERNATIONAL LAW	SWEENEY, OLIVER & LEECH	12.00
1480	JUVENILE JUSTICE	MILLER, D., D. & P.	12.00
1331	LABOR LAW	COX, BOK & GORMAN	14.00
1333	LABOR LAW	LESLIE	12.50
1332	LABOR LAW	MELTZER & HENDERSON	14.00
1330	LABOR LAW	MERRIFIELD, S. & C.	13.00
1471	LAND FINANCE (REAL ESTATE TRANS.)	AXELROD, BERGER & JOHNSTONE	13.00
1620	LAND FINANCE (REAL ESTATE TRANS.)	NELSON & WHITMAN	15.00
1470	LAND FINANCE	PENNEY, B. & C.	12.00
1450	LAND USE	WRIGHT & GITELMAN	15.00
1420	LEGISLATION	NUTTING & DICKERSON	12.00
1590	LOCAL GOVERNMENT LAW	VALENTE	16.00
1520	MEDICINE	SHARPE, FISCINA & HEAD	15.00
1600	NEGOTIABLE INSTRUMENTS	WHALEY	9.00
1570	NEW YORK PRACTICE	PETERFREUND & McLAUGHLIN	19.00
1541	OIL & GAS	KUNTZ, L., A. & S.	13.00
1540	OIL & GAS	WILLIAMS, M., M. & W.	11.00
1580	PATENT LAW	CHOATE & FRANCIS	18.00
1431	PRODUCTS LIABILITY	KEETON, MONTGOMERY & GREEN	14.00
1430	PRODUCTS LIABILITY	NOEL & PHILLIPS	15.50
1090	PROF. RESPONSIBILITY (ETHICS)	PIRSIG & KIRWIN	10.00
1033	PROPERTY	BROWDER, C., N., S. & W.	15.50
1030	PROPERTY	CASNER & LEACH	15.00
1031	PROPERTY	CRIBBET, JOHNSON, FINLEY & SMITH	16.50
1035	PROPERTY	DUKEMINIER & KRIER	13.00
1034	PROPERTY	HAAR & LIEBMAN	14.50
1036	PROPERTY	KURTZ & HOVENKAMP	14.50
1032	PROPERTY	RABIN	14.00
1620	REAL ESTATE TRANSFER & FINANCE	NELSON & WHITMAN	15.00
1254	REMEDIES (EQUITY)	LAYCOCK	14.50
1253	REMEDIES (EQUITY)	LEAVELL, LOVE & NELSON	15.00
1252	REMEDIES (EQUITY)	RE	18.50
1255	REMEDIES (EQUITY)	SHOBEN & TABB	16.50
1250	REMEDIES (EQUITY)	YORK, BAUMAN & RENDLEMAN	18.00
1312	SECURED TRANS. (COMM. LAW)	JORDAN & WARREN	14.00
1270	SECURITIES REGULATION	JENNINGS & MARSH	14.00
1271	SECURITIES REGULATION	RATNER	13.00
1215	TAXATION (BASIC FED. INC.)	ANDREWS	14.00
1217	TAXATION (ESTATE & GIFT)	BITTKER & CLARK	10.00
1212	TAXATION (FED. INC.)	FREELAND, LIND & STEPHENS	13.00
1211	TAXATION (FED. INC.)	GRAETZ	12.00
1214	TAXATION (ESTATE & GIFT)	KAHN & WAGGONER	12.00
1210	TAXATION (FED. INC.)	KLEIN, BITTKER & STONE	13.50
1216	TAXATION (FED. INC.)	KRAGEN & McNULTY	11.00
1218	TAXATION (CORPORATE)	LIND, S., L. & R.	9.00
1213	TAXATION (FED. WEALTH TRANS.)	SURREY, M. & G.	11.00
1281	TRADE REGULATION (ANTITRUST)	HANDLER, B., P. & G.	11.50
1006	TORTS	DOBBS	16.00
1003	TORTS	EPSTEIN, GREGORY & KALVEN	16.50
1004	TORTS	FRANKLIN & RABIN	12.50
1001	TORTS	HENDERSON & PEARSON	14.50
1002	TORTS	KEETON, K., S. & S.	16.00
1000	TORTS	PROSSER, WADE & SCHWARTZ	18.00
1005	TORTS	SHULMAN, JAMES & GRAY	16.00
1230	TRUSTS	BOGERT & OAKS	14.50
1231	TRUSTS (DECEDENTS ESTATES)	WELLMAN, WAGGONER & BROWDER	13.00
1410	U.C.C.	EPSTEIN, MARTIN, H. & N.	10.00
1580	WATER LAW	TRELEASE & GOULD	14.00
1223	WILLS, TRUSTS & EST. (DEC. EST.)	DUKEMINIER & JOHANSON	14.50
1220	WILLS	MECHEM & ATKINSON	15.00

CASENOTES PUBLISHING CO. INC. ● P.O. BOX 3946 ● BEVERLY HILLS, CA 90212 ● (213) 475-1141
PLEASE PURCHASE FROM YOUR LOCAL BOOKSTORE.   IF UNAVAILABLE, YOU MAY ORDER DIRECT. *
4TH CLASS POSTAGE (ALLOW TWO WEEKS) $1.00 PER ORDER; 1ST CLASS POSTAGE $3.00 (ONE BOOK), $2.00 EACH (TWO OR MORE BOOKS)
* CALIF. RESIDENTS PLEASE ADD SALES TAX   (SERIES XXII)

New OUTLINE Series

casenote LAW OUTLINES

NEW from casenotes

▶ **WRITTEN BY NATIONALLY RECOGNIZED AUTHORITIES IN THEIR FIELD.**

▶ **CONTAINS:** *TABLE OF CONTENTS; CAPSULE OUTLINE; FULL OUTLINE; PRACTICE EXAMS; SUBJECT GLOSSARY; TABLE OF CASES; TABLE OF AUTHORITIES; CASEBOOK CROSS-REFERENCE CHART; INDEX.*

▶ **THE TOTAL LAW SUMMARY UTILIZING THE MOST COMPREHENSIVE STUDY APPROACH IN THE MOST EFFECTIVE, EASY-TO-READ FORMAT.**

Available 1990

	Retail Price
#5000—TORTS by **George C. Christie**, James B. Duke Professor of Law, Duke University. Editor: *Cases and Materials on the Law of Torts;* **Jerry J. Phillips**, W.P. Toms Professor of Law & Chair, Committee on Admissions, University of Tennessee. Co-editor: *Cases and Materials on Torts and Related Law* (with Noel). Co-editor: *Products Liability Cases and Materials* (with Noel)	$16.95
#5010—CONTRACTS by **Daniel Wm. Fessler**, Professor of Law, University of California, Davis. Co-editor: *Cases and Materials on Contracts* (with Loiseaux)	$16.95
#5020—CRIMINAL LAW by **Joshua Dressler**, Professor of Law, Wayne State University. Author: *Understanding Criminal Law* (Matthew Bender: 1987). *Understanding Criminal Procedure* (publication: 1990)	$14.95
#5040—CIVIL PROCEDURE by **John B. Oakley**, Professor of Law, University of California, Davis. Co-author: *An Introduction to the Anglo-American Legal System* (with Bodenheimer & Love). Chair: AALS Section on Civil Procedure, 1979–80. **Rex R. Perschbacher**, Professor of Law, University of California, Davis. Co-editor: *Cases and Materials on Civil Procedure* (with Crump, Dorsaneo & Chase). Author: *California Trial Technique*	$16.95
#5050—CORPORATIONS AND ALTERNATIVE BUSINESS VEHICLES by **Lewis D. Solomon**, Professor of Law, George Washington University. Co-editor: *Corporations: Law and Policy: Problems and Materials* (with D. Schwartz & J. Bauman). Author: *Corporate Mergers, Acquisitions & Divestitures* and **Daniel Wm. Fessler**, Professor of Law, University of California, Davis. Editor: *Alternatives to Incorporation for Persona in Quest of Profit, Cases and Materials on Partnerships, Limited Partnerships, Joint Ventures and Related Agency Concepts, 2d ed. 1986* and **Arthur E. Wilmarth, Jr.**, Associate Professor of Law, George Washington University	$17.95
#5060—EVIDENCE by **Kenneth W. Graham, Jr.**, Professor of Law, University of California, Los Angeles. Co-author: *Federal Practice and Procedure: Evidence* (with Wright), vols. 21–24 (1977–1988)	$16.95
#5080—CONSTITUTIONAL LAW by **Gary Goodpaster**, Professor of Law & Associate Dean, Academic Affairs, University of California, Davis; Fulbright Professor of Law, Hong Kong University (1987–88)	$18.95
#5210—FEDERAL INCOME TAXATION by **Joseph M. Dodge**, W.H. Francis, Jr. Professor of Law, The University of Texas at Austin. Editor: *Federal Taxation of Estates, Trusts and Gifts: Principles and Planning Boot Distributions. Federal Income Taxation: Principles, Policy, Planning. Transfers With Retained Interests and Powers*	$17.95
#5220—WILLS, TRUSTS & ESTATES by **William M. McGovern**, Professor of Law, University of California, Los Angeles. Editor: *Cases and Materials on Wills, Trusts and Future Interests; An Introduction to Estate Planning.* Co-author: *Wills, Trusts and Estates* (with S. Kurtz & J. Rein)	$16.95

...and more to come

EFFECTIVE July 1, 1990

COMMON LATIN WORDS AND PHRASES ENCOUNTERED IN THE LAW

A FORTIORI: Because one fact exists or has been proven, that therefore a second fact which is related to the first fact must also exist. This term is most often used when making arguments based upon logic.

A PRIORI: From the cause to the effect. A term of logic used to denote that when one cause, fact, or position is shown to exist, another particular cause, fact or position must necessarily follow.

AB INITIO: From the beginning; a condition which has existed throughout, as in a marriage which was void *ab initio*.

ACTUS REUS: The guilty act; in criminal law, such action sufficient to trigger criminal liability.

AD VALOREM: According to value; an *ad valorem* tax is imposed upon an item located within the taxing jurisdiction calculated by the value of such item.

AMICUS CURIAE: Friend of the court. Its most common usage takes the form of an amicus curiae brief, filed by a person who is not a party to an action, but is nonetheless allowed to offer an argument supporting his legal interests.

ARGUENDO: In arguing. A statement, possibly hypothetical, made for the purpose of argument.

BILL QUIA TIMET: A bill to quiet title (establish ownership) to real property.

BONA FIDE: True, honest or genuine. May refer to the genuiness of a person's legal position (such as a bona fide purchaser for value), or a particular document (such as a bona fide last will and testament).

CAUSA MORTIS: With approaching death in mind. A gift causa mortis is a gift given by a party who feels certain that death is imminent.

CAVEAT EMPTOR: "Let the buyer beware," is the literal translation. This maxim is reflected in the rule of law that a buyer purchases at his own risk because it is his responsibility to examine, judge, test, and otherwise inspect what he is buying.

CERTIORARI: A writ of review. Petitions for review of a case by the United States Supreme Court are most often done by means of a writ of certiorari.

CONTRA: On the other hand. Opposite. Contrary to.

CORAM NOBIS: Before us; writs of error directed by a court to another branch of the same court.

CORAM VOBIS: Before you; writs of error by an appellate court to a lower court to correct a factual error.

CORPUS DELICTI: The body of the crime; the requisite elements of a crime amounting to objective proof that a crime has been committed.

CUM TESTAMENTO ANNEXO, ADMINISTRATOR (ADMINISTRATOR C.T.A.): With will annexed; an administrator c.t.a. settles an estate pursuant to a will in which he is not appointed.

DE BONIS NON, ADMINISTRATOR (ADMINISTRATOR D.B.N.): Of goods not administered; an administrator d.b.n. settles a partially settled estate.

DE FACTO: In fact; in reality; actually. Existing in fact but not officially approved or engendered.

DE JURE: By right; lawful. "As a matter of law" is what this term commonly connotes, in contrast to the term "de facto" (which generally connotes something existing in fact but not legally sanctioned or authorized). For example, *de facto* segregation would refer to segregation brought about by housing patterns, etc., while *de jure* segregation would refer to segregation created by law.

DE MINIMUS: Of minimal importance; insignificant; a trifle; not worth bothering with.

DE NOVO: Anew; a second time; afresh. A trial de novo is a new trial held at the appellate level as if the case originated there and the trial at a lower level had not taken place.

DICTA: Generally used as an abbreviated form of *obiter dicta,* a term describing those portions of a judicial opinion incidental or not necessary to resolution of the specific question before the court. Such nonessential statements and remarks are not considered to be binding precedent.

DUCES TECUM: Refers to a particular type of writ or subpoena requesting a party or organization to produce certain documents in their possession.

EN BANC: Full bench. Where a court sits with all justices present rather than simply a quorum.

EX PARTE: For one side or one party only. An ex parte proceeding is one undertaken for the benefit of only one party, and proceeds without notice to, or an appearance by an adverse party.

EX POST FACTO: After the fact. An ex post facto law is a law which retroactively changes the consequences of a prior act.

EX REL.: (abbr. for ex relatione) Upon relation or information. When the state brings an action in which it has no interest against an individual at the instigation of one who has a private interest in the matter.

FORUM NON CONVENIENS: Inconvenient forum. Although a court may have jurisdiction over the case, the action should be tried in a more conveniently located court, one to which parties and witnesses may more easily travel, for example.

GUARDIAN AD LITEM: A guardian of an infant as to litigation, appointed to represent the infant and pursue his rights.

HABEAS CORPUS: "You have the body" is the literal translation. The modern writ of *habeas corpus* is a writ directing that a person (body) being detained (such as a prisoner) be brought before the court so that the legality of his detention can be judicially ascertained.

IN CAMERA: In private, in chambers. When a hearing is held before a judge in his chambers or when all spectators are excluded from the courtroom.

IN FORMA PAUPERIS: In the manner of a pauper. A party who proceeds *in forma pauperis* because of his poverty may be allowed to bring suit without liability for costs.

INFRA: Below, under. The opposite of *supra,* above.

IN LOCO PARENTIS: In the place of a parent.

IN PARI DELICTO: Equally wrong; a court of equity will not grant requested relief to an applicant who is *in pari delicto,* or as much at fault in the transactions giving rise to the controversy as is the opponent of the applicant.

IN PARI MATERIA: On like subject matter or upon the same matter. Statutes relating to the same person or things are said to be *in pari materia.* It is a general rule of statutory construction that such statutes should be construed together, i.e. looked at as if they together constituted one law.

IN PERSONAM: Into or against the person. Jurisdiction over the person of an individual.

IN RE: In the matter of.

IN REM: A term that signifies an action against the *res,* or thing. An action *in rem* is basically one that is taken directly against property, in contradistinction to an action *in personam* or action against the person.

INTER ALIA: Amongst other things. Used to show that the whole of a statement, pleading, list, or statute, for example, has not been set forth in its entirety.

INTER PARTES: Between the parties. May refer to contracts, conveyances or other transactions having legal significance.

INTER VIVOS: Between the living. An inter vivos gift is a gift made by a living grantor, as distinguished from bequests contained in a will, which pass upon the death of the testator.

IPSO FACTO: By the mere fact itself.

JUS: Law or the entire body of law.

LEX LOCI: The law of the place; the notion that the rights of parties to a legal proceeding are governed by the law of the place where those rights arose.

MALUM IN SE: Evil or wrong in and of itself; inherently wrong. This term describes an act that is wrong by its very nature as opposed to one which would not be wrong but for the fact that there is a specific legal prohibition against it *(malum prohibitum)*.

MALUM PROHIBITUM: Wrong because prohibited, but not inherently evil. Used to describe something which is wrong because it is expressly forbidden by law but which is not in and of itself evil, e.g. speeding.

MANDAMUS: We command. A writ directing an official to take certain action.

MENS REA: A guilty mind; a criminal intent. A term used to signify the mental state that accompanies a crime or other prohibited act. Some crimes require only a general *mens rea* (general intent to do the prohibited act), but others (like assault with intent to murder) require the existence of a specific *mens rea*.

MODUS OPERANDI: Method of operating; generally refers to the manner or style of a criminal in committing crimes, admissible in appropriate cases as evidence of the identity of a defendant.

NEXUS: A connection to.

NISI PRIUS: The courts of first impression. The court where issues of fact are tried before a judge or jury.

N.O.V. (NON OBSTANTE VERDICTO): Notwithstanding the verdict. A judgment n.o.v. is a judgment given in favor of one party despite the fact that a verdict was returned in favor of the other party, the justification being that the verdict either had no reasonable support in fact or was contrary to law.

NUNC PRO TUNC: Now for then. This phrase refers to actions which may be taken, and then have full retroactive effect.

PENDENTE LITE: Pending the suit; pending litigation underway.

PER CAPITA: By head; beneficiaries of an estate, if they take in equal shares, take *per capita*.

PER CURIAM: By the court; signifies an opinion ostensibly written "by the whole court" and with no identified author.

PER SE: By itself; in itself; inherently.

PER STIRPES: By representation. Used primarily in the law of wills to show that when a person, generally because of death, is unable to take that which is left to him by the will of another, his heirs shall divide such property between them rather than take under the will individually.

PRIMA FACIE: On its face; at first sight. A *prima facie* case is one that is sufficient on its face, meaning that the evidence supporting it is adequate to establish the case until contradicted or overcome by other evidence.

PRO TANTO: For so much; as far as it goes. Often used in eminent domain cases when property owner receives partial payment for his land without prejudice to his right to bring suit for the full amount he claims his land to be worth.

QUANTUM MERUIT: As much as he deserved. Today, this term refers to recovery based on the doctrine of unjust enrichment in those cases in which a party rendered valuable services or furnished materials that were accepted and enjoyed by another under circumstances that would reasonably notify the recipient that the rendering party expected to be paid. In essence, the law implies a contract to pay the reasonable value of the services or materials furnished.

QUASI: Almost like; as if; nearly. This term is essentially used to signify that one subject or thing is almost analogous to another but that material differences between them do exist. For example, a quasi-criminal proceeding is one that is not strictly criminal but which shares so many of the same characteristics that it is sufficiently like a criminal proceeding to require that some of the same safeguards apply (e.g., procedural due process must be followed in a parol hearing).

QUID PRO QUO: Something for something. In contract law, the consideration, something of value, passed between the parties to render the contract binding.

RES GESTAE: The things done; in evidence law, this principle justifies the admission of a statement, which otherwise would be hearsay, when it is made so closely to the event in question as to be said to be a part of it or with such spontaneity as not to have the possibility of falsehood.

RES IPSA LOQUITUR: The thing speaks for itself. This doctrine gives rise to a rebuttable presumption of negligence when the instrumentality causing the injury was within the exclusive control of the defendant, and the injury was one which does not normally occur unless a person has been negligent.

RES JUDICATA: A matter adjudged. Doctrine which provides that once a court of competent jurisdiction has rendered a final judgment or decree on the merits, that judgment or decree is conclusive upon the parties to the case and their privies and prevents them from engaging in any other litigation on the points and issues determined therein.

RESPONDEAT SUPERIOR: Let the master reply. This doctrine holds the master liable for the wrongful acts of his servant (or the principal for his agent) in those cases in which the servant (or agent) was acting within the scope of his authority at the time of the injury.

STARE DECISIS: To stand by or adhere to that which has been decided. The common law doctrine of *stare decisis* attempts to give security and certainty to the law by following the policy that once a principle of law as applicable to a certain set of facts has been set forth in a decision, it forms a precedent which will subsequently be followed even though a different decision might be made were it the first time the question had arisen. Of course, *stare decisis* is not an inviolable principle, but is departed from in instances where there is good cause (e.g. considerations of public policy led the Supreme Court to disregard prior decisions sanctioning segregation).

SUPRA: Above. A word referring a reader to an earlier part of a book.

ULTRA VIRES: Beyond the power. This phrase is most commonly used to refer to actions taken by a corporation which are beyond the power or legal authority of the corporation.

ADDENDUM OF FRENCH DERIVATIVES

IN PAIS: Not pursuant to legal proceedings.

CHATTEL: Tangible personal property.

CY PRES: Doctrine permitting courts to apply trust funds to purposes not expressed in the trust, but necessary to carry out the settlor's intent.

PER AUTRE VIE: For another's life; in Property Law, an estate may be granted which will terminate upon the death of someone other than the grantee.

PROFIT 'A PRENDRE: A license to remove minerals or other stone from land.

VOIR DIRE: Process of questioning jurors as to their predispositions about the case or parties to a proceeding and removing those jurors displaying bias or prejudice.

TABLE OF CASES

TABLE OF CASES — Cont.

PEOPLE v. ZACKOWITZ
N.Y. Ct. of Apls.
254 N.Y. 192, 172 N.E. 466 (1930).

NATURE OF CASE: Appeal from first-degree murder conviction.

FACT SUMMARY: Zackowitz (D) claimed that evidence relating to his possession of other weapons at home should not have been admitted at his murder trial because its sole purpose was to give the impression he had a general criminal disposition.

CONCISE RULE OF LAW: Unless the defendant has made his general character an issue in a criminal prosecution, evidence thereon is inadmissible (unless admissible for some other purpose).

FACTS: After engaging in a verbal confrontation with Coppola, who made insulting remarks to his wife on a Brooklyn street, Zackowitz (D) returned home. There, his wife informed him that Coppolla had specifically offered her two dollars to sleep with him. Zackowitz (D) then returned to the street where Coppolla was repairing a car. A fight ensued, and Zackowitz (D) shot and killed Coppola with a .25-calibre pistol he had on him. Zackowitz (D) told the police he had obtained the pistol at home, before he went back to confront Coppola. At trial, however, he insisted that he had had the pistol on his person the entire evening. The People (P) were permitted to put into evidence the fact that Zackowitz (D) had a radio box, three pistols, and a teargas gun at his apartment. In appealing his first-degree murder conviction, Zackowitz (D) maintained this evidence was inadmissible because it was designed to show he had a general criminal disposition.

ISSUE: Unless a criminal defendant has put his general character at issue, is evidence thereon admissible at a criminal trial?

HOLDING AND DECISION: (C.J. Cardozo) No. The character of a criminal defendant is never an issue in criminal prosecution unless the defendant makes it one, which Zackowitz (D) did not do. Nonetheless, the court permitted introduction of evidence designed to show that he was a man of evil life—a man of murderous heart, of criminal disposition, and therefore more likely to commit the crime charged. There could have been no other purpose because these other weapons Zackowitz (D) had at home had no connection with the crime with which he was charged. Thus, the evidence was not admissible. Judgment reversed; new trial ordered.

DISSENT: (J. Pound) The evidence was presented to show Zackowitz (D) had an opportunity to select a weapon to carry out his threats, did so, then killed Coppola - not to show Zackowitz's (D) character.

EDITOR'S ANALYSIS: The exclusion of evidence as to the "bad character" of the defendant (including evidence of his other crimes) is relevant but is kept out because, as McCormick puts it, "in the setting of jury trial the danger of prejudice outweighs the probative value." Some courts have recognized that a judge trying a case is less likely to give undue weight to such evidence.

PATTERSON v. NEW YORK
432 U.S. 197 (1977)

NATURE OF CASE: Appeal from a conviction of second-degree murder.

FACT SUMMARY: Patterson (D) alleged as an affirmative defense that he was emotionally disturbed at the time of the killing.

CONCISE RULE OF LAW: So long as the state proves every element of the charge beyond a reasonable doubt, the defendant may be required to prove an affirmative defense.

FACTS: Patterson (P), after separating from his wife, killed her new boyfriend. Patterson (P) was charged with second degree murder. Patterson (P) raised a statutorily authorized affirmative defense that he had been emotionally disturbed at the time. If proved, this would have reduced the offense to manslaughter. The jury convicted Patterson (D) of second-degree murder and he appealed on the grounds that the state had failed to prove, beyond a reasonable doubt, that he was not emotionally disturbed at the time. The state alleged that the burden of proving an affirmative defense was on Patterson (D). Since it had proved every element of its case beyond a reasonable doubt, the burden was on Patterson (D) to show, by a preponderance of the evidence, that mitigating circumstances warranted a lesser charge.

ISSUE: Where an affirmative defense does not include an element of the crime is the defendant required to bear the burden of proof?

HOLDING AND DECISION: (J. White) Yes. Due process considerations only require the state to prove each element of the charge beyond a reasonable doubt. They do not require the state to prove the non-existence of all affirmative defenses or mitigating factors. Here, emotional distress is not an element of the charge of second-degree murder. The state proved every element of its case. It was up to Patterson (D) to prove that he was entitled to a lesser charge. Merely because a state makes a defense available does not require it to negate the existence of the defense. Affirmed.

DISSENT: (J.J. Powell) The court is focusing on the wording of a statute which just as easily could have required a showing that no mitigating factors such as emotional distress be present. If this were the case, the burden would fall on the state to negate the existence of the defense. Constitutional protections should not be left to the whim and caprice of chance as to how a statute is drawn. Such a formalistic approach is indefensible.

EDITOR'S ANALYSIS: In Mullaney v. Wilbur 421 U.S. 684 (1975), the Court held that Maine's murder law could not shift the burden to the defendant of showing that heat of passion or sudden provocation existed. This was included within the state's definition of mens rea. However, in Rivera v. Delaware - U.S. - (1976), the Court held that the burden of proof was on the defendant to establish his affirmative defense of insanity. The rationale was substantially the same as herein.

NOTES:

DUNCAN v. LOUISIANA

U.S.SUP.CT., 1968, 391 U.S. 145, S.Ct.1444,20 L.Ed.2d 491

NATURE OF CASE: Appeal from conviction for simple battery.

FACT SUMMARY: Duncan (D), a black youth, was convicted on disputed evidence, without a jury, of simple battery on a white youth.

CONCISE RULE OF LAW: Because trial by jury in criminal cases is fundamental to the American scheme of justice, the Fourteenth Amendment guarantees a right of jury trial in all criminal cases which, were they to be tried in federal court, could come within the Sixth Amendment's guarantee.

FACTS: Upon disputed evidence, Duncan (D), a black youth, was convicted of simple battery upon a white youth. It was agreed that he at least touched the other boy on the elbow, but unclear whether he slapped him. Duncan's (D) request for a jury trial was denied. Under Louisiana law, a jury trial is guaranteed in cases where capital punishment or imprisonment at hard labor may be imposed. Simple battery is punishable as a misdemeanor with up to two years' imprisonment and a $300 fine. Duncan (D) appealed, claiming denial of a jury trial was a denial of due process in violation of the Sixth and Fourteenth Amendments.

ISSUE: Is the right to a jury trial so fundamental a principle of liberty and justice as to be guaranteed in state courts by the Fourteenth Amendment?

HOLDING AND DECISION: (J. White) Yes. The test for determining whether rights found in the Fifth and Sixth Amendments should apply to the states by the Fourteenth Amendment is to determine whether that right is basic in our system of jurisprudence; a fundamental right essential to a fair trial. The right to a jury trial is such a right. The right to a jury trial has historically received protection in English and American law. It protects against unfounded criminal charges brought to eliminate enemies, judges too responsive to higher authority, and overzealous prosecutors. This does not mean that an accused cannot choose to waive a jury trial. Also, crimes carrying possible penalties up to six months do not require a jury trial if otherwise a petty offense. The possible penalty for a particular crime is of major importance in determining whether it is serious or not. The possible penalty may, in itself, if so severe, require a jury trial upon request. It was error to deny a jury trial here.

CONCURRENCE: (J. Black with whom J. Douglas joins) The history of the Fourteenth Amendment shows that it was intended to guarantee the rights of all the first eight amendments upon the states, although selective incorporation of those rights is the next best alternative.

CONCURRENCE: (J. Fortas) While a jury trial may be fundamental, it is not necessarily so that all aspects of federal jury trials, e.g., 12 jurors, unanimity, etc., are also fundamental.

DISSENT: (J. Harlan with whom J. Stewart joins) When the criminally accused argues that his state conviction lacked due process of law, the question is actually whether he was denied an element of fundamental procedural fairness. A criminal trial can be fundamentally fair without a jury.

EDITOR'S ANALYSIS: Few Justices have gone as far as Justices Black and Douglas in arguing that the Fourteenth Amendment was designed to extend the Bill of Rights to the states. Even so, the historical support for that view is strong, particularly in the statements of the Senator who introduced the Amendment. The prevailing view, however, is that of selective incorporation. Only those rights found in the Bill of Rights deemed to be "fundamental," "basic," or "essential" have been held to apply to the states. Over the years, the vast majority of rights found in the first eight amendments have been extended by the court to the states. Yet it is strange to think that for the good part of a century after adoption of the Fourteenth Amendment and 150 years after adoption of the Bill of Rights, rights guaranteed for trials in federal court were not necessarily guaranteed in the same type of case in state courts, unless the constitution of the state in question also guaranteed those rights.

NOTES:

UNITED STATES v. DOUGHERTY
473 F. 2d 1113 (D.C. Circuit, 1972).

NATURE OF CASE: Appeals from conviction for unlawful entry and malicious destruction of property.

FACT SUMMARY: Dougherty (D) contends that the trial judge erred in refusing to instruct the jury of its right to acquit without regard to the law and the evidence.

CONCISE RULE OF LAW: While the jury's prerogative to disregard the court's instructions even as to matters of law does exist and is approved of, the jury should not be formally informed of that power by the judge.

FACTS: Dougherty (D) and eight others broke into Dow Chemical Company offices and destroyed property as part of an attack on Dow's role in supporting U.S. military action in Vietnam. The trial judge refused to instruct the jury of its right to acquit Dougherty (D) without regard to the law and the evidence.

ISSUE: Should the jury be instructed of its power to nullify the law in a particular case?

HOLDING AND DECISION: (J. Leventhal) No. An undoubted jury prerogative to disregard the law has evolved. It is derived from the jury's power to bring in a verdict of not guilty in a criminal case that is not reversible by the court. However, the fact that this power exists and is approved of as a necessary counter to hardened judges and arbitrary prosecutors does not mean that the jury must be informed by the judge of its power. The prerogative is reserved for the exceptional case and the judge's instruction acts as a generally effective constraint. To hold otherwise would unnecessarily burden the jury system, since the jury, that must be unanimous, would not merely have to come to a united determination of the facts, but also of the law. It would also burden the individual jurors. "For it is one thing for a juror to know that the law condemns, but he has a factual power of lenity. To tell him expressly of a nullification prerogative, however, is to inform him, in effect, that it is he who fashions the rule that condemns."

DISSENT: (C.J. Bazelon) Nullification serves the important function of permitting the jury to bring to bear on the criminal process a sense of fairness and particularized justice. Pretending the jury does not have this power may allow it to avoid its responsibility. Further, the use of the nullification power provides important feedback on the standards of the criminal laws. For example, the reluctance of juries to hold defendants responsible for unmistakable violation of the prohibition laws told us much about the morality of those laws.

EDITOR'S ANALYSIS: The ability of the jury system to render a fair verdict for militant, radical, and minority defendants has been strongly questioned. Some of the criticism has been dissipated by the refusal of juries to convict in cases such as Huey Newton's, Bobby Seale's, and Angela Davis'. William Kunstler, defense attorney for many militants, commented, "For many, the inability of prosecutors in recent trials of radicals to convince any - or even most - of their respective panels that the defendants were guilty has been regarded as a stunning vindication of our legal system. For others, including myself, these results only indicate that just verdicts are, under certain conditions, attainable."

NOTES:

NIX v. WHITESIDE

U.S.Sup.Ct. (1986) 106 S.Ct. 988

NATURE OF CASE: Appeal of order granting habeas corpus.

FACT SUMMARY: Whiteside's (D) attorney refused to permit him to commit perjury when testifying in his defense.

CONCISE RULE OF LAW: A defendant is not denied the right to counsel when his attorney prevents him from committing perjury.

FACTS: Whiteside (D) stabbed an individual, killing him. He was charged with murder. He claimed he acted in self-defense. One week before the trial, Whiteside (D) told his attorney that he saw the decedent with a gun or something metallic. The defense attorney disbelieved him and urged him not to testify regarding this at trial. Whiteside (D) insisted that he would do so. The attorney threatened that he would inform the court that he believed Whiteside (D) not to be telling the truth. Whiteside (D) agreed not to mention the object and did not so testify. Convicted, he appealed, arguing he had been denied the right to counsel. The state appellate and supreme courts affirmed. The Eighth Circuit granted habeas corpus, however, holding that Whiteside (D) had been denied the right to counsel. The Supreme Court accepted review.

ISSUE: Is a defendant denied the right to counsel when his attorney prevents him from committing perjury?

HOLDING AND DECISION: (C.J. Burger) No. A defendant is not denied the right to counsel when his attorney prevents him from committing perjury. For counsel to be denied, it must be shown that counsel was so inept as not to be functioning as counsel. An attorney's duty to his client goes only so far as to include legitimate, lawful conduct. It is universal among the jurisdictions, as well as in the Model Code of Professional Responsibility, that an attorney should not solicit or tolerate perjury. It is also, of course, incumbent upon a witness not to lie. In this case, therefore, the attorney's actions, at most, deprived Whiteside (D) of the ability to do that which he was not entitled to do. This being so, the conduct of the attorney was not deficient; in fact, it would have been a dereliction of duty for the attorney to have done otherwise. Therefore, in no way was Whiteside (D) denied effective counsel. Reversed.

CONCURRENCE: (J. Brennan) The Court has no constitutional authority to establish conduct for lawyers practicing in state courts.

CONCURRENCE: (J. Blackmun) To the extent the Court seems to adopt a set of rules of professional responsibility, it encroaches upon state authority.

CONCURRENCE: (J. Stevens) A lawyer's certainty that a change in his client's recollection is a harbinger of intended perjury—as well as judicial review of such apparent certainty—should be tempered by the realization that the most honest witness can later recall facts not at first remembered.

EDITOR'S ANALYSIS: Only five justices joined Chief Justice Burger's opinion, making it the opinion of a bare majority. The four justices declining to join, however, appeared to do so on the basis that the opinion could be read as adopting the Model Code of Professional Responsibility, something they considered improper. It would seem that all nine justices agreed with the rule of the case.

NOTES:

REGINA v. DUDLEY AND STEPHENS
QUEENS BENCH DIV., 1884. 14 Q.B.D. 273.

NOTES:

NATURE OF CASE: Appeal of jury's special verdict finding Dudley (D) and Stephens (D) guilty of murder.

FACT SUMMARY: Dudley (D) and Stephens (D) killed Parker, with whom they were stranded on the high seas in a lifeboat, in order to survive off Parker's remains after having run out of food and water.

CONCISE RULE OF LAW: Homicide may not be excused when the person killed is an innocent and unoffending victim.

FACTS: Dudley (D), Stephens (D) Brooks and Parker, crew members of an English yacht, were cast adrift on the high seas 1,600 miles from land in an open lifeboat. They had no water and two one-pound tins of turnips. After 12 days adrift, they were without food. Dudley (D) and Stephens (D) suggested to Brooks that one of the four may be sacrificed so that the others might survive. Brooks dissented, and Parker, a 17-year old boy, was never consulted. On the twentieth day, Dudley (D) and Stephens (D) killed Parker, who was too weak either to resist or assent. Four days after Parker's death, the surviving three were rescued. They would not have survived had they not fed off Parker's remains.

ISSUE: Was the homicide excusable by the necessity of saving some of the crewmen?

HOLDING AND DECISION: (C.J. Lord Coleridge) No. An innocent person may not be killed in order to save the life of another. Where the victim has not assaulted or otherwise endangered the killer, the killer has not, by necessity, been placed in a position which permits him to kill the innocent victim. The extreme necessity of hunger does not justify larceny, nor can it justify murder. While, generally, the preservation of one's own life is a duty; in some cases, the highest duty may be to sacrifice it. Neither can the temptation caused by hunger be called an excuse.

EDITOR'S ANALYSIS: While this case actually discusses a defense to murder, necessity (which here did not excuse the murder), the case appears here in the casebook more for its moral discussion of why the defendants, unwillingly placed in a tragic situation, must be punished for their act. The court notes that "Law and morality are not the same, and many things may be immoral which are not necessarily illegal," but that law would be divorced from morality if the temptation to kill, which arose, could be an excuse for the actual killing. Even if the temptation were a valid excuse, who is to determine who must die so that the others might live? Note that the death sentence was later commuted by the crown to six months' imprisonment.

UNITED STATES v. BERGMAN
416 F. Supp. 496 (S.D.N.Y.1976)

NATURE OF CASE: Action for defrauding of the federal government.

FACT SUMMARY: Bergman (D) argued that no purpose would be served by sentencing him to jail.

CONCISE RULE OF LAW: A jail sentence may be given as a general deterrent to others to prevent future commissions of similar offenses.

FACTS: Bergman (D), a distinguished rabbi and civic leader, was found to have been guilty of a conspiracy to defraud the federal government in connection with a nursing home scheme. A plea bargain was entered to plead guilty to two counts carrying a maximum of eight years in prison. Bergman (D) alleged that no purpose would be served in incarcerating him. Bergman (D) was 64 and not in good health. The government (P) alleged that incarceration was necessary as a general deterrent to others and so as not to depreciate the seriousness of the offense.

ISSUE: May a jail sentence be imposed as a general deterrent to the future misconduct of others?

HOLDING AND DECISION: (J. Frankel) Yes. Jail sentences should not be imposed to rehabilitate anyone. This concept is no longer accepted. Bergman (D) need not be incarcerated to protect society, since it is doubtful he would commit any further offenses. However, jail sentences serve other interests which make its imposition mandatory herein. First, it will serve as a general deterrent to others. This is not cruel and unusual punishment; it serves a valid governmental interest and has been recognized for centuries. Next, it is necessary, based on the seriousness of the crime. There is no reason not to jail Bergman (D) for an offense others are being incarcerated for. This would depreciate the seriousness of the offense. The fact that other alternatives exist, such as public work, would not be a punishment for the offense. Bergman's (D) age and health are merely factors in determining the length of the term. We are not bowing to public pressures, and the embarrassment Bergman (D) has already suffered is immaterial.

EDITOR'S ANALYSIS: Generally, the maximum sentence is fixed by law. The judge has almost absolute discretion in fixing any sentence he chooses up to and including the maximum fixed by statute. Some offenses may require a mandatory jail term. For example, California requires mandatory jail time for the second drunk driving conviction within a five-year period. Claims that the wide variance in discretion is cruel and unusual punishment have been rejected except for crimes involving the death penalty.

NOTES:

STATE v. CHANEY
Alaska Sup. Ct. (1970) 447 P.2d 441.

NATURE OF CASE: Petition seeking disapproval of sentence imposed upon convictions of rape and robbery.

FACT SUMMARY: Chaney (D), convicted of rape and robbery, was sentenced to one year in prison, a sentence the prosecution considered too lenient.

CONCISE RULE OF LAW: A criminal sentence should be sufficiently harsh so as to effectuate the societal purposes of incarceration.

FACTS: Chaney (D) was convicted of forcible rape and robbery. Although he argued consent, the jury convicted him. Following the conviction, the court imposed a one-year sentence, further commenting that an early parole would be appropriate. The state filed a petition seeking disapproval of the sentence by the state Supreme Court. (Under Alaska rules, the sentence once made could not be enhanced, but the Supreme Court could approve or disapprove of a sentence, as a guide to future prosecutions.)

ISSUE: Should a criminal sentence be sufficiently harsh so as to effectuate the societal purposes of incarceration?

HOLDING AND DECISION: (J. Rabinowitz) Yes. A criminal sentence should be sufficiently harsh so as to effectuate the societal purposes of incarceration. Incarceration exists for the purposes of rehabilitation, public safety, and deterrence. If a criminal sentence fails to promote these objectives, incarceration is purposeless. Here, the sentence imposed was very light, and the court-mentioned possibility of early parole further weakened the sentence. It is not hard to envision that, in the future, a would-be perpetrator of similar offenses would decide that the potential benefits of the unacceptable behavior outweigh the risks of such a light sentence. This being so, the purposes of incarceration are not being promoted here. Sentence disapproved.

EDITOR'S ANALYSIS: The primary purpose served by incarceration has shifted over the years. Originally, the primary purpose was punishment/deterrence. Towards the middle of the twentieth century, rehabilitation became the principal objective. In the last decade, punishment has again asserted a pre-eminent place in sentencing standards.

NOTES:

BOWERS v. HARDWICK
U.S. Sup. Ct. (1986) 478 U.S. 186.

NATURE OF CASE: Appeal from invalidation of a sodomy statute.

FACT SUMMARY: The Court of Appeals held a state statute prohibiting private sexual conduct of a particular type was invalid.

CONCISE RULE OF LAW: There is no fundamental constitutional right to engage in homosexual acts.

FACTS: Georgia (P) enacted a statute prohibiting sodomy. Hardwick (D) sued to invalidate the statute on the basis that he had a fundamental due process right to engage in private consensual homosexual activities including sodomy. The trial court upheld the statute, and the Court of Appeals reversed. The Supreme Court granted certiorari.

ISSUE: Is there a fundamental constitutional right to engage in homosexual acts?

HOLDING AND DECISION: (J. White) No. There is no fundamental constitutional right to engage in homosexual acts. Sodomy has long been the subject of criminal statutes and is well-rooted in the common law. There is no basis to expand the list of protected groups to include homosexuals. Nothing in the Constitution suggests this specifically or by implication. Thus, the statute was valid. Reversed.

CONCURRENCE: (C.J. Burger) History requires the result in this case.

DISSENT: (J. Blackmun) The right to be left alone is fundamental and must be protected.

EDITOR'S ANALYSIS: While the sexual rights of individuals have been expanded greatly, there is still a reluctance to announce a general legal right to sexual freedom. Consensual acts have been legalized in many states, yet some statutes such as the one in this case still survive. Often the law treads in essentially moral areas, giving rise to difficult decisions. Justice Blackmun's dissent has been widely praised for its cogent arguments upholding the view of the Court of Appeals.

NOTES:

MARTIN v. STATE

ALABAMA CT. OF APPLS., 1944. 31 Ala. App. 334, 17 So. 2d 427.

NATURE OF CASE: Appeal of a conviction for drunkenness on a public highway.

FACT SUMMARY: Martin (D), after being arrested at his home, was taken by officers on to the highway, where he manifested a drunken condition.

CONCISE RULE OF LAW: Criminal liability must be based on conduct which includes a voluntary act or omission to act which it was physically possible to have performed.

FACTS: Martin (D), who was convicted of being drunk on a public highway, was arrested at his home by officers who then took him on to the highway, where he allegedly used loud and profane language and otherwise manifested a drunken condition. He was charged with violation of a statute which proscribed such acts in a public place where more than one person is present.

ISSUE: Did Martin's (D) conduct include a voluntary act or omission to act which it was physically possible to have performed?

HOLDING AND DECISION: (J. Simpson) No. The statute presupposes that the violator voluntarily appears drunk in public. Being involuntarily and forcibly brought into a public place when drunk by an arresting officer is not a voluntary breach of the law and is not punishable.

EDITOR'S ANALYSIS: This case introduces the concept of actus reus, wrongful conduct. For conduct to be wrongful, it must either be a voluntary act or omission to act. This in itself is not sufficient to establish liability, but is an essential element for liability to arise. The law rests on the supposition that only voluntary acts or omissions are punishable, and while involuntary acts may be threatening, they are not of such nature so as to require correction by the penal system.

NOTES:

PEOPLE v. NEWTON
CA.DIST.CT.OF APPLS., 1970.8 Cal.App.2d 559, 87 Cal. Rptr.394.

NOTES:

NATURE OF CASE: Appeal from a conviction for voluntary manslaughter.

FACT SUMMARY: Newton (D), involved in an altercation with a police officer following his arrest, was shot and possibly acted unconsciously in shooting the officer while in a state of shock resulting from his (Newton's [D]) gunshot wound.

CONCISE RULE OF LAW: Criminal liability must be based on conduct which includes a voluntary act or omission to act which it was physically possible to have performed.

FACTS: Huey P. Newton (D) was charged with murder and convicted of voluntary manslaughter in the death of Officer Frey. Newton (D), after being arrested by Frey, became involved in a struggle with him for the officer's gun. Newton (D) was shot in the midsection but managed to grab the gun and fire several point-blank shots into Frey, who was killed. Newton (D) testified that he basically remembered nothing that occurred after he was shot except for some events at an emergency hospital where he sought treatment until recovering full consciousness at a second hospital. Expert medical testimony established that a profound reflex shock reaction would very likely result from a gunshot wound to a body cavity and could last up to a half hour.

ISSUE: Was it error to fail to instruct the jury on the matter of unconsciousness as a defense to the charge of criminal homicide?

HOLDING AND DECISION: (J. Rattigan) Yes. Where not self-induced, unconsciousness is a complete defense to a charge of criminal homicide. Unconsciousness need not be a state commonly associated with the term, i.e., coma, but can apply where the subject can act physically but is not, in fact, aware of this act at the time of acting. An instruction to that effect can arise upon an inference of unconsciousness arising out of only the actor's own testimony that he did not recall the events. As the failure to so instruct the jury did not result from invited error, i.e., a deliberate tactical purpose by Newton's (D) counsel not to have an instruction regarding unconsciousness, the judgment must be reversed.

EDITOR'S ANALYSIS: Actus reus, wrongful conduct, does not include an involuntary act. An act can be involuntary when either one is forced to do something against his will or is not consciously aware of his act. Thus, an act which is a reflex, spasm, or convulsion, or even sleepwalking, would not be conscious, and hence, not voluntary. But an involuntary act does not include such acts where the doer simply cannot remember it or because he could not control his impulse to do it.

R

Exception

STATE ex rel. POPE v. SUPERIOR COURT
Sup. Ct. of Ariz.
113 Ariz. 22, 545 P.2d 946 (1976).

NATURE OF CASE: Special action requesting reconsideration of rules of evidence in rape cases.

FACT SUMMARY: Pope (P) asked the Arizona Supreme Court to reconsider existing law regarding the admissibility in rape prosecutions of evidence as to the prosecutrix's unchaste character.

CONCISE RULE OF LAW: With limited exceptions, the general rule is that evidence as to the unchaste character of the prosecutrix is not admissible in a rape prosecution.

FACTS: Pope (P), the County Attorney of Mohave County, brought a special action in which he requested that the Supreme Court of Arizona reconsider existing law regarding the admissibility of evidence of the prosecutrix's unchaste character in rape prosecutions.

ISSUE: In general, is evidence regarding the unchaste character of the prosecutrix admissible in prosecutions for forcible rape?

HOLDING AND ISSUE: (J. Gordon) No. While the court follows the notion that such evidence is generally inadmissible, almost every jurisdiction permits the substantive use of evidence concerning the unchastity of a prosecutrix where the defense of consent is raised in a forcible rape prosecution. A majority of states limit the scope of this character evidence to a showing of the general reputation of the prosecutrix for unchastity, but a minority also allow the presentation to extend to specific prior acts of unchastity. This court feels that such evidence is generally inadmissible, but that there are exceptions where such evidence is sufficient probative to compel its admission despite its inflammatory affect, e.g. where the prosecution offers evidence of the prosecutrix's chastity; where the defendant alleges the prosecutrix actually consented to an act of prostitution (making her prior acts of prostitution relevant); or where the defense is attempting to show the prosecutrix has made unsubstantiated charges of rape in the past. When it is urged that such evidence is admissible under one of these exceptions, a hearing should be held by the court outside the presence of the jury, prior to the presentation of the evidence. If the evidence proffered falls within an exception, the court should allow its admission if it is not too remote and appears credible.

CONCURRENCE: (J. Hays) I do not believe that there should be any exception to the general rule that evidence of the prosecutrix's unchaste character is inadmissible. Reputation evidence is questionable at best and should not be given special standing in the limited field of rape.

EDITOR'S ANALYSIS: A recent development in this area of the law is the enactment of "victim shield laws" in many jurisdictions. They put limits on the admissibility of evidence regarding the prosecutrix's past sexual behavior. Some are rather restrictive, but others provide for exceptions to the general rule of inadmissibility.

JONES v. UNITED STATES

U.S. CT. OF APPLS., D.C. Cir., 1962, 308 F, 2d 307.

NOTES:

NATURE OF CASE: Appeal from conviction for involuntary manslaughter.

FACT SUMMARY: Jones was found guilty of the involuntary manslaughter of Green, a 10-month old baby belonging to Shirley Green, who placed her baby in Jones' (D) care.

CONCISE RULE OF LAW: Under some circumstances, the omission of a legal duty owed by one individual to another, where such omission results in the death of the one to whom the duty is owing, will make the other chargeable with manslaughter.

FACTS: Anthony Green, the 10-month-old illegitimate child of Shirley Green, was placed in the care of Jones (D), a family friend. The baby died of neglect and malnutrition. Jones (D) was convicted of involuntary manslaughter. There was a conflict in the evidence over whether Jones (D) was paid to take care of the baby. Medical evidence clearly showed the baby to have been shockingly neglected. Jones (D) had ample means to provide food and medical care. Jones (D) took exception to the trial court's failure to instruct the jury that it must find beyond a reasonable doubt, as an element of the crime, that she was under a legal duty to provide for the baby.

ISSUE: Will omission of a legal duty owed by one individual to another, where such omission results in the death of the one to whom the duty is owing, make the other chargeable with manslaughter?

HOLDING AND DECISION: (J. Wright) Yes. The omission of a legal duty owed by one individual to another, where such omission results in the death of the one to whom the duty is owing, will make the other chargeable with manslaughter. The duty must be imposed by law or contract. The omission must be the immediate cause of death. Breach of a legal duty can arise in four situations: (1) where a statute imposes the duty; (2) where one is in a certain status relationship to another; (3) where one has assumed a contractual duty to care for another; and (4) where one has voluntarily assumed the care of another. Whether Jones (D) fits any of those four situations is a question for the jury. Evidence was in conflict particularly on the third and fourth situations. Failure to instruct the jury on a critical element of the crime requires a reversal of the conviction with the matter to be remanded for a new trial.

EDITOR'S ANALYSIS: A tentative draft of the Model Penal Code dealing with the issue confronted in the instant case states, "Liability for the commission of an offense may not be based on an omission unaccompanied by action unless: (a) the omission is expressly made sufficient by the law defining the offense; or (b) a duty to perform the omitted act is otherwise imposed by law, M.P.C., Tent. Draft No. 4 (1955), Section 2.01 (3). Here, whether there was a duty was an element of the crime. Failure to find beyond a reasonable doubt on any element of a crime prohibits a conviction. Note that the duty must be legal, not merely moral.

Case R applied by jury

Proposed R

General principle of Crim law, for most cases.

13

BARBER v. SUPERIOR COURT

Cal. Dist. Ct. of Appeal (1983) 147 Cal.App. 3d 1006, 195 Cal. Rptr. 484.

NATURE OF CASE: Appeal from reinstatement of dismissal of murder charges.

NOTES:

FACT SUMMARY: When Clarence Herbert, permanently comatose following surgery, was taken off of artificial respiration and nutrition, leading to death, Barber (D), his physician, was charged with murder.

CONCISE RULE OF LAW: Absent objection from the spouse of one permanently comatose, a doctor is under no legal duty to keep the patient alive through forced respiration and nutrition.

FACTS: Clarence Herbert underwent surgery following a heart attack and lapsed into a coma from which medical authorities gave virtually no chance of his recovering. He was not completely brain-dead. His family expressed a desire that he be taken off all life support equipment, including nutrition. This was done, and Herbert died. The Government (P) then charged Barber (D), the attending physician, with murder. The complaint was dismissed, and then reinstated. Barber (D) appealed.

ISSUE: Absent objection from the spouse of one permanently comatose, is a doctor under a legal duty to keep the patient alive through forced respiration and nutrition?

HOLDING AND DECISION: (J. Compton) No. Absent objection from the spouse of one permanently comatose, a doctor is under no legal duty to keep the patient alive through forced respiration and nutrition. As Herbert was not clinically dead at the time support was withdrawn, the court must decide whether such withdrawal was unlawful. The best way to analyze this is in terms of a benefits versus burdens analysis. Where there is a reasonable chance of recovery, the benefits outweigh the burdens. Where, as here, there is no such chance, extraordinary measures confer no such benefit. Both respiration and nutrition are medical procedures that can be classified as extraordinary support. Thus, a doctor may, without objection from the patient's survivor, cease such support. Reversed.

EDITOR'S ANALYSIS: The issue here has been grappled with by courts for some time, and they have understandably had difficulty with it. Criminal law was developed in times when such situations were unthinkable. This area is appropriate for legislative action, but as yet there has been little.

REGINA v. CUNNINGHAM
CT.OF CRIM.APP.,1957. 41 Crim.App.R.155, (1957) 3 week. L.R. 76.

NOTES:

NATURE OF CASE: Appeal from conviction for unlawfully and maliciously injuring another person.

FACT SUMMARY: Cunningham (D) intentionally stole a gas meter out of a house. A woman in the house was made ill by the escaping gas.

CONCISE RULE OF LAW: "Malice" in a statutory crime means foresight of the consequences and requires either an actual intention to do the particular kind of harm that in fact was done or recklessness as to whether such harm should occur or not.

Def.
Elements

FACTS: Cunningham (D) wrenched a gas meter from the pipes and stole it. He had not turned off the gas, and escaping gas seeped into Wade's bedroom, injuring her and endangering her life.

ISSUE: Can a defendant be said to have maliciously done some harm where he did not intend to do the particular kind of harm done or did not foresee that the particular harm might be done?

HOLDING AND DECISION: (J. Byrne) No. The word "maliciously" in a statutory crime postulates foresight of the consequences. It requires either an actual intention to do the particular kind of harm that, in fact, was done or recklessness as to whether such harm should occur or not, as where the accused foresees that the particular kind of harm might be done and yet goes on to take the risk of it. Malice is neither limited to nor does it require any ill will towards the person injured. Nor does the word mean wicked. In this case, the fact that Cunningham (D) acted unlawfully or wickedly in stealing the gas meter does not mean that he acted maliciously in causing Wade's injury. It should have been left to the jury to decide whether Cunningham (D) foresaw that the removal of the meter might cause injury to someone. His conviction is reversed.

Def. continued

→ *No crime—since elements not fulfilled.*

→ *Jury Issue*

EDITOR'S ANALYSIS: An intention to cause one type of crime cannot serve as a substitute for the required intention in another type of crime. Hence, where a defendant throws a rock with an intent to hit another and misses, unintentionally breaking a window, he is not guilty of malicious destruction of property. Likewise, where a defendant intending to steal rum from a ship, lights a match in order to see, thereby causing a fire which destroys the ship, he is not guilty of intent-to-burn arson. However, such defendants might be convicted on the basis of having acted recklessly or negligently. As these cases demonstrate, the transferred intent doctrine is applicable only within the limits of the same crime. *NOTE*

→ *Unlike in tort, there is no transferability of intent between crimes, because the elements of each differ (different) So, one should pursue the crime which occurred according to the relevant elements, and seek relief for related damages w/a civil/torts action.*

See p. 227

REGINA v. PRINCE

Ct. of Cr.Cas.Res. L.R. 2 Cr.Cas.Res. 154 (1875).

NATURE OF CASE: Appeal from a misdemeanor conviction.

FACT SUMMARY: Prince (D), who was under the reasonable belief that Annie Phillips was 18, was convicted of violating a law making it a misdemeanor for anyone to lawfully take or cause to be taken an unmarried girl under age 16 out of the possession and against the will of her father.

CONCISE RULE OF LAW: A reasonable but mistaken belief that the girl was 16 or older is not a defense against a charge that one violated the law which makes it a misdemeanor to unlawfully take any unmarried girl under age 16 out of the possession and against the will of her father.

FACTS: At the time Prince (D) took young Annie Phillips away, he was under the reasonable belief that she was 18 years old - which is what she had told him. Actually, she was only 14. Prince (D) was convicted of violating the law which made it a misdemeanor for anyone to "unlawfully take or cause to be taken any unmarried girl, being under the age of 16 years, out of the possession and against the will of her father or mother, or of any person having the lawful care or charge of her."

ISSUE: Is the reasonable but mistaken belief that the girl was 16 or older a defense against the charge that one violated a law making it a misdemeanor to unlawfully take any unmarried girl under 16 out of the possession and against the will of her father?

HOLDING AND DECISION: (J. Denman) No. The fact that one was under the reasonable but mistaken belief that the girl was at least 16 is not a defense against the charge that one violated the law making it a misdemeanor to unlawfully take any unmarried girl under 16 out of the possession and against the will of her father. The conviction must stand. Affirmed.

CONCURRENCE: (Branwell, B.) What the defendant would have us do is read into the statute in question language requiring that a person not believe the girl he takes is over 16 years of age when he takes her. These words are not there, and the question is, whether we are bound to construe the statute as though they were, on account of the rule that the mens rea is necessary to make an act a crime. It is my opinion that we are not. The legislature has enacted that if anyone does a particular wrongful act— i.e., takes a female of such tender years that she is properly called a girl, can be said to be in another's possession, and in the other's care or charge—he does it at the risk of her turning out to be under 16. This position gives full scope to the doctrine of mens rea. The defendant can be convicted of violating this law despite the fact that he was under the reasonable belief the girl he took was over 16; the doctrine of mens rea is not threatened or controverted, because the defendant has done the act forbidden— an act wrong in itself. I do not say illegal, but wrong. If the taker believed he had the father's consent, though wrongly, he would have no mens rea; so if he did not know she was in anyone's possession, nor in the charge or care of anyone. In those cases, unlike the one at bar, he would not know he was doing the act forbidden by that statute—an act which, if he knew she was in the possession and in the care or charge of anyone, he would know

was a crime or not, according as she was under 16 or not. He would not know he was doing an act wrong in itself, whatever was his intention, if done without lawful cause. It seems to me impossible to say that where a person takes a girl out of her father's possession, not knowing whether she is or is not under 16, that he is not guilty; and equally impossible when be believes, but erroneously, that she is old enough for him to do a wrong act with safety. Affirmed.

DISSENT: (Brett, J.) There can be no conviction for crime in England in the absence of a criminal mind or mens rea. The maxim as to mens rea applies whenever the facts which are present in the prisoner's mind, and which he has reasonable ground to believe, and does believe to be the facts, would, if true, make his act no criminal offence at all. I come to the conclusion that a mistake of facts on reasonable grounds, to the extent that if the facts were as believed the acts of the prisoner would make him guilty of no criminal offence at all, is an excuse, and that such excuse is implied in every criminal charge and every criminal enactment in England.

EDITOR'S ANALYSIS: Many defendants have attempted to defeat statutory rape charges by claiming as a defense their erroneous belief that the "victim" was over the designated age of consent. The still-predominant view is that such a mistake is no defense (even if reasonable) - that one simply runs a risk of engaging in sexual activity with a young person, that that person will turn out to be below the age of consent. This is much the same attitude expressed in the Prince case. Some courts have, however, recognized such a defense to statutory rape charges - if the mistakes as to the "victim's" age was reasonable. Under the provisions of the Model Penal Code, such reasonable belief is not an affirmative defense where, as Professor Kadish explains, criminality turns on the child's being below the age of 10, but where the critical age is higher. Some jurisdictions have adopted this approach in their codes.

NOTES:

PEOPLE v. OLSEN
Cal.Sup.Ct. (1984) 36 Cal.3d 638, 685 P.2d 52.

NATURE OF CASE: Appeal from conviction for committing a lewd act on child under 14.

FACT SUMMARY: Olsen (D) was convicted of committing a lewd act on a child under 14 years of age whom he believed to be, and who looked, older.

CONCISE RULE OF LAW: A reasonable mistake as to the victim's age is not a defense to a charge of committing a lewd act on a child under 14 years of age.

FACTS: While exactly what happened was in dispute, Olsen (D) at some point had sexual intercourse with a girl just under 14. She had told Olsen (D) she was over 16, and she looked it. Olsen (D) was charged with a violation of Penal Code §288(a), committing a lewd act on a child under 14, which carried a greater penalty than statutory rape. The court rejected his defense of reasonable mistake as to age, and the Court of Appeals affirmed.

ISSUE: Is a reasonable mistake as to the victim's age a defense to a charge of committing a lewd act on a child under 14 years of age?

HOLDING AND DECISION: (C.J. Bird) No. A reasonable mistake as to the victim's age is not a defense to the charge of committing a lewd act on a child under 14 years of age. While statutory rape is not a strict liability offense in California, the law has always recognized a special need to protect its younger children. The fact that this offense carries a greater maximum penalty than statutory rape demonstrates this. Also, the fact that the code provides that reasonable mistake as to age can be a basis for probation rather than incarceration demonstrates that the legislature did not want reasonable mistake to be a defense. Affirmed.

DISSENT AND CONCURRENCE: (J. Grodin) Strict liability offenses in all traditional crimes should be abolished.

EDITOR'S ANALYSIS: California is one of a handful of jurisdictions that make statutory rape a non-strict liability offense. A reasonable belief as to the minor's majority is a viable defense. Most jurisdictions, in imposing strict liability, have made the policy judgment that the protection of its children is so grave a matter as to justify this harsh rule.

UNITED STATES v. FEOLA
U.S. Sup. Ct. (1975) 420 U.S. 672.

NATURE OF CASE: Appeal from conviction for conspiracy to assault a federal officer.

FACT SUMMARY: Feola (D) was convicted of conspiracy to assault a federal officer when he had not known of the victim's official status.

CONCISE RULE OF LAW: Knowledge that the intended victim is a federal officer is not a requisite for conspiracy to assault a federal officer.

FACTS: Feola (D) and several others ostensibly entered into a drug deal with undercover federal officers. In actuality, they intended to assault and rob the putative drug buyers. When they attempted to carry out their plan, they were arrested by the officers. They were convicted of conspiracy to violate 18 U.S.C. § 111, which proscribed assault upon federal officers. Feola (D) appealed, contending that he had not known that the would-be victims were federal officers. The Court of Appeals reversed. The Supreme Court granted review.

ISSUE: Is knowledge that the intended victim is a federal officer a requisite for conspiracy to assault a federal officer?

HOLDING AND DECISION: (J. Blackmun) No. Knowledge that the intended victim is a federal officer is not a requisite for conspiracy to assault a federal officer. If all Congress wished to protect by virtue of the law were federal functions, then knowledge of the victim's official status would be a proper element of the offense. If Congress wished to protect federal officers, however, this scienter requirement would frustrate the statute's purpose. The legislative history indicates that Congress intended to protect federal officers as well as federal functions, so the scienter requirement should not be read into the statute. Reversed.

DISSENT: (J. Stewart) It is more blameworthy to assault one known to be an officer than one not so known, and in the absence of a clear congressional intent to provide otherwise, the former should be more heavily sanctioned.

EDITOR'S ANALYSIS: Had the scienter requirement been accepted by the Court, a certain asymmetry would have been created. Assault upon a federal officer does not require knowledge of the victim's official status. The decision here kept the mental state requirements the same as between the substantive offense and conspiracy thereto.

NOTES:

REGINA v. MORGAN
House of Lords (1976) A.C. 182.

NATURE OF CASE: Appeal from rape for conviction.

FACT SUMMARY: The appellants contended that their mistaken belief in Mrs. Morgan's consent to sexual intercourse shielded them from criminal culpability of rape.

CONCISE RULE OF LAW: A defendant may not be convicted of rape if he believed that the woman consented, even if such belief was unreasonable.

FACTS: Morgan (D) invited three males back to his house to have sexual intercourse with his wife. Morgan (D) told the three individuals that although his wife may protest, she in fact would want them to have sexual intercourse with her. The four arrived at the Morgan home and engaged in forcible sexual intercourse with Morgan's (D) wife, over her objections. The four were arrested and charged with conspiracy and rape. The three male defendants argued that based upon Morgan's (D) representations they believed that Mrs. Morgan consented to the sexual intercourse, therefore they did not have the sufficient state of mind to commit the crime of rape. All four were convicted and appealed. The trial court certified the question whether or not an unreasonable belief that consent existed will abrogate a rape conviction.

[handwritten note: H set conditions that would be fulfilled, causing D's to think their actions were actually w/out consent. This prevented the ct. from finding mens rea of intent]

ISSUE: Does an unreasonable belief in the consent to sexual intercourse shield a defendant from a rape conviction?

HOLDING AND DECISION: (Lord Hailshim) Yes. Any belief in the victim's consent to sexual intercourse shields a defendant from a rape conviction. The crime of rape involves the intent to have unconsented sexual intercourse. The question to be determined is whether or not consent existed. Whether such belief was reasonable or not is not the appropriate question. The question for the prosecution to prove to the jury is whether or not the consent existed. In this case, it is clear from the facts that consent was in existence, therefore the requisite state of mind was not present. The rape convictions must stand, however, based upon procedural grounds.

CONCURRENCE: (Lord Fraser): While the majority of the court is correct in that a belief in the consent of the victim is sufficient to negate the requisite intent to commit the crime of rape, whether or not such belief is reasonable or not is irrelevant to the discussion. However, based upon the procedural requirements of the Criminal Appeal Act of 1968, the appeal should have been refused.

EDITOR'S ANALYSIS: The Morgan decision understandably evoked a considerable amount of controversy after it came down. It essentially changed the law, in that previously it was felt that only a reasonable belief in the consent of the victim would abrogate a rape conviction. However, analyzing the case strictly on a mens rea basis, the court came to what it felt was a logical conclusion that the requisite intent was not present. The severe penalties for rape militated against the wide application of a reasonableness test.

[handwritten note: U.S. Presently, in some juris, consent will negate intent only if it is reasonable. In other juris, consent does not negate intent, which must be found from the circumstances]

COMMONWEALTH v. SHERRY
Mass. Sup Jud. Ct. (1982) 386 Mass. 682, 437 N.E.2d 224.

NATURE OF CASE: Appeal of rape conviction.

FACT SUMMARY: Sherry (D), charged with rape, argued that he had believed the victim to have consented to intercourse.

CONCISE RULE OF LAW: A subjective belief that the victim has consented is no defense to a rape charge. → *Opposite to 66!*

FACTS: Sherry (D) and two male companions left a party with a woman. Whether she left voluntarily or was coerced was unclear. When the four arrived at the home of one of the men, they smoked marijuana and conversed for a while. Eventually the woman had intercourse with the three men, sequentially. The woman pressed charges, and the three were charged with rape. Sherry (D) and the other two defendants claimed that the woman had consented. The court refused to offer an instruction permitting a subjective belief in consent to be a defense. Sherry (D) et al. were convicted and appealed.

ISSUE: Is a subjective belief that the victim has consented a defense to a rape charge?

HOLDING AND DECISION: (J. Liacos) No. A subjective belief that the victim has consented is not a defense to a rape charge. It has never been held that the subjective mindset of an alleged perpetrator was crucial in passing upon consent; the prosecution would have a serious burden of proof were this so. Rather, it is proper for the jury to consider the entire sequence of events from an objective perspective. Here, the instruction the court gave did in fact create an objective standard, and this was proper. Affirmed.

EDITOR'S ANALYSIS: There is no uniform rule on this issue among the jurisdictions. A fully subjective approach is found in few, if any jurisdictions. Some permit a good-faith-belief-in-consent defense, but those that do require the good faith belief to be reasonable.

NOTES:

PEOPLE v. MARRERO
N.Y. Ct. of App. (1987) 69 N.Y.2d 382, 507 N.E.2d 1068.

NATURE OF CASE: Appeal of conviction for illegal firearms possession.

NOTES:

FACT SUMMARY: Marrero (D), charged with illegal firearms possession, argued that he mistakenly believed himself to be exempt from the ambit of the statute proscribing possession.

CONCISE RULE OF LAW: A good faith mistaken belief as to the meaning of a criminal statute is no defense to a violation of the statute.

FACTS: Marrero (D) was a corrections officer in a federal prison. He was found to be carrying a handgun in public and was charged with violating a statute criminalizing such possession. He argued that he mistakenly believed that a subdivision exempting state correctional officers also applied to him. He was convicted, and the appellate division affirmed. He appealed.

ISSUE: Is a good faith mistaken belief as to the meaning of a criminal statute a defense to a violation of the statute?

HOLDING AND DECISION: (J. Bellacosa) No. A good faith mistaken belief as to the meaning of a criminal statute is no defense to a violation of the statute. To admit the excuse of ignorance of law would work to encourage ignorance when policy should favor knowledge. While this rule will no doubt result in occasional unfair outcomes, the larger societal interest in promoting knowledge of the law is more important. Here, Marrero (D) was ignorant of the law, and this will not excuse him. Affirmed.

DISSENT: (J. Hancock) The ancient rule that "ignorance of the law is no excuse" may have been proper in times when almost all laws proscribed conduct *malum in se*. Today, however, a vast array of laws prohibit conduct only *malum prohibitum*, and an arbitrary rule disallowing a good faith mistake defense is unfair.

EDITOR'S ANALYSIS: "Ignorance of the law is no excuse" is something of a cliché and is generally true. It is not universal, however. The Model Penal Code rule, accepted in numerous jurisdictions, permits the defense when mistake negates the purpose or belief necessary to establish a material element.

LIPAROTA v. UNITED STATES
471 U.S. 419.

NATURE OF CASE: Appeal from conviction for violating food stamp regulations.

FACT SUMMARY: Liparota (D) illegally purchased food stamps without realizing the illegality of the act.

CONCISE RULE OF LAW: To convict an individual for violating food stamp regulations requires the government to prove that the accused was aware that the conduct was illegal.

FACTS: Liparota (D), a restaurant owner, made several purchases of food stamps from an undercover government agent. He was charged with a violation of 7 U.S.C. 2024(b), which proscribed the knowing acquisition of food stamps in an unauthorized manner. The trial court held that "knowing" only meant that the accused knew what he was doing. The trial court rejected Liparota's (D) contention that the statute required knowledge by the accused that he was breaking the law. Liparota (D) was convicted, and the Court of Appeals affirmed.

ISSUE: To convict an individual for violating food stamp regulations, must the government prove that the accused was aware that the conduct was illegal?

HOLDING AND DECISION: (J. Brennan) Yes. To convict an individual for food stamp regulation violations, the government must prove that the accused was aware that the conduct was illegal. The normal rule in criminal cases is that all crimes, other than certain regulatory offenses, must involve a knowledge, either actual or constructive, of the illegality of one's act. Strict liability offenses tend to be either ones with mild punishment or involve acts which are obviously illegal. The offense here can lead to incarceration, no mild punishment. Unlike some strict liability offenses, such as violations of gun registration laws or pure drug laws, the violation here was not so obviously illegal as to charge the accused with knowledge of the law. Thus, in the absence of an explicit provision in the statute making the offense strict liability, the Court will not impute one. Reversed.

DISSENT: (J. White) The language of the statute implies that all the accused needed to know was the nature of the act he committed. The Court's opinion ignores the long-established rule that ignorance of the law is no excuse.

EDITOR'S ANALYSIS: More than any other area of law, criminal law is highly concerned with mental states. There are two basic categories of intent: general and specific. More severe crimes are generally held to require specific intent, which requires more proof, but this is not always the case.

UNITED STATES v. ALBERTINI
U.S. Ct. of App., 9th Cir. (1987) 830 F.2d 985.

NATURE OF CASE: Appeal of conviction for trespassing on restricted federal property.

FACT SUMMARY: Albertini (D), relying on a later-reversed Court of Appeals opinion, violated an order not to enter certain federal property.

CONCISE RULE OF LAW: One may rely on a later-reversed declaration that his conduct is lawful.

FACTS: Albertini (D), in defiance of a base commander order, entered a military base for the purpose of protesting. He was convicted of violating 18 U.S.C. § 1832, which prohibited trespassing onto federal property. His conviction was reversed by the Ninth Circuit. In reliance on this, he again entered the base. The Supreme Court later reversed the Ninth Circuit and reinstated the conviction. He was then convicted again, based on the subsequent entry. He appealed.

ISSUE: May one rely on a later-reversed declaration that his conduct is lawful?

HOLDING AND DECISION: (J. Goodwin) Yes. One may rely on a later-reversed declaration that his conduct is lawful. Although the ex post facto clause in the Constitution applies to the legislature and not the courts, the principle upon which it is based - the notion that persons have a right to fair warning of that conduct which may give rise to criminal liability - is fundamental to our concept of constitutional liberty. When one relies on an official pronouncement that certain conduct is lawful, he may not be prosecuted if that pronouncement is later overruled. This was precisely the case here: Albertini(D) relied on a subsequently overruled decision that legitimized his conduct. Therefore, he may not be held liable for the conduct. Reversed.

EDITOR'S ANALYSIS: Generally speaking, a mistake of law is not a defense to a conviction. This was the Government's (P) position in regards to this appeal. However, the "official pronouncement" exception to this rule is well recognized in the law.

LAMBERT v. CALIFORNIA
355 U.S. 225, 78 Sup. Ct. 240, 2 L.Ed. 2d 228.

NOTES:

NATURE OF CASE: Appeal from conviction for violation of registration statute.

FACT SUMMARY: Lambert (D) was convicted for violating a statute which required all persons who had previously been convicted of a felony to register with the police.

CONCISE RULE OF LAW: Failure to act may not be punishable under a criminal statute unless it is shown that the defendant knew or should have known of the duty established by the statute and the penalty for failure to comply with the statute.

FACTS: A city ordinance defined a convicted person as any person who has been convicted of a felony in California, or convicted of any offense in any other state which would have been punishable as a felony under California law. Another ordinance required any convicted person who stayed more than five days in Los Angeles or who had visited Los Angeles more than five times within a 30-day period, to register with the Chief of Police; failure to register was a continuing offense, with each day's failure to register treated as a separate offense. Lambert (D) was arrested on suspicion of another crime and was charged with violating the registration statute.

ISSUE: Is it a violation of due process to apply a registration statute to a person who has no knowledge of his duty to register?

HOLDING AND DECISION: (J. Douglas) Yes. It is a maxim of criminal law that ignorance of the law is no offense; but under this statute, the violation is wholly passive. Mere presence in the city is the test of violation, and there is no requirement that the convicted person have any knowledge of the registration statute. The only purpose of this ordinance was for the administrative convenience of the police. Due process requires notice of a possible offense, particularly in a situation where the mere failure to act will result in a penalty. Here, although Lambert's (D) failure to act was totally innocent, when she was informed of the existence of the statute, she was given no chance to comply with the requirement and avoid punishment. Therefore, to comply with due process, it must be shown that the defendant had actual knowledge of the duty to register, or that there was a probability of such knowledge. Otherwise, Lambert (D) cannot be punished for conduct which would have been innocent if done by other members of the community.

[handwritten margin notes: "Note specific character of violation", "DP standard", "Test of Notice per DPC"]

DISSENT: (J. Frankfurter) Many laws enacted under the police power of the state require no knowledge of the existence of the law on the part of the defendant. The majority bases its decision on a wholly untenable distinction between affirmative and passive acts.

EDITOR'S ANALYSIS: In such cases as this, which concern wholly passive acts, and in other cases which involve statutes concerning freedom of speech, the court has readily read into such statutes a requirement of knowledge of the existence of the statute or some other form of scienter.

[handwritten note: "Exceptions to the Knowledge is not required rule"]

UNITED STATES v. BARKER
U.S.Ct.App., D.C.Cir.(1976) 546 F.2d 940.

NATURE OF CASE: Appeal of federal conspiracy conviction.

FACT SUMMARY: Barker (D) and Martinez, mistakenly believing they were acting pursuant to the lawful instructions of White House aide E. Howard Hunt, burglarized the office of Daniel Ellsberg's psychiatrist.

CONCISE RULE OF LAW: The mistaken reliance of a criminal actor on a representation by a government official that he can authorize such an actor to commit an act which would otherwise be a crime is a legally cognizable "mistake of fact," which will relieve such an actor of any criminal responsibility if it "negatives the mental element" of the crime he commits thereby.

FACTS: Bernard Barker (D) and Eugenio Martinez, both former employees of the CIA, were contacted by White House aide E. Howard Hunt, their former CIA boss, in 1971 and asked to burglarize the office of Daniel Ellsberg's psychiatrist, Dr. Fielding. Since Hunt clearly worked for the White House, Barker (D) and Martinez simply accepted, as fact, his ostensible authority to authorize them to engage in such activity. Subsequently, they were tried and convicted of the burglary under 18 U.S.C. §241, for conspiracy to violate the Fourth Amendment rights of Fielding thereby. This appeal followed.

ISSUE: Should an individual be relieved of responsibility for a criminal act because it was undertaken at the request of a government official?

HOLDING AND DECISION: (J. Wilkey) Yes. The mistaken reliance of a criminal actor on a representation by a government official that he can authorize such an actor to commit an act which would otherwise be a crime is a legally cognizable "mistake of fact," which will relieve such an actor of any criminal responsibility if it "negatives the mental element" of the crime he commits thereby. As long as a mistake of fact is reasonable, it may relieve an actor of responsibility. Here, especially, when the strong policy of the law toward encouraging cooperation with officials is considered, Barker's (D) reliance on Hunt's authority should insulate him from criminal responsibility.

CONCURRENCE: (J. Merhige) Reliance on an official interpretation of the law has long been recognized as a defense.

DISSENT: (J. Leventhal) The mistake here was a mistake of law regarding Barker's (D) right to burglarize, not a mistake of fact, and no amount of judicial interpretation can alter that. Mistake of law is not a defense, except in certain very limited circumstances (e.g., in response to a call for assistance in making an arrest by a police officer). The ALI recognizes no such exception for the solicitation of felonious conduct, however, and the "official interpretation" exception is limited to far more legitimate pronouncements (e.g., search warrants). Finally, even if the broader "mistake" rule, which the court today promulgates, is adopted, it could not be responsibly claimed that Barker's (D) reliance negatives the "specific intent to violate Fielding's constitutional rights," as required by 18 U.S.C. §214.

EDITOR'S ANALYSIS: In this case, the court acts to adopt the suggestion of many writers that the traditional mistake of law (is not a defense) and mistake of fact (is a defense) rules be discarded and replaced by a rule which would make any mistake a defense if it "negatived the mental element" of a crime - i.e., prevented the formation of whatever specific intent was required as an element of the crime committed (e.g., burglary requires the specific intent to commit a felony at common law). This case also points up the major problem with the law/fact characterization dichotomy. Note that even the ALI does not escape such characterization problems, however. The ALI states that the mistake defense is unavailable if what the actor thought mistakenly he was doing was a crime. Even though Barker (D) here was "authorized" to break in, he knew that what he was doing was technically against the law.

NOTES:

MORISETTE v. UNITED STATES
SUP.CT. of the U.S., 1952. 342 U.S. 246, 72 S. Ct. 246.

NATURE OF CASE: Appeal of conviction for unlawful conversion of government property.

FACT SUMMARY: Morisette (D) converted spent Air Force shell casings, found on a military target range, into scrap metal which he sold.

CONCISE RULE OF LAW: Crimes which are mala in se (bad in themselves) necessarily include the element of mens rea and no statutory strict liability version of them is permissible.

FACTS: Morisette (D) discovered a number of spent military shell casings while deer hunting in an area marked "Danger — Keep Out — Bombing Range." Seeing them merely dumped in heaps, he thought they had been abandoned. He thereupon loaded three tons of them on a truck, took them to a farm where he flattened them with a tractor, and then finally took them to a nearby town where he sold them for scrap for $84. He was charged under a federal statute which makes knowing conversion of government property a crime. Previous decisions had pointed out the right of the government to regulate its property on a strict liability basis. As a result, when Morisette (D) attempted to prove that he had no intent to convert the scrap unlawfully because he felt it had been abandoned, his offer was refused by the trial court stating, "The question of intent is whether or not he intended to take the property." In other words, no mens rea scienter need be shown to establish felonious intent. His conviction was affirmed subsequently. Now, he appeals to the U.S. Supreme Court.

Strict liability Instruction

ISSUE: May a person be held criminally responsible on a strict liability basis for a crime which is mala in se?

HOLDING AND DECISION: (J. Jackson) No. Crimes which are mala in se (bad in themselves) necessarily include an element of mens rea and no strict liability version of them is permissible. In short, felonious intent may not be presumed from the intentional doing of the act plus the proscribed result. At common law, where all crimes were mala in se, the mens rea requirement of scienter was always necessary. This rule has been followed even where modern statutory definitions of the common law crimes have omitted mention of it. Here, conversion, as a common law crime, always included scienter as a necessary element and mere omission from the statutory definition of it does not justify its abandonment.

The underlying rationale here is that the purpose of exempting regulatory crimes from the requirements of mens rea (that no evil purpose can exist to do an act which is not evil in itself) is not served when crimes are mala in se, such as conversion. The Court also points out that the previous decisions permitting strict liability involved regulatory (mala prohibita) statutes, where such is properly applied.

EDITOR'S ANALYSIS: This case points up the general technical rationale for excluding malum in se crimes from strict liability. At common law, all such crimes had a mens rea requirement. The point here is that the statute is really a version of a common law crime. Allowing the omission of an element of the definition of a crime alters the nature of the crime and creates a new one.

NOTE

UNITED STATES v. PARK
U.S. Sup. Ct. (1975) 421 U.S. 658.

NOTES:

NATURE OF CASE: Appeal of conviction for violation of the federal Food, Drug and Cosmetic Act.

FACT SUMMARY: Park (D), president of Acme Markets, Inc. (D), was prosecuted for violations of the Food, Drug and Cosmetic Act.

CONCISE RULE OF LAW: The manager of a corporate defendant may be prosecuted under the federal Food, Drug and Cosmetic Act absent affirmative wrongdoing.

FACTS: Park (D) was president of Acme Markets, Inc. (D). FDA inspectors found substantial quantities of food warehoused by Acme (D) to be rodent-infested. Following several subsequent inspections, which demonstrated the problem to be unresolved, Acme (D) and Park (D) were charged with violations of the federal Food, Drug and Cosmetic Act. Acme (D) pleaded guilty; Park (D) was convicted. The Court of Appeals reversed, holding that a strict liability offense such as a violation of the Act required some affirmative wrongdoing. The Government (P) petitioned for certiorari.

ISSUE: May the manager of a corporate defendant be prosecuted under the federal Food, Drug and Cosmetic Act absent affirmative wrongdoing?

HOLDING AND DECISION: (C. J. Burger) Yes. The manager of a corporate defendant may be prosecuted under the federal Food, Drug and Cosmetic Act absent affirmative wrongdoing. It must be remembered that a corporation can act only through the individuals acting on its behalf. The Act imposes an affirmative duty on one providing a product within its ambit to seek out and implement measures to prevent violations of the Act. In the case of corporations, the only effective way to ensure that this occurs is to hold those responsible for a corporation's violations to the same standard as the corporation itself. This being so, the affirmative wrongdoing requirement grafted on by the Court of Appeals was improper. Reversed.

[handwritten margin note:] → Policy

[handwritten margin note:] → Rule

DISSENT: (J. Stewart) The instructions given by the District Court did not comport with the rule fashioned by the Court today. The Court's rule would impose liability only if the defendant had a position of responsibility in the corporation related to the violation. The District Court's instruction would impose liability on an individual with responsibilities in the corporation not so related.

[handwritten margin note:] unlike the DC, fed cts rule only to applies to persons related to offense by their positions not to any person in management regardless of title.

EDITOR'S ANALYSIS: The federal Food, Drug and Cosmetic Act is a 'strict liability' offense. No proof of mental state is required. This type of offense is at odds with the traditional view of criminal culpability. Nonetheless, a good portion of 'general welfare' laws impose strict liability.

STATE v. GUMINGA
Minn. Sup. Ct. (1986) 395 N.W.2d 344.

NOTES:

NATURE OF CASE: Certified question of law related to a prosecution for violation of a state liquor control statute.

FACT SUMMARY: Guminga (D), a tavern owner, was prosecuted under a statute providing vicarious criminal liability for the acts of one's employees.

CONCISE RULE OF LAW: A person may not be vicariously liable for the acts of his employees that he did not ratify.

FACTS: Guminga (D) was a tavern owner. As part of an undercover investigation, a minor ordered alcohol, and was served. The waitress was arrested for violation of a state statute making it a misdemeanor to serve liquor to minors. Guminga (D), although he did not ratify the waitress' actions, was also prosecuted. Guminga (D) contended this violated due process. The trial court certified this issue for answer by the State Supreme Court.

ISSUE: May a person be vicariously liable for the acts of his employees that he did not ratify?

HOLDING AND DECISION: (J. Yetka) No. A person may not be vicariously liable for the acts of his employees that he did not ratify. Due process analysis of a statute involves a balancing of the public interest advanced and the intrusion on personal liberty. The public interest of preventing intoxication among minors is important. However, the private interests involve loss of liberty, damage to reputation, and possible future disabilities. This is too great a burden to place on one not ratifying the proscribed conduct, particularly since there are civil remedies, such as fines or license revocation, to compel compliance. For this reason, the statute is unconstitutional.

DISSENT: (J. Kelley) The imposition of light criminal sanctions is a penalty reasonably related to achieving the strong social policy of avoiding intoxication of minors.

EDITOR'S ANALYSIS: Vicarious liability, called the doctrine of *respondeat superior,* is an accepted part of tort law. For the most part, it has also made its way into criminal jurisprudence. The analysis of the court in this instance is accepted in a minority of jurisdictions, however.

REGINA v. CITY OF SAULT STE. MARIE
Can. Sup. Ct. (1978) 85 D.L.R.3d 161.

NOTES:

NATURE OF CASE: Not stated in casebook excerpt.

FACT SUMMARY: Not stated in casebook excerpt.

CONCISE RULE OF LAW: It is a defense to charges of violating public welfare laws that the accused took reasonable steps to avoid the violation.

FACTS: Not stated in casebook excerpt.

ISSUE: Is it a defense to charges of violating public welfare laws that the accused took reasonable steps to avoid the violation?

HOLDING AND DECISION: (J. Dickson) Yes. It is a defense to charges of violating public welfare laws that the accused took reasonable steps to avoid the violation. The justifications usually given for imposing strict liability are that doing so will ensure a high standard of care, and that administrative efficiency mandates dispensing with a mental state element. However, the arguments to the contrary have greater force. First, there is no empirical evidence that strict liability results in greater care. Indeed, the possible injustice of a conviction of those who legitimately tried to comply with the law may breed cynicism and disrespect for the law. Also, it seems profoundly improper to attach the stigma of a conviction on one fault-free. While it would be too much a burden on the prosecution to require the establishment of a mens rea in these cases, it appears that justice would be served by allowing the accused to prove that he took reasonable steps to comply with the law.

EDITOR'S ANALYSIS: Canada has proven to take a less sanguine view of strict liability offenses than has its southern neighbor. In 1985, the Canadian Supreme Court held such offenses unconstitutional. The U.S. Supreme Court has been asked to do this, but has never done so.

SOLEM v. HELM
U.S. Sup. Ct. (1983) 103 S. Ct. 3001.

NATURE OF CASE: Appeal of life sentence given under a recidivist statute.

FACT SUMMARY: Helm (D) was sentenced to life imprisonment under South Dakota's recidivist statute.

CONCISE RULE OF LAW: A statute allowing for life imprisonment without parole for a series of nonviolent felonies is unconstitutional as cruel and unusual punishment.

FACTS: Helm (D) had been convicted of three burglaries, larceny, false pretenses, and drunk driving. He was then convicted of writing a bad check. Under South Dakota's recidivist statute, an individual could be sentenced to life without possibility of parole. Helm (D) was so sentenced. The South Dakota Supreme Court upheld the sentence, and Helm (D) appealed.

ISSUE: Is a statute allowing for life imprisonment without parole for a series of nonviolent felonies unconstitutional as cruel and unusual punishment?

HOLDING AND DECISION: (J. Powell) Yes. A statute allowing for life imprisonment without parole for a series of nonviolent felonies is unconstitutional as cruel and unusual punishment. A criminal sentence must be proportionate to the harm done. The standard by which the severity of punishment should be judged must be arrived at by comparing it with other punishment in both the same and different jurisdictions. Here, all the felonies were nonviolent. A review of the jurisdictions shows that the punishment here is much more severe than punishment in almost all other jurisdictions. A similar punishment in other jurisdictions generally requires much more egregious conduct. Therefore, the sentence here was excessive. Reversed.

DISSENT: (C.J. Burger) The Court completely departs from precedent. Additionally, the Court has left no standard to guide future lawmakers. Finally, the Court is mistaken in considering burglary and drunk driving as minor felonies.

EDITOR'S ANALYSIS: It is difficult to square this decision with Rummel v. Estelle 445 U.S. 263 (1980). The Court there held that a defendant could properly be sentenced to life after three nonviolent offenses. The Court said the difference was that [Rummel] did not have the "without parole" aspect, but never really explained why that was constitutionally significant.

STATE v. BAKER
Kansas Ct. of Apl. 571 P.2d 65 (1977).

NATURE OF CASE: Appeal from conviction of speed-law violation.

FACT SUMMARY: Baker (D) appealed his conviction for driving 77 miles per hour in a 55 mile per hour zone on the grounds that it was not a "voluntary" act on his part because his cruise control stuck in the "accelerate" position and caused the car to exceed the speed limit.

CONCISE RULE OF LAW: The absence of a voluntary act on the part of the defendant constitutes a defense even as to a strict liability offense.

FACTS: The trial court in which Baker (D) was convicted of going 77 miles per hour in a 55 miles per hour zone prevented him from presenting evidence that his cruise control had stuck in the "accelerate" position and had caused his car to accelerate beyond the posted speed limit before he managed to deactivate it as a defense. On appeal, Baker (D) maintained that the evidence was not offered to negate an intent or culpable state of mind on his part, since the statute makes speeding a strict liability offense, but to show that his speeding was not a voluntary act, and that there was, therefore, no criminal liability.

ISSUE: Is the absence of a voluntary act on the part of the defendant a legitimate defense as to a strict liability offense?

HOLDING AND DECISION: (J. Spencer) Yes. The absence of a voluntary act on the part of the defendant constitutes a defense even as to a strict liability offense. If Baker (D) were able to establish that his act of speeding was the result of an unforeseen occurrence or circumstance, which was not caused by him and which he could not prevent, such would constitute a valid defense to the charge. But, the evidence proffered suggests a malfunction of a device attached to the motor vehicle he was operating and over which he had or should have had absolute control. Baker (D) does not suggest that the operation of his motor vehicle on the day of his arrest was anything but a voluntary act on his part, nor that anyone other than himself activated the cruise control, which may have caused his excessive speed. Malfunction of a cruise control device to which Baker (D) voluntarily delegated partial control of his automobile is not a circumstance which would prevent his being convicted of violating the speed law. Affirmed.

EDITOR'S ANALYSIS: Baker (D) would have fared better had his brakes failed with no prior warning or his throttle unexpectly malfunctioned. Both such circumstances were found in other cases to establish that there was no covert voluntary act on the part of the defendant and thus nothing for which he could be held liable.

SHAW v. DIRECTOR OF PUBLIC PROSECUTIONS

HOUSE OF LORDS, 1961 (1962) A.C. 220.

NATURE OF CASE: Appeal of conviction for conspiracy to corrupt public morals.

FACT SUMMARY: Shaw (D) was convicted for publishing a prostitute directory.

CONCISE RULE OF LAW: Common-law courts have an inherent power to enforce the supreme and fundamental purposes of the law, regardless of the existence or non-existence of a specific statute. Where public policy demands the judicial fashioning of a particular offense to protect the public welfare, only the jury may determine whether the resultant offense is sufficiently free of uncertainty to be enforceable.

FACTS: After a statute made it impossible for prostitutes to use the streets of England for the solicitation of business, Shaw (D) decided to publish a "Ladies Directory," containing names, addresses, nude photos, and available sexual practices of individual prostitutes. He was indicted and convicted for "conspiracy to corrupt public morals." On appeal, he contends that the fact that this offense is not a statutory one makes its broad, vague proscriptions unenforceable at law.

ISSUE: May the courts proscribe and punish conduct which threatens the public welfare absent a specific statute empowering them to do so?

HOLDING AND DECISION: (Viscount Simonds) Yes. Common-law courts have an inherent power to enforce the supreme and fundamental purposes of the law, regardless of the existence or non-existence of a specific statute. Where public policy requires the judicial fashioning of a particular offense to protect the public welfare, only the jury may determine whether the resultant offense is sufficiently free of uncertainty to be enforceable. It is true that it is the responsibility of the legislature, not the courts, to make new laws. The law against conspiracies to corrupt public morals is well recognized, however. The fact that Shaw's (D) conduct here is novel, and heretofore has never been specifically addressed by any law, is irrelevant in the face of the overriding public policy requirement of preventing his immoral conduct. The court here has merely filled in a gap in the law. The appeal must be dismissed.

CONCURRENCE: (Lord Morris) One Lord points out that the jury will prevent injustice from arising out of the vagueness of the charge here by applying current community standards to their consideration of it.

DISSENT: (Lord Reid) One justice points out that the relevant conspiracy statute here does not expressly contain a proscription against the corruption of public morals. Especially in light of the sensitivity of questions involving public morals, he feels only the legislature (i.e., the House of Commons) should create laws on such questions. He would allow the appeal, accordingly.

EDITOR'S ANALYSIS: The common-law doctrine pointed up in this case (and accepted in some U.S. jurisdictions) is particularly relevant to the consideration of so-called morality of victimless crimes. Originally, the province of the ecclesiastical courts of England, such laws have now been increasingly attacked in this country as a violation of due process (i.e., void for vagueness). Notable exceptions to this trend, however, include Commonwealth v. Mochan, a 1955 Pennsylvania case, in which Mochan was convicted for making obscene telephone calls despite the lack of a relevant statute (i.e., as a crime against public morals). But note that this was not a victimless crime. Distinguish the rule in Shaw from an analogous one in many jurisdictions. That rule states that a prosecutor may proceed against a defendant for violation of a common-law crime (e.g., burglary) where the exact conduct of the defendant falls short of the requirements for a particular criminal statute.

NOTES:

3 Standards

i.
ii
iii

1) Establish a principle
2) Jury determines whether certainty of violation

KEELER v. SUPERIOR CT.
Calif. Supreme Court (1970) 2 Cal.3d 619, 470 P.2d 617.

NOTES:

NATURE OF CASE: Appeal from an information charging murder.

FACT SUMMARY: The State (P) contended Keeler (D) was guilty of murder for killing a fetus which was ultimately stillborn.

CONCISE RULE OF LAW: An unborn, viable fetus is not a human being for purposes of the murder statute.

FACTS: Keeler (D), after divorcing his wife, struck her in the abdomen, knowing she was pregnant with another man's child. The fetus was delivered stillborn with a fractured skull. Keeler (D) was charged with murder, and he moved to dismiss the information on the basis that the fetus was not a human being as defined by the murder statute. The motion was denied, and he petitioned the California Supreme Court for a writ of prohibition.

ISSUE: Is an unborn, viable fetus a human being for purposes of the murder statute?

HOLDING AND DECISION: (J. Mosk) No. An unborn, viable fetus is not a human being for purposes of the murder statute. The murder statute is of ancient origins and must be construed in light of the definition of "human being" at common law. A viable fetus was not considered a life in being at the time the statute was enacted. Thus, it would be overreaching to create a new crime on this basis. Therefore, the writ is issued.

DISSENT: (J. Burke) This opinion is based solely upon historical understanding and does not reflect reasoned thought.

EDITOR'S ANALYSIS: The vagueness of the statute as applied to the fact situation was the basic problem for the the Court here. Justice Stewart, dissenting in *Parker v. Levy*, 417 U.S. 773, 774-775 (1974), made two important points about the vagueness problem. Vague statutes fail to provide fair notice of just what conduct is prohibited. Secondly, by failing to provide explicit standards for those who enforce them, vague statutes offend due process by allowing discriminatory and arbitrary enforcement.

NASH v. UNITED STATES
SUPREME COURT OF UNITED STATES, 1912, 229 U.S. 373.

NOTES:

NATURE OF CASE: Appeal of Sherman Act conviction.

FACT SUMMARY: A Sherman Act conviction against Nash (D) involved a determination of whether his acts were prejudicial to the public interest either "by intent of the(ir) inherent nature."

CONCISE RULE OF LAW: A criminal statute is not unconstitutionally vague merely because it permits conviction to be based upon a determination by the trier of fact that the wrongdoer, in a particular case, has unreasonably calculated his conduct to be outside the proscriptions of the statute.

FACTS: Nash (D), a businessman was convicted under the Sherman Anti-Trust Act for conspiracy in restraint of trade and conspiracy to monopolize trade. By that Act, contracts or combinations are declared criminal which " . . . by reason of intent or the inherent nature of the contemplated acts," are prejudicial to the public interest (i.e., restrain or monopolize trade). On appeal, Nash (D) contends that, by permitting a jury to convict him of miscalculating the "inherent nature" of an act, the statute is unconstitutionally vague, in that it gives him no notice of what conduct it proscribed.

ISSUE: Is a criminal statute unconstitutionally vague because the trier of fact under it may be required to determine whether a particular wrongdoer's act was so unreasonable, in light of that statute, as to qualify under it as criminal?

HOLDING AND DECISION: (J. Holmes) No. A criminal statute is not unconstitutionally vague merely because it permits conviction to be based upon a determination by the trier of fact that the wrongdoer, in a particular case, has "unreasonably" calculated his conduct to be outside the proscriptions of the statute. The very meaning of the fiction of "implied malice" at common law was that a man could be forced to answer, even with his life, for consequences of his acts which he never intended. The criterion in such cases was simply whether "... common social duty would, under the circumstances, have suggested a more circumspect conduct." This social duty, though undefinable with precision, is nevertheless enforceable under the law. There is nothing constitutionally defective about allowing a jury to determine whether a particular defendant has fallen short of it. All men are on notice of it. Conviction affirmed.

EDITOR'S ANALYSIS: Justice Holmes' opinion in [Nash], supra, has served as the justification for a wide range of "negligent," "reckless," and "careless" act criminal statutes. Note how such crimes border on strict liability (i.e., no mens rea element). The Sherman Act, by focusing on the consequences of particular acts, would be a strict liability crime but for the "by reason of intent or the inherent nature" clause. Compare this case, however, with [Winters], supra p. 182. In that case, the statute involved attempted to predicate liability on a potential consequence, without giving adequate guidelines as to what acts gave rise to it. Such a statute cannot qualify even as strict liability, because of its failure to give notice.

PAPACHRISTOU v. CITY OF JACKSONVILLE
405 U.S. 156, 92 Sup.Ct. 839, 31 L.Ed. 2d 110.

NATURE OF CASE: Appeal from conviction for violation of vagrancy statute.

FACT SUMMARY: Papachristou (D) was arrested while driving in her car and charged with "prowling by auto."

CONCISE RULE OF LAW: Vagrancy statutes will be held unconstitutionally void for vagueness if they fail to give adequate notice of impermissible conduct and allow discriminatory enforcement.

FACTS: A Jacksonville ordinance, in archaic language, forbade such activities as wandering without any purpose, being a habitual loafer, frequenting places where alcohol is served and being able to work but living on the earnings of their wives. Papachristou (D) and her co-defendants were arrested while driving from a restaurant to a nightclub and charged under the statute with "prowling by auto." Other defendants were arrested while waiting on a street corner for a ride from a friend. Another defendant was charged with being a "common thief" because he was reputed to be a thief. Other defendants were arrested for loitering because they stood where the police told them not to stand, for driving at a high rate of speed, and other innocuous conduct.

ISSUE: Is the vagrancy statute, due to its broad and archaic language, a violation of the Due Process Clause?

HOLDING AND DECISION: (J. Douglas) Yes. The vagrancy statute is void for vagueness because it fails to give a person notice that his conduct is a violation of the statute and because it encourages arbitrary arrests. The statute includes perfectly innocent actions, such as walking the streets at night and being unemployed. Such activities are part of the amenities of life, and freedom of movement is necessary to an individual's feelings of independence. The statute is generalized and all-inclusive, allowing conviction for almost any kind of conduct. Also, it allows unfettered discretion on the part of the police, permitting arrest on mere suspicion of future criminal conduct. The result of the statute is to allow the arrest of poor people and nonconformists who do not correspond to the police's idea of the correct lifestyle.

EDITOR'S ANALYSIS: The Florida statute is void because it is overbroad and includes innocent activities, as well as conduct which could be punishable under a more narrowly drawn statute, within its sweep. The overbreadth is due to vagueness; the language is so imprecise that one can't conform one's conduct to the commands of the statute and allows arrest of those whose presence is a mere annoyance to the authorities. This statute is unconstitutional on its face for the reason that it provides no clear standards of prohibited conduct, allowing arbitrary enforcement, and is overbroad in that it includes constitutionally-protected activities.

STATE v. RUSK
Ct.of Apls.of Md. 289 Md. 230, 424 A.2d 720 (1981).

NATURE OF CASE: Appeal from a rape conviction.

FACT SUMMARY: Rusk's (D) second degree rape conviction was reversed by the Court of Special Appeals, which said it could not see in any of the victim's testimony "any resistance on her part to the sex acts" and "no fear as would overcome her attempt to resist or escape."

CONCISE RULE OF LAW: The lack of consent element essential to a rape conviction can be established by proof of resistance or by proof that the victim failed to resist because of a genuine, reasonably grounded fear.

FACTS: Rusk (D) was convicted of raping a 21-year-old. She testified that Rusk (D) took her car keys after she drove him at night to an unfamiliar part of the city where he lived and the "look" on his face when he told her to come up to his place scared her to the point that she complied instead of running or blowing her horn or seeking some other method of escape. She also testified that she remained seated in his apartment, even though he left the room for one to five minutes, and that she did not notice a telephone in the room. Allegedly, he pulled her by the arms to the bed and began to undress her. She admitted to removing his pants because "he asked her to do it" and to engaging in sexual activity after Rusk (D) allegedly "began to lightly choke her" in response to her starting to cry after he gave no response to her querry as to whether or not he would let her go without killing her if she did what he wanted. The Court of Special Appeals reversed his conviction, stating it did not see in any of the "victim's" testimony "any resistance on her part to the sex acts" and "no fear as would overcome her attempt to resist or escape."

ISSUE: Can one establish that the sexual act was without the consent of the victim and thus constituted rape, by showing that the victim resisted or failed to resist because of a genuine, reasonably grounded fear?

HOLDING AND DECISION: (C.J. Murphy) Yes. Lack of consent, which is an essential element of rape, is generally established through proof of resistance or by proof that the victim failed to resist because of fear. The degree of fear necessary to obviate the need to prove resistance, and thereby establish lack of consent, was defined in the following manner: "The kind of fear which would render resistance by a woman unnecessary to support a conviction of rape includes, but is not necessarily limited to, a fear of death or serious bodily harm, or a fear so extreme as to preclude resistance, or a fear which would well nigh render her mind incapable of continuing to resist, or a fear that so overpowers her that she does not dare resist." It is clear that the fear had to be genuine, but undecided whether a real but unreasonable fear of imminent death or serious bodily harm would suffice. The vast majority of jurisdictions have required that the victim's fear be reasonably grounded in order to obviate the need for either proof of actual force on the part of the assailant or physical resistance on the part of the victim. In general, that is the correct standard. Such principles notwithstanding, it seems to this court that the Court of Special Appeals was in error in this case in that it substituted its view of the evidence for that of the judge and jury. Just where persuasion ends and force begins in cases like the present is essentially a factual issue. Considering all of the evidence, with particular focus upon the actual force applied by Rusk (D) to the victim's neck, this court concludes that the jury could rationally find that the essential elements of second degree rape had been established and that Rusk (D) was guilty of that offense beyond a reasonable doubt. Conviction affirmed.

DISSENT: (J. Cole) In concluding that the reasonableness of the victim's fear was plainly a question of fact for the jury to determine, the majority has skipped over the crucial issue. It seems to me that whether the prosecutrix's fear is reasonable becomes a question only after the court determines that the defendant's conduct under the circumstances was reasonably calculated to give rise to a fear on her part to the extent that she was unable to resist. There is simply no evidence in this case to suggest that the actions taken by Rusk (D) were anything other than a pattern of conduct consistent with the ordinary seduction of a female acquaintance who at first suggests her disinclination. While the prosecutrix did claim she started to cry and that Rusk (D) "started lightly to choke" her, whatever that means it is obvious that the choking was not of any significance. There are no acts or conduct on the part of Rusk (D) to suggest that the prosecutrix's fears were created by Rusk (D) or that he made any objective, identifiable threats to her which would give rise to her failure to flee, summon help, scream, or make physical resistance. The State (P) simply failed to prove the essential element of force beyond a reasonable doubt. A prosecutrix cannot transform a seducer into a rapist by simply asserting that she was scared. While courts no longer require a female to resist to the utmost or to resist where resistance would be foolhardy, they do require her acquiescence in the act of intercourse to stem from fear generated by something of substance. A female must resist unless the defendant has objectively manifested his intent to use physical force to accomplish his purpose. The law regards rape as a crime of violence. The majority today attenuates this proposition. It declares the innocence of an at best distraught young woman. It does not demonstrate the defendant's guilt of the crime of rape.

EDITOR'S ANALYSIS: There is no jurisdiction in this country that still adheres to the stringent traditional notion that the victim must have resisted "to the utmost." In its heyday, that notion led courts to insist that the victim resist to the extent of her physical capacity and that her struggle be continued throughout the encounter. The only case in which utmost resistance was not required was when the victim was in fear of grave harm. While lack of resistance might still be used by a defendant as evidence that the victim consented, some state codes and the Model Penal Code have taken the focus off of the victim's lack of consent and placed it on the actor's use of force in compelling her to submit to intercourse by defining the crime of rape in these terms.

NOTES:

PEOPLE v. EVANS

Sup. Ct., N.Y. County, Trial Term

85 Misc. 2d 1088, 379 N.Y.S.2d 912 (1975).

NATURE OF CASE: Prosecution for rape.

FACT SUMMARY: According to Evans (D), the words his "victim" misinterpreted as a threat by him—causing her to submit to sexual intercourse—were not so intended but were part of his seduction of her.

CONCISE RULE OF LAW: A defendant is not guilty of rape if words he uses in attempting to seduce a woman are misinterpreted as a threat by her so that she acquiesces to sexual intercourse.

FACTS: Evans (D) used the ruse that he was a psychologist doing an article and conducting a sociological experiment to persuade a 20-year-old college sophomore he met at LaGuardia airport to accept a ride from him into Manhattan and to come with him to an apartment there. When she resisted his advances, he told her she had failed the experiment, pointing out she had come to a strange man's apartment and could not even be sure he was really a psychologist. He then made the statements, "I could kill you; I could rape you; I could hurt you physically." Trying another tactic, he gave her a story about how she reminded him of his lost love—who had driven her car off a cliff. Sexual intercourse took place, the girl later claiming Evans' (D) words had so frightened her that she had been afraid to resist. Evans (D) claimed he might be guilty of seduction, which was no crime, but was not guilty of rape in that he never intended to threaten her.

ISSUE: Is a defendant guilty of rape if the words he uses to seduce a woman are interpreted by her, but not meant by him, as a threat designed to "compel" her to engage in sexual intercourse without resistance?

HOLDING AND DECISION: (J. Greenfield) No. If a defendant engages in fraud, trick, or stratagem to seduce a woman, it does not become rape because the words he used to achieve his goal are interpreted by her, but not meant by him, as a threat designed to "compel" her to engage in sexual intercourse without resistance. The controlling state of mind is that of the defendant who is charged with rape. If one who is attempting a seduction utters words which are taken as a threat by the person who hears them, but are not intended as a threat by the person who utters them, there would be no basis for finding the necessary criminal intent to establish culpability under the law. Since Evans' (D) statements are susceptible to diverse interpretations, the court cannot say beyond a reasonable doubt that the guilt of Evans (D) has been established with respect to the crime of rape. The court can find neither forcible compulsion nor threat beyond a reasonable doubt -despite Evans' (D) reprehensible conduct.

EDITOR'S ANALYSIS: Some jurisdictions abandoned the common law approach, which was that seduction was not a criminal act, and made it a statutory offense. One primary difference between seduction and rape is that in seduction the woman's consent, either implied or explicit, is procured—although by artifice, deception, flattery, fraud, or promise.

PEOPLE v. LIBERTA
New York Ct. App. (1984) 64 N.Y.2d 152, 474 N.E.2d 567.

NOTES:

NATURE OF CASE: Appeal from rape conviction.

FACT SUMMARY: Liberta (D) contended the statute prohibiting rape was unconstitutional because it applied only to males.

CONCISE RULE OF LAW: A rape statute must apply equally to both sexes.

FACTS: Liberta (D) was under under court order to stay away from his wife, Denise. He violently raped her and was convicted of rape. He appealed on the basis of the marital exemption in the statute and its unconstitutional application only to conduct by males.

ISSUE: Must a rape statute apply equally to the conduct of both sexes?

HOLDING AND DECISION: (J. Wachtler) Yes. A rape statute must apply equally to both sexes. This statute renders forcible rape by males criminal. It is thus unconstitutionally underinclusive. It can be remedied by interpreting it to include female forcible rape. By doing so, instead of invalidating it *in toto*, the conviction can be, and is, affirmed.

EDITOR'S ANALYSIS: The court also struck down the marital exemption. This was originally based on protecting the chastity of and the concomitant property value of the wife to her father or husband. With the increase in domestic violence and the expansion of women's rights, this view was found to be archaic and, thus, invalid.

UNITED STATES v. WILEY
U.S.Ct. of Apls., D.C. Cir.
492 F.2d 547 (1974).

NATURE OF CASE: Appeal from a rape conviction.

FACT SUMMARY: At issue in Wiley's (D) appeal from a rape conviction was the lack of independent evidence corroborating the testimony of the "victim."

CONCISE RULE OF LAW: The District of Columbia retains a corroboration requirement for rape cases, which is met when there is independent corroborative evidence that would permit the jury to conclude beyond a reasonable doubt that the victim's account of the crime was not a fabrication.

FACTS: The lack of evidence corroborating the testimony of the prosecutrix was made an issue in Wiley's (D) appeal from a rape conviction.

ISSUE: Is there a corroboration requirement in rape cases?

HOLDING AND DECISION: Yes. The District of Columbia is among those jurisdictions which retains a corroboration requirement in rape cases. In this instance, the complainant's testimony was not adequately corroborated by independent evidence. Conviction reversed.

CONCURRENCE: (J. Bazelon) Although 35 states have rejected the corroboration requirement for rape, the District of Columbia is among those jurisdictions that has retained one. It does so in the absence of legislation, as do about half the states retaining the requirements. The precise formulation of the corroboration requirement varies enormously from state to state, ranging from a requirement of corroboration for force, penetration, and identity, to minimal corroboration of any part of the complainant's testimony. The justifications advanced for such requirements are: (1) that false charges of rape are more prevalent than false charges of other crimes, (2) that rape is a charge unusually difficult to defend against, (3) that the penalties for rape tend to be severe, and (4) that there has been a racist cast to the enforcement of rape laws. It is also said that traditional sex stereotypes have helped shape the rape laws. Separating the valid from the invalid justifications is not easy, especially since society is changing in many of its fundamental aspects. Be that as it may, for the immediate present, the flexible corroboration rule developed by this court provides the best accommodation of numerous conflicting considerations. To guard against the possible dangers of fabrication, the jurisdiction retains a corroboration rule which provides that "independent corroborative evidence will be regarded as sufficient when it would permit the jury to conclude beyond a reasonable doubt that the victim's account of the crime was not a fabrication."

EDITOR'S ANALYSIS: Specific corroboration is no longer a requirement in most American jurisdictions. It was even abandoned by the D.C. Circuit in 1977. There was no common law requirement of corroboration for any sex offense.

STATE v. DeLAWDER
Md.Ct. of Spec.Apls.
28 Md.App.212, 344 A.2d 446 (1975).

NATURE OF CASE: Action seeking postconviction relief.

FACT SUMMARY: DeLawder (D) had tried to introduce evidence of the prosecutrix's prior sexual activity with others to show she was pregnant and fabricated the rape story out of fear of her mother's reaction.

CONCISE RULE OF LAW: A defendant's constitutional right to engage in effective cross-examination is denied when he is not permitted to introduce evidence of the prosecutrix's prior sexual activities so as to establish an alleged bias, prejudice, or ulterior motive and thus attack her credibility as a witness.

FACTS: After being convicted of having carnal knowledge of a female under 14 years of age, DeLawder (D) sought postconviction relief. At his trial, he had not been permitted to introduce evidence of the "victim's" prior acts of sexual intercourse to support his contention that at the time of their alleged encounter, she was already pregnant as the result of voluntary sexual activity with others; that she feared telling her mother this, and that she therefore fabricated the story that DeLawder (D) had raped her.

ISSUE: Is it unconstitutional to deny a rape defendant the right to introduce evidence of the prosecutrix's prior sexual activities as they relate to an alleged bias, prejudice, or ulterior motive that would undermine her credibility as a witness?

HOLDING AND DECISION: (C.N. Onth) Yes. A defendant has a constitutional right to engage in effective cross-examination of the witnesses against him. That right is denied when, as here, a defendant is kept from introducing evidence or asking questions concerning the past sexual activity of the prosecutrix as they relate to an alleged bias, prejudice, or ulterior motive that would undermine her credibility as a witness. Defense counsel should have been permitted to expose to the jury the facts from which jurors, as the sole triers of fact and credibility, could appropriately draw inferences relating to the reliability of the prosecutrix as a witness. The desirability that the prosecutrix fulfill her public duty to to testify, free from embarrassment and with her reputation unblemished, must fall before the right of an accused to seek out the truth in the process of defending himself. The conviction must not be permitted to stand.

EDITOR'S ANALYSIS: A Wisconsin court did not accept the same type of argument when advanced by a defendant who sought to introduce prior sexual history to show the prosecutrix had contracted a venereal disease from others and fabricated the rape accusation because she was afraid she had infected her boyfriend [Milenovic v. State], 86 Wis.2d 272 (1978). In fact, it criticized the DeLawder court's "unwarranted assumption" that the prosecutrix's mother was unaware of her daughter's pregnancy at the time of the alleged encounter with the defendant.

GOVERNMENT OF THE VIRGIN ISLANDS v. SCUITO
U.S. Ct. of Apls., 3d Cir.
623 F.2d 869 (1980).

NATURE OF CASE: Appeal from a conviction for forcible rape.

FACT SUMMARY: Scuito (D) charged that the trial judge had abused his discretion in not ordering a psychiatric examination of the woman who claimed that Scuito (D) had forcibly raped her.

CONCISE RULE OF LAW: The decision whether or not to order a psychiatric examination of the prosecutrix in a rape case is one that is entrusted to the sound discretion of the trial judge.

FACTS: In appealing his conviction for forcible rape, Scuito (D) maintained that the trial judge abused or failed to exercise his discretion in denying his motion for a psychiatric examination of the prosecutrix. In an affadavit supporting the motion, Scuito's (D) attorney had made specific representations that community members had witnessed her "spaced out" behavior and knew she was in the habit of using controlled substances; that she had admitted at the first trial a devotion to the writings of Timothy Leary; that she habitually appeared in public in see-through top garments; and that this was all behavior indicative of a personality that fantasizes to extremes and indulges in and seeks altered states of consciousness.

ISSUE: Is it within the judge's discretion to decide whether the prosecutrix in a rape case should be ordered to undergo a psychiatric examination?

HOLDING AND DECISION: (J. Adams) Yes. The decision to order an examination of the prosecutrix in a rape case is one that has been entrusted to the sound discretion of the trial judge in light of the particular facts of each case. It is not an unbounded discretion, for there are countervailing considerations weighing heavily against such an order: it may seriously impinge on a witness' right to privacy; the trauma that attends the role of complainant to sex offense charges is sharply increased by the indignity of such an examination; it could serve as a tool of harassment; and the impact of all these considerations may well deter the victim of such a crime from lodging any complaint at all. The trial judge did not abuse his discretion or fail to exercise it in this case when, in refusing to order such an examination, he relied on the spirit of Fed.R.Evid. 412 - whose letter does not apply to the motion that was made but whose purpose was to protect rape victims from the degrading and embarrassing disclosure of intimate details about their private lives. To the extent admissible, evidence of the prosecutrix's indulging in drugs or dressing provocatively could be introduced by direct evidence rather than expert testimony of a psychiatrist. Affirmed.

EDITOR'S ANALYSIS: Wigmore has taken the extreme position that "No judge should let a sex offense charge go to the jury unless the female complainant's social history and mental makeup have been examined and testified by a qualified physician." No jurisdiction has followed his suggestion.

COMMONWEALTH v. CARROL

SUP.CT. OF PENN., 1963. 412 Pa. 525, 194 Atl.2d 911.

NATURE OF CASE: Appeal from conviction for first degree murder.

FACT SUMMARY: After prolonged arguing with his allegedly nagging and sadistic wife, Carrol (D) grabbed the loaded gun near their bed and shot her twice in the back of the head while she was lying on the bed with her back to him.

CONCISE RULE OF LAW: The specific intent to kill may be found from a defendant's words or conduct or the surrounding circumstances together with all reasonable inferences therefrom, and may be inferred from the intentional use of a deadly weapon on a vital part of another's body.

FACTS: Carrol's (D) wife suffered from mental disorders which sometimes took the form of sadistic discipline toward their children. Carrol (D) had a very good reputation among his neighbors. Carrol's (D) wife strongly objected to his work which required him to be away from home four nights of the week and asked him to put a loaded gun near their bed so she would feel safe. One night after a violent argument, while his wife lay on their bed with her back to him, Carrol (D) grabbed the gun, brought it down, and shot her twice in the back of the head. A psychiatrist testified that, in his opinion, it was an impulsive automatic reflex homicide as opposed to an intentional premeditated one. He said that his opinion was that if the gun had fallen to the floor, or if Carrol (D) had had to load the gun, he wouldn't have committed the killing. Carrol (D) contends that the crime was second, rather than first, degree murder.

ISSUE: Does evidence of a defendant's good character, together with psychiatric testimony that a homicide was not premeditated or intentional, require the court to fix the degree of guilt no higher than second degree murder?

HOLDING AND DECISION: (J. Bell) No. The specific intent to kill, necessary to a first degree murder, may be found from a defendant's words or conduct or the surrounding circumstances, together with all reasonable inferences therefrom, and may be inferred from the intentional use of a deadly weapon on a vital part of another's body. Carrol (D) urges that there was insufficient time for premeditation in light of his good reputation. He argues that, based on the rule that "No time is too short for a wicked person to frame the scheme of murder in his mind," conversely a long time is necessary to find premeditation in a "good" person. However, whether the premeditation and the killing were within a brief space of time or a long space of time is immaterial if the killing was, in fact, intentional, willful, deliberate and premeditated. As to the psychiatric testimony, a psychiatrist's opinion of a defendant's impulse or lack of intent is entitled to very little weight when a defendant's own actions or testimony or confession or the facts themselves belie the opinion, as is true in this case. The judgment below is affirmed.

EDITOR'S ANALYSIS: There is a continuing debate as to what part the space of time between the forming of an intent and a killing is to play in determining the murder degree. In [People v. Bender], 163 P.2d 8, the court reduced the judgment of first degree murder to second degree murder. The trial court had instructed the jury that no appreciable space of time need be shown to sustain a verdict of first degree murder. The State Supreme Court responded, "If an act is deliberate and premeditated, even though it is executed in the very moment it is conceived, with absolutely no appreciable time for consideration, then it is difficult to see wherein there is any field for the second degree classification...Such a slaying was never intended to be placed in the same class as murder which is truly cold-blooded or committed during arson, rape, robbery, etc., or by means of poison, lying in wait, or torture."

NOTES:

PEOPLE v. ANDERSON

SUP. CT. OF CALIF., 1968. 70 Cal.2d 15, 447 P.2d 942.

NATURE OF CASE: Appeal from a conviction for first degree murder.

FACT SUMMARY: Anderson (D) killed the ten-year-old daughter of the woman with whom he had been living for about eight months by mutilating the child with a knife, leaving about 60 wounds over the entire body.

CONCISE RULE OF LAW: A finding of premeditation and deliberation for first degree murder cannot be sustained in the absence of any evidence of (1) defendant's actions prior to the killing, (2) a "motive" or "reason from which the jury could" reasonably infer defendant's intent to kill, or (3) a manner of killing from which the jury could reasonably infer was deliberately calculated to cause death.

FACTS: Anderson (D), who had been living with the family of the deceased for about eight months, was left alone with Mrs. Hammond's daughter, Victoria, 10 years old. She was last seen alive by a classmate about 3:45 P.M. that day in front of her house. Anderson (D) had been drinking heavily the previous two days. Victoria's 10-year-old brother returned home from school about 3:30 P.M. and found nothing unusual. He left before 4:00 P.M., but while in the basement he did hear noises of objects being moved around upstairs. Mrs. Hammond returned at about 5:30 P.M. and, noticing blood on the couch, was told by Anderson (D) that Kenneth, the son, had cut himself. He had earlier told Kenneth that Victoria had cut herself. Kenneth returned at 6:30 P.M., and Mrs. Hammond, seeing that he had not cut himself, asked Kenneth to help her find Victoria whom Anderson (D) said was eating dinner at a friend's. As Kenneth passed Victoria's room, he found her bloody, nude body under boxes and blankets on the floor. Police found blood in every room but the kitchen which Anderson (D) apparently mopped. Over 60 wounds over the entire body were found including vaginal lacerations which were post mortem. Anderson's (D) blood alcohol level was high enough to meet drunk driving levels.

ISSUE: Was there evidence of premeditation and deliberation sufficient enough to support a charge of first degree murder?

HOLDING AND DECISION: (J. Tobriner) No. The evidence only supports a finding of second degree murder. The words "deliberate" and "premeditated" are to be given their ordinary dictionary meanings. For a killing to be first degree murder, there must be a pre-existing intent to kill which must be the subject of actual deliberation or forethought. There are three categories of evidence which indicate premeditation and deliberation: (1) facts which show the defendant was engaged in planning activities prior to the killing; (2) facts which show defendant's prior relationship and/or conduct from which could be inferred an intent to kill, which inference together with facts of type (1) or (3) would support a second inference that the killing was thought out beforehand, rather than a hastily-executed impulse; or (3) facts of the killing from which it could be inferred that the manner of killing was preconceived, designed to show forethought, e.g., ambush, time bomb, etc.

EDITOR'S ANALYSIS: While premeditation and deliberation are often lumped together as a single concept, they are distinguishable. Premeditation conveys the idea that the killing was given a second thought, while deliberation means that the defendant was acting calmly, "in cold blood," rather than passionately or impulsively. Note that a killing committed during any of the following felonies is first degree murder under the felony-murder rule: burglary, rape, robbery or arson. Note that those felonies are of a type not committed impulsively. Second degree murder may be intentional but is not premeditated or deliberated, or death results when only serious bodily injury was intended.

NOTES: *Not premed or deliberate here, although harm or death is intentional.*

MAHER v. PEOPLE

SUP. CT. OF MICH., 1862. 10 Mich.212, 81 Am.Dec.781.

NATURE OF CASE: Appeal from conviction for assault with intent to kill.

FACT SUMMARY: The court rejected evidence offered by Maher (D) which tended to show that shortly before the assault, Hunt, the victim, had intercourse with Maher's (D) wife.

CONCISE RULE OF LAW: If a killing, though intentional, is committed in the heat of passion, produced by a reasonable provocation and before a reasonable time has lapsed for the passion to cool and is the result of temporary excitement rather than one's personal depravity, it is manslaughter, rather than murder.

FACTS: Maher (D) was charged with an assault with an intent to kill Hunt (the victim). Maher (D) offered evidence showing that he saw his wife and Hunt go into the woods half an hour before he assaulted Hunt. When they came out, he followed Hunt and attacked him. On his way to do so, a friend informed him that Hunt and his [Maher's (D)] wife had had sexual intercourse in the woods the preceding day. The evidence was rejected by the court. Maher (D) was charged with assault with intent to kill.

ISSUE: Is the question of what constitutes a reasonable provocation sufficient to reduce a killing from murder to manslaughter a question of fact to be determined by the facts of each case?

HOLDING AND DECISION: (J. Christiancy) Yes. If a killing, though intentional, is committed in the heat of passion, produced by a reasonable provocation and before a reasonable time has lapsed for the passion to cool and is the result of temporary excitement rather than one's personal depravity, it is manslaughter rather than murder. In determining what constitutes reasonable provocation, the standard to be used is that of the average reasonable person. This is essentially a question of fact and is to be decided with reference to the facts of each case. The rejected evidence in this case tends to show adulterous relations between Hunt and Maher's (D) wife shortly before the assault. This is sufficient evidence of provocation to go to the jury. A new trial is granted.

DISSENT: (J. Manning) To reduce a homicide to manslaughter, the provocation must have occurred in the defendant's presence.

EDITOR'S ANALYSIS: Contrary to Maher, the traditional common-law view did not permit a jury to return a verdict of manslaughter in all situations in which it found reasonable provocation. Only in certain narrowly-defined circumstances could a jury find "legally sufficient" provocation. The principal "legally sufficient" provocation was an actual physical battery, although there were others such as personal witnessing of a wife in the act of adultery. This view is generally followed in the U.S., although there is some movement toward expanding legally sufficient provocation to include words.

PEOPLE v. CASASSA
N.Y. Ct. of App. (1980) 49 N.Y.2d 668, 404 N.E.2d 1310.

NATURE OF CASE: Appeal of conviction for second degree murder.

FACT SUMMARY: Casassa (D), charged with murder, contended that whether he was under extreme disturbance should be analyzed subjectively.

CONCISE RULE OF LAW: Whether a defendant was so emotionally disturbed as to lessen murder to manslaughter involves both an objective and subjective analysis.

FACTS: Casassa (D) became romantically obsessed with a neighbor. After she consistently rejected his advances, he confronted her with a knife, stabbing her to death. He was charged with murder. The trial court rejected his argument that whether he was under an extreme emotional disturbance sufficient to mitigate the homicide to manslaughter should be viewed from an entirely subjective viewpoint. Instead, the court, sitting without a jury, found the reaction to have been so peculiar to Casassa (D) that it would have been unreasonable to mitigate the crime. The court therefore convicted Casassa (D) of second-degree murder. Casassa appealed.

ISSUE: Does the question of whether a defendant was so emotionally disturbed as to lessen murder to manslaughter involve both an objective and subjective analysis?

HOLDING AND DECISION: (J. Jasen) Yes. Whether a defendant was so emotionally disturbed as to lessen murder to manslaughter involves both an objective and subjective analysis. The applicable penal code permits the affirmative defense where "the defendant acted under the influence of extreme emotional disturbance for which there was a reasonable explanation or excuse." This language clearly introduces both subjective and objective elements into the analysis. It is subjective as to whether or not the defendant was in fact under an extreme emotional disturbance. It is objective as to whether or not the disturbance was reasonable. The court here appears to have used this standard, and found Casassa's (D) disturbance not to have been based on reasonable grounds. This was a proper analysis. Affirmed.

[handwritten: Subjective / Objective]

EDITOR'S ANALYSIS: The language adopted by the New York Legislature here basically comports with the Model Penal Code. The test here can be seen to have grown out of the classic "heat of passion" manslaughter test. The test here differs from heat of passion mainly in that the homicide does not necessarily have to be basically contemporaneous to the triggering event, as heat of passion almost always requires.

[handwritten: Note difference between Maher + MPC]

DIRECTOR OF PUBLIC PROSECUTORS v. CAMPLIN
House of Lords (1978) 2 All E.R. 168.

NATURE OF CASE: Action to decide a point of law subsequent to the appellate court's substituting a conviction for manslaughter for the jury's conviction for murder.

FACT SUMMARY: Camplin (D), who was convicted by a jury of murder, insisted that the proper test for determining whether there was "reasonable" provocation had not been applied.

CONCISE RULE OF LAW: When the defense of provocation is raised, the jury must decide whether a "reasonable man" would react to the provocation as the accused did - which involves ascertaining what the reaction of an ordinary person of the same sex and age as the defendant would be under the circumstances.

FACTS: Camplin (D), a 15-year-old, was convicted of murder by a jury. Although it differed from what he had told the police, the story Camplin (D) told in the witness box was that the victim, a middle-aged Pakistani, had buggered him in spite of his resistance and had then laughed at him. Whereupon Camplin (D) lost his self-control and split the victim's skull with a heavy kitchen utensil, like a rimless frying pan. In addressing the jury on the defense of provocation, Camplin's (D) counsel suggested that when they attempted to answer the question whether the provocation relied on was enough to make a "reasonable man" do as Camplin (D) had done, they ought not to consider the reaction of a reasonable adult, but of a reasonable boy of 15. The judge, believing this to be wrong in law, instructed the jury that they were to consider not what would be the reaction of a reasonable boy of 15, but of a "reasonable man" in like circumstances. Feeling this was a misdirection, the Court of Appeals substituted a conviction for manslaughter. Thereafter, the House of Lords attempted to answer this question of law.

ISSUE: When the defense of provocation is raised, must the jury, in deciding whether a "reasonable man" would react to the provocation as the accused did, be guided by what the reaction would be of an ordinary person of the defendant's sex and age?

HOLDING AND DECISION: (Lord Diplock) Yes. When considering a defense of provocation, the jury must decide whether a "reasonable man" would react to the provocation as the accused did. That is, it must consider what would be the reaction under the same circumstances of an ordinary person of the same sex and age as the defendant.

As it stands, the law of provocation recognized a dual test. The provocation must not only have caused the accused to lose his self-control, but also must be such as might cause a reasonable man to react to it as the accused did. To require old heads on young shoulders is inconsistent with the law's compassion of human infirmity to which Sir Michael Foster ascribed the doctrine of provocation more than two centuries ago. It is legitimate to take the age of the accused into account in directing the jury on the "reasonable man" test that must be applied when the defense of provocation is raised by a defendant. In my opinion, a proper direction to the jury must explain to them that the "reasonable man" referred to is a person having the power of self-control to be expected of an ordinary person of the sex and age of the accused; but, in other respects, sharing such of the accused's characteristics

as they think would affect the gravity of the provocation to him, and that the question is not merely whether such a person would, in like circumstances, be provoked to lose his self-control, but whether he also would react to the provocation as the accused did.

LORD SIMON: The concept of the "reasonable man" was imported into the branch of the law dealing with the defense of provocation to avoid the injustice of a man being entitled to rely on his exceptional excitability (whether idiosyncratic or by cultural environment or ethnic origin) or pugnacity or ill-temper or on his drunkenness, etc. I think that the standard of self-control, which the law requires before provocation is held to reduce murder to manslaughter, is still that of the reasonable person; but that, in determining whether a person of reasonable self-control would lose it in the circumstances, the entire factual situation, which includes the characteristics of the accused, must be considered.

EDITOR'S ANALYSIS: At common law, words unaccompanied by violence could never amount to provocation. While that aspect of the doctrine of provocation has changed, the requirement that the defendant acted in an objectively reasonable way to the provocation has survived. New Hampshire took the very rare step of totally eliminating the objective element from the doctrine of provocation by omitting any requirement of reasonableness. Under its statute, murder is reduced to manslaughter if a person kills another "under the influence of extreme mental or emotional disturbance." The Model Penal Code has not dropped the objective element, but it has qualified it in providing: "Criminal homicide constitutes manslaughter when: ...(b) a homicide which would otherwise be murder is committed under the influence of extreme mental or emotional disturbance for which there is a reasonable explanation or excuse. The reasonableness of such explanation or excuse shall be determined from the viewpoint of a person in the actor's situation under the circumstances as he believes them to be." This is much the same position that was taken by the House of Lords in the [Camplin] case.

NOTES:

STATE v. BARNETT
S.C. Sup. Ct. (1951) 218 S.C.415, 63 S.E.2d 57.

NOTES:

NATURE OF CASE: Appeal of conviction of involuntary manslaughter.

FACT SUMMARY: Barnett (D) was convicted of involuntary manslaughter following a vehicular homicide, where he was shown to be negligent as opposed to reckless or acting intentionally.

CONCISE RULE OF LAW: Negligence alone will support an involuntary manslaughter conviction where the homicide involved a motor vehicle.

FACTS: Barnett (D) was involved in a motor vehicle accident, resulting in a death. He was charged with involuntary manslaughter. The court instructed the jury that negligence alone could support a conviction. Barnett (D) was convicted and he appealed, contending that negligence alone could not support a conviction.

ISSUE: Will negligence alone support an involuntary manslaughter conviction where the homicide involved a motor vehicle?

HOLDING AND DECISION: (J. Oxner) Yes. Negligence alone will support an involuntary manslaughter conviction where the homicide involved a motor vehicle. The old rule that criminal liability could arise from negligence alone has been largely abandoned. However, in this state at least, where the negligence involved a necessarily dangerous instrumentality, criminal liability may arise for negligence alone. A motor vehicle, in the opinion of this court, is such an instrumentality. The purpose of this rule is to compel those using such instrumentalities to exercise utmost care. Here, the homicide resulted from Barnett's (D) use of an auto, so he was properly charged. Affirmed.

Policy

DISSENT: (J. Taylor) Criminal liability for simple negligence is too harsh.

EDITOR'S ANALYSIS: At early common law, criminal liability was not greatly differentiated from tort liability. Eventually, a higher standard of culpability was read into criminal law. Almost all jurisdictions require something more than negligence today. Few, if any, follow the rule stated here.

COMMONWEALTH v. WELANSKY
Mass. Sup. Jud. Ct. (1944) 316 Mass. 383, 55 N.E.2d 902.

NOTES:

NATURE OF CASE: Appeal from conviction for involuntary manslaughter.

FACT SUMMARY: Welansky (D), owner of a nightclub, had failed to alleviate serious fire hazards that existed prior to a deadly blaze that erupted one night.

CONCISE RULE OF LAW: A manslaughter conviction may be based on omissions as well as affirmative acts.

FACTS: Welansky (D) owned a fashionable Boston nightclub. Access was limited, with only one main door, and the few emergency exits were either blocked or barred so as to prevent dinner patrons from leaving without paying. One evening a fire broke out, which quickly swept through the overcrowded facilities. Escape proved impossible for many, and dozens of patrons and employees were killed. Welansky (D) was convicted of involuntary manslaughter, and he appealed.

ISSUE: May a manslaughter conviction be based on omissions as well as affirmative acts?

HOLDING AND DECISION: (J. Lummus) Yes. A manslaughter conviction may be based on omissions as well as affirmative acts. Involuntary manslaughter consists of wanton or reckless conduct resulting in a homicide. Where one has a duty to act, such recklessness may exist in the failure to perform the duty. Here, Welansky (D) was under a duty to provide for the safety of his patrons. The jury found his failure to have done so to have gone beyond mere negligence into recklessness. Considering the numerous safety hazards that existed at the club, the record supports the verdict. Affirmed.

EDITOR'S ANALYSIS: The "wanton and reckless" standard is a common one among the jurisdictions for supporting manslaughter. It implies something worse than a mere failure to act prudently, yet falls short of intentional behavior. It is often defined as a conscious disregard of a known risk.

STATE v. WILLIAMS

WASHINGTON CT. OF APP., 1971. 4 Wash.App. 908, 484 P.2d 1167.

NOTES:

NATURE OF CASE: Appeal of manslaughter conviction.

FACT SUMMARY: Mr. and Mrs. Williams (D) failed to obtain medical aid for their 17-month-old child and he died as a result.

CONCISE RULE OF LAW: Where the failure of a person to act while under the duty to do so is the proximate cause of the death of another, that person may be convicted of involuntary manslaughter, even though his conduct was no more than ordinary negligence.

FACTS: Mrs. Williams (D) had a son by a previous marriage before she married Mr. Williams (D). When the lad, only 17 months old, developed a toothache, neither she nor her husband considered it serious enough to seek out medical help. As the tooth became worse and abscessed, however, the Williamses (D) became apprehensive but did not seek medical (or dental) care for the boy, fearing that the Welfare Department might take him away if they saw how bad he looked. Eventually, the boy developed gangrene (the smell from which was clearly noticeable), and pneumonia, from which he died about ten days later. The Williamses (D) were convicted of manslaughter on these facts. They appealed.

ISSUE: May ordinary negligence serve as the basis for convicting someone of involuntary manslaughter?

HOLDING AND DECISION: (C.J. Horowitz) Yes. Where the failure of a person to act while under a duty to do so is the proximate cause of the death of another, that person may be convicted of involuntary manslaughter, even though his conduct was no more than ordinary negligence. There is no question but that the Williamses (D) were under a duty to obtain medical care for their seriously ill son, and their fear of the Welfare Department does not excuse this duty. The tough question here is whether the seriousness of the child's illness became sufficiently apparent to them early enough for their failure to do anything about it to be declared the proximate cause of the boy's death. Medical experts, however, testified that the gangrenous condition of the boy's cheek must have been apparent (both by sight and smell) to his parents for some ten days before he died. Clearly, they were on notice as to the seriousness of their son's illness in time to prevent him from dying of it. Conviction affirmed.

EDITOR'S ANALYSIS: This case points up a modern departure from the common-law rule that involuntary manslaughter required an act of gross negligence (i.e., criminal negligence). Ordinary negligence may arise either by act or, as above, by omission while under a duty to act. As in tort, its general formulation is the "failure of a man of reasonable prudence to exercise due care under the circumstances." Note, however, that this "objective" (i.e., what a reasonable man would do) standard runs the risk of undermining individualized justice by sanctioning punishment, regardless of the subjective knowledge of the wrongdoer. In [Williams], supra, for example, it appeared that the parents were illiterates - wholly ignorant of the most rudimentary principles of health care - who honestly did not know their son was in trouble.

[Handwritten margin notes:]

— I

(H) Ordinary negligence = involuntary manslaughter
v. Criminal negligence is no longer requisite
A lower threshold of harm and heightened duty of care is imposed.

} OLD CLR

Policy
↓
Result

COMMONWEALTH v. MALONE

SUP.CT. OF PENNSYLVANIA, 1946. 354 Pa. 180, 47 A.2d 445.

NATURE OF CASE: Appeal from conviction of second degree murder.

FACT SUMMARY: Malone (D), aged 17, killed his friend by shooting him in the head during a game of "Russian poker."

CONCISE RULE OF LAW: When an individual commits an act of gross recklessness for which he must reasonably anticipate that death to another is likely to result, he exhibits that wickedness of disposition, hardness of heart, and cruelty which proves that he possessed malice.

FACTS: Malone (D), aged 17, obtained a gun. His friend, Long, aged 13, obtained a cartridge. Malone (D) suggested they play Russian poker. Long consented. Malone (D) put the gun to Long's head, fired three times, and killed him. They were on friendly terms at the time, and Malone (D) testified that he had no intention of harming Long. Malone (D) contends he was only guilty of involuntary manslaughter.

ISSUE: Is the malice which is an essential element of murder necessarily a malevolence toward the deceased particularly?

HOLDING AND DECISION: (C.J. Maxey) No. The malice on the part of a killer is not necessarily malevolent to the deceased particularly but "any evil design in general, the dictate of a wicked, depraved and malignant heart." When an individual commits an act of gross recklessness for which he must reasonably anticipate that death of another is likely to result, he exhibits that wickedness of disposition, hardness of heart, cruelty, recklessness of consequences, and a mind regardless of social duty which proves that he possessed malice. The killing of Long by Malone (D) resulted from an act intentionally done by Malone (D) in reckless and wanton disregard of the consequences. The killing was therefore murder, for malice is evidenced by the intentional doing of an uncalled-for act in callous disregard of its likely affect on others. The fact that there was no motive for this murder does not exculpate Malone (D). Conviction affirmed.

EDITOR'S ANALYSIS: Outrageously reckless homicide, such as that in [Malone], is commonly made murder by express statutory provisions. A common statute included in its definition of murder, acts greatly dangerous to the lives of others, and evidencing a depraved mind regardless of human life, although without any preconceived purpose to deprive any particular person of life. These statutes make murder of this kind first degree murder. The qualifications in such statutes that the act be dangerous to the lives of others has led to the doctrine in many states that this type of murder exists only when persons, in addition to those killed, were endangered. A variant of this view is that while persons other than the deceased need not be put in jeopardy, it is necessary that the act be committed without a special design with respect to the deceased.

UNITED STATES v. FLEMING
U.S. Ct.of App., 4th Cir.(1984) 739 F.2d 945.

NOTES:

NATURE OF CASE: Appeal from conviction for second degree murder.

FACT SUMMARY: Fleming (D) was convicted of murder subsequent to a vehicular homicide without evidence of intent to kill.

CONCISE RULE OF LAW: Second degree murder does not require an intent to kill.

FACTS: Fleming (D), with a blood alcohol level of over .30, drove for several miles at speeds of over 50 mph in excess of the posted limit, at times driving on the wrong side of the road to avoid traffic. He lost control of his vehicle and hit another vehicle head-on, killing the occupant. He was tried and convicted of second degree murder. He appealed, contending that the record could support only a manslaughter conviction.

ISSUE: Does second degree murder require an intent to kill?

HOLDING AND DECISION: (C.J. Winter) No. Second degree murder does not require an intent to kill. The mental state required for murder is "malice aforethought." This standard does not require an intent to kill; it may also be satisfied by wanton conduct grossly deviating from a reasonable standard of care such that it may be inferred that the defendant was aware of a serious risk of death or serious bodily harm. Here, the record is clear that Fleming's (D) conduct went beyond merely driving under the influence; the driving was so reckless that a serious accident was highly probable. The jury found this to constitute malice aforethought, and the record supports this finding. Affirmed.

EDITOR'S ANALYSIS: There is a good deal of overlap between involuntary manslaughter and second degree murder. They both involve wanton and reckless conduct. The distinction is not clear and varies among the jurisdictions. The risk of harm and the defendant's awareness thereof appear to be the crucial factors, but where involuntary manslaughter ends and second degree murder begins is not clear.

STATE v. HUPF
SUP.CT.OF DELAWARE, 1953. 48 Del. 254, 101 A.2d 355.

NATURE OF CASE: Appeal from conviction for involuntary manslaughter.

FACT SUMMARY: The car Hupf (D) was driving collided with another car and killed a person. Hupf (D) admitted four vehicle code violations.

CONCISE RULE OF LAW: Death resulting proximately from the commission of an unlawful act which is not a felony nor which tends toward great bodily harm constitutes manslaughter, and reckless or conscious disregard for the lives of others need not be proved.

FACTS: The car Hupf (D) was driving collided with another car. Hupf's (D) passenger was killed as a result of the collision. Hupf (D) admitted four vehicle code violations, and the State (P) established that the death was the proximate result of the violations. The State (P) did not establish a reckless disregard for the life and safety of others.

ISSUE: Does a homicide resulting proximately from violation of a penal law, not amounting to a felony, constitute involuntary manslaughter without proof of rash or reckless conduct amounting to gross negligence?

HOLDING AND DECISION: (C.J. Southerland) Yes. The classic definition of involuntary manslaughter is Blackstone's: "The unlawful killing of another, involuntarily but in the commission of some unlawful act." Under this definition, the State (P) need not prove conscious or reckless disregard of the lives and safety of others where a death had proximately resulted from violation of a penal law, which is not a felony, in order to prove involuntary manslaughter. Hupf (D) argues that this rule is too harsh when applied to automobile drivers, since it stamps as a felon any driver who, without conscious wrongdoing, violates one of the many vehicle provisions and is in an accident resulting in a death. However, the doctrine of proximate cause imposes an important limitation. The mere violation of the statute is not enough to constitute manslaughter. The violation must be the proximate cause of death and that causal connection must be affirmatively shown.

EDITOR'S ANALYSIS: Most jurisdictions punish, as involuntary manslaughter, death-causing conduct in the commission of an unlawful act (generally, a misdemeanor). This is especially true if the act is malum in se (wrong in itself) or if that act involves a danger of death or serious bodily injury to others. If the unlawful act is malum prohibitum (wrong only because prohibited by law), the defendant is generally not held guilty of manslaughter unless the death is the foreseeable consequence of his committing the act, as was the case in [Hupf].

REGINA v. SERNE
CENTRAL CRIMINAL COURT, 1887. 16 Cox Crim. Cas. 311.

NATURE OF CASE: Indictment for murder.

FACT SUMMARY: It is alleged that Serne (D) set a house on fire and caused his son to burn to death.

CONCISE RULE OF LAW: Any act known to be dangerous to life and likely, in itself, to cause death, done for the purpose of committing a felony, which causes death is murder.

FACTS: It is alleged that Serne (D) deliberately set his house on fire to collect insurance on it. Serne (D), his wife, two daughters, two sons and a servant were in the house at the time of the fire. One son burned to death.

ISSUE: Is one guilty of murder who commits an act, known to be dangerous to life and likely to cause death, when the act is a felony and when the commission of that act causes death?

HOLDING AND DECISION: (J. Stephen) Yes. The law that says any act done with the intent to commit a felony and which causes death amounts to murder should be narrowed. It is more reasonable to say that any act known to be dangerous to life and likely to cause death, done for the purpose of committing a felony, which causes death, should be murder. It is alleged that Serne (D) deliberately set fire to his house while six other people were sleeping in it and that he must have known that he was placing all of those people in a deadly risk. If these alleged facts are true, it does not matter whether Serne (D) set fire to his house with his family in it and a boy burned to death. He is as guilty of murder as if he had stabbed the boy.

EDITOR'S ANALYSIS: At early common law one whose conduct brought about an unintended death in the commission of a felony was guilty of murder. Today, the law of felony murder varies substantially throughout the U.S., largely as a result of efforts to limit the scope of the rule. Some U.S. jurisdictions have limited the rule by permitting its use only as to certain types of felonies. Others have done so by a more strict interpretation of the requirement of proximate cause. Some give a narrower construction of the time period during which the felony is being committed, and others require that the underlying felony be independent of the homicide.

PEOPLE v. PHILLIPS
SUP. CT. OF CAL., 1966. 64 Cal.2d 574, 414 P.2d 353.

NOTES:

NATURE OF CASE: Appeal from conviction for second degree murder.

FACT SUMMARY: Phillips (D), a chiropractor, persuaded a child's parents not to have her submit to an operation for cancer, but to have her treated by him. She died as a result.

CONCISE RULE OF LAW: Only felonies which are inherently dangerous to human life can support the application of the felony murder rule.

In Abstract view

FACTS: A medical center told a child's parents that immediate removal of the child's cancerous eye was necessary to save or prolong her life. Phillips (D), a chiropractor, induced the parents not to consent to the operation and told them he could cure the child without surgery. He charged $700 for his treatment. The child died. It is argued that since the death occurred in the perpetration of a felony (i.e., grand theft), Phillips (D) is guilty of felony murder.

ISSUE: Can one be found guilty of felony murder for death caused by the perpetration of a felony which is not inherently dangerous? — *In Abstract*

HOLDING AND DECISION: (J. Tobriner) No. Only felonies which are, in themselves, inherently dangerous to human life can support the application of the felony murder rule. Grand theft by false pretenses is not such a felony. The prosecution argues that in determining whether the felony committed by Phillips (D) was inherently dangerous, the court should look to the facts of this case and hold that Phillips' (D) conduct was inherently dangerous. To do so would mean that the felony murder could be applied to the perpetration of any felony during which a defendant may have acted in such a manner as to endanger life. In assessing the danger to human life inherent in any felony, we look to the elements of the felony in the abstract, not the particular facts of the case.

→ Policy in CA which opposes Serne rule

EDITOR'S ANALYSIS: LaFave says that on principle the approach applied in [Phillips] is incorrect if the purpose of the felony murder rule is to hold felons accountable for unintended deaths caused by their dangerous conduct. "If the armed robber is to be held guilty of felony murder because of a death caused by the accidental firing of her gun, it seems no more harsh to apply the felony murder rule to the thief whose fraudulent scheme includes inducing the victim to forego a life-prolonging operation." He adds, though, that the rule is more understandable if viewed as an attempt by courts to limit the scope of the felony murder rule.

PEOPLE v. SMITH
CA. Sup. Ct. (1984) 345 Cal. 3d 798, 678 P.2d 886.

NATURE OF CASE: Appeal of second-degree murder conviction.

FACT SUMMARY: Smith (D) was convicted under the felony-murder rule when the underlying felony was child abuse.

CONCISE RULE OF LAW: Felony-murder may not be applied where the underlying felony is child abuse.

FACTS: Smith (D) had a two-year old daughter. One evening, pursuant to disciplinary action against the child, she delivered a severe beating, which resulted in fatal injuries. Smith (D) and her housemate, Foster (D) who also administered a beating, were convicted of child abuse and second-degree murder under the felony-murder rule. They appealed the murder conviction to the Court of Appeal, which affirmed. The State Supreme Court granted review.

ISSUE: May felony-murder be applied where the underlying felony is child abuse?

HOLDING AND DECISION: (J. Mosk) No. Felony-murder may not be applied where the underlying felony is child abuse. The felony-murder rule is disfavored, as it erodes the relation between criminal liabilty and moral culpability. For this reason, this court has made the rule inapplicable where it is based upon a felony which is an integral part of the homicide. To hold otherwise prevents the jury from passing on the issue of malice aforethought, which is central to murder as we define it. This court has already held that the rule cannot be applied to homicide resulting from felonious assault, as the assault is integral to the homicide. The same logic applies to child abuse, which is a variation on felonious assault. For this reason, the felony-murder rule is improperly applied in this instance, and the conviction must be reversed.

EDITOR'S ANALYSIS: In *People v. Shockley*, 79 Cal. App. 3d 669 (1978), a child died as a result of abuse consisting of malnutrition and dehydration. The felony-murder rule was applied there. The court here did not overrule *Shockley*, but stated that in a direct assault the felony is more integral to the homicide than in a passive situation such as neglect.

[Handwritten margin notes:]
→ Policy
R
EX → Prosecutors must directly charge murder, cannot bootstrap murderous homicide from lesser felony facts that ended w/ a murder

→ Distinguish Direct Assault — F/M - No from Passive Assault → F/M - yes

54

STATE v. CANOLA

Sup.Ct. OF N.J., 73 N.J. 206, 374 A.2d 20 (1977).

NATURE OF CASE: Appeal from affirmation of a felony-murder conviction.

FACT SUMMARY: Canola (D) was convicted of felony-murder because one of his cohorts in the commission of an armed robbery was killed by a bullet fired by the owner of the store being robbed.

CONCISE RULE OF LAW: The felony-murder rule does not extend to render a felon liable for the death of a co-felon effected by one resisting the felony.

FACTS: While Canola (D) and three confederates were in the process of robbing a store, the store owner and an employee engaged one of the robbers in a physical skirmish in an effort to resist the robbery. Hearing a call for assistance, another of the robbers began shooting. The store owner returned the gunfire. In the exchange, both the owner and one of the robbers, Lloredo, were fatally shot—the latter by the firearm of the owner. The Appellate Division upheld Canola's (D) conviction under the felony-murder rule for the murder of the store owner and his conviction under the same rule for the murder of his co-felon, Lloredo. The Supreme Court of New Jersey granted a petition for certification addressed to the latter count.

ISSUE: Does the felony-murder rule apply to make a felon liable for the death of his co-felon at the hands of the intended victim of the felony?

HOLDING AND DECISION: (J. Conford) No. The English courts never applied the felony-murder rule to hold a felon guilty of the death of his co-felon at the hands of the intended victim of the felony. Traditionally, it is concerned solely with situations where the felon or a confederate does the actual killing. It appears to this Court to be regressive to extend the application of the rule beyond its classic common-law limitation to acts by the felon and his accomplices, to lethal acts of third persons not in furtherance of the felonious scheme. Judgment modified to strike the conviction.

CONCURRENCE: (J. Sullivan) I agree with the result, but not the reasoning. The thrust of our felony murder statute is to hold the criminal liable for any killing which ensues during the commission of a felony, even though the felon, or a confederate, did not commit the actual killing. The only exception I would recognize would be the death of a co-felon, which could be classified as a justifiable homicide and not within the purview of the statute.

EDITOR'S ANALYSIS: This case expresses what is the majority rule—that the felony murder rule renders a defendant guilty for a killing that grows out of the commission of the felony only if it is directly attributable to the act of the defendant or those associated with him in the felonious scheme. Acceptance has not been forthcoming as to the opposing view, which would extend the rule to cover any death proximately resulting from the unlawful activity, including the death of a co-felon.

TAYLOR v. SUPERIOR COURT

Calif.Sup.Ct.(1970) 3 Cal.3d 578, 477 P.2d 131.

NOTES:

NATURE OF CASE: Appeal from denial of motion to set aside the information on a murder charge.

FACT SUMMARY: Taylor (D) was charged with the murder of his accomplice in a robbery attempt.

CONCISE RULE OF LAW: Where a felon or his accomplice, with a conscious disregard for life, intentionally commits an act that is likely to cause death, and a victim kills in reasonable response to such act, that felon will be guilty of murder.

FACTS: Taylor (D) was the getaway driver in a robbery. His two accomplices, Daniels and Smith, went into a liquor store to rob it while brandishing guns and repeatedly threatening to kill the storeowner. Daniels chattered insanely during the holdup and was extremely agitated. He talked of having a gun and blowing the heads off the owners if they did not obey. Smith was intent and apprehensive, as if he were waiting for something big to happen. Finally, one of the proprietors pulled out a gun and shot Smith, who shot back. Daniels was hit but made it out the door. Smith died as a result of the shooting, and Taylor (D), the driver, was later apprehended and charged with the murder of Smith.

ISSUE: Can an accomplice to a robbery be said to have murdered another accomplice where that accomplice was killed by the victim of the robbery?

HOLDING AND DECISION: (J. Burke) Yes. Where a felon or his accomplice, with a conscious disregard for life, intentionally commits an act that is likely to cause death, and a victim kills in reasonable response to such an act, that felon will be guilty of murder. This is not a felony-murder theory, but rather is based upon vicarious liability for the intentional acts of an accomplice. Mens rea in such cases is supplied by the felon's "conscious disregard for life" - as determined by whether the conduct of the robbers was sufficiently provocative of lethal resistance to support a finding of malice. (The provocation may be less than firing a gun at the victim.) Here, Smith and Daniels repeatedly talked about killing and were highly agitated. It is reasonable to find from this provocation that the robbers initiated the gun battle. As such, their accomplice Taylor (D) is vicariously responsible for the murder which they caused.

DISSENT: (J. Peters) The culpability of criminal defendants should be determined by their own acts, not by the fortuitous acts of their victims.

EDITOR'S ANALYSIS: In some jurisdictions, where a killing, although proximately caused by an independent felony (e.g., robbery) is actually committed by a bystander, victim or police officer, the felons do incur liability via the felony-murder rule. This case circumvents the felony-murder rule by basing it on vicarious liability. In [People v. Washington], 62 Cal. 2d 777, a case with almost identical facts to those supra, the court held that the felony-murder rule was inapplicable to deaths which resulted from victim-initiated gun battles in which a victim shot and killed someone. This decision was widely criticized, however, as ignoring the basic rationale for the felony-murder rule.

→ Distinguished from Canola

→ Contra to Taylor

GREGG v. GEORGIA
428 U.S. 153 (1976).

NATURE OF CASE: Appeal from a death sentence.

FACT SUMMARY: Gregg (D) alleged that the death penalty was per se unconstitutional.

CONCISE RULE OF LAW: The death penalty is not per se unconstitutional and is permissible if the statute has sufficient controls to avoid capricious or indiscriminate sentencing.

FACTS: Gregg (D) was convicted of murder and was sentenced to death. Gregg (D) argued that the death sentence was cruel and inhuman punishment and was a per se violation of the Eighth Amendment. Gregg (D) relied on [Furman v. Georgia], 408 U.S. 238 (1972), which struck down the Georgia death penalty statute on the grounds that there were inadequate standards and guidelines to avoid capricious and indiscriminate impositions of a death sentence. The State (P) argued that it had cured the constitutional defects by requiring the jury to find that one of ten specific factors exist before the penalty is imposed. The statute also provided for review of all such sentences by the Supreme Court to determine if the sentence was justified and if one of the statutory factors was present. Gregg (D) argued that several of the factors were vague, and the ability to plea bargain and the vagaries of jury sentencing practices rendered the statute unconstitutional.

ISSUE: Is the imposition of the death penalty cruel and unusual punishment constituting a per se violation of the Eighth Amendment?

HOLDING AND DECISION: (J. Stewart) No. The Eighth Amendment merely requires that punishments not be excessive, i.e. unnecessary and wanton infliction of pain, and that the punishment not be grossly out of proportion with the crime. The Eighth Amendment reflects current social trends. Legislatures, and not the courts, are the determiners of such trends in most cases. Almost every state revised their capital offense statutes after [Furman] and retained, in some form or another, a death penalty. [Furman] merely stated that there must be standards and guidelines to prevent indiscriminate or capricious sentencing. It did not prohibit the imposition of the death penalty. Traditionally, we have recognized death penalties for specific crimes since the beginning of the country and even before. The retention of the penalty by most states after [Furman] indicates that current social trends and morality still favor it. It may have a deterrent effect on some who might otherwise commit murder. The Georgia (P) statute contains sufficient safeguards to prevent capricious or indiscriminate results. Prior cases involving ambiguous portions of the statute have established that the State Supreme Court is carefully construing these requirements to prevent abuses, and one of the factors was even declared unconstitutionally vague. The fact that in the interests of justice and compassion some individuals are shown mercy, will not invalidate the statute. The conviction is affirmed, as death penalties are not, per se, unconstitutional and the Georgia (P) statute gives defendants adequate protection.

DISSENT: (J. Marshall) If the American people were adequately acquainted with the information critical to a judgment on the morality of the death penalty, they would consider that penalty shocking, unjust, and unacceptable. As to the two purposes the death penalty supposedly serves - general deterrence and retribution - the evidence shows that capital punishment is not necessary to deter crime in our society and it simply defies belief to suggest that the death penalty is necessary to prevent the American people from taking the law into their own hands.

EDITOR'S ANALYSIS: In [Jurek v. Texas], 428 U.S. 262 (1976), the defendant challenged the death penalty statute of Texas. The procedure limited capital punishment to five knowing types of homicide. The jury had to also find that the murder was deliberate and with reasonable expectation of death; whether the defendant was a likely continuing threat to the community; and whether any justification or provocation was present. The Court found that the sentencing procedure satisfied the demands of the Eighth Amendment.

NOTES:

McCLESKEY v. KEMP
U.S. Sup. Ct. (1987) 107 S. Ct. 1756.

NATURE OF CASE: Review of death sentence imposed after a murder conviction.

FACT SUMMARY: In challenge to a death penalty, McCleskey (D) produced statistics demonstrating a tendency towards bias in its application.

CONCISE RULE OF LAW: The death penalty is not unconstitutional because of statistics demonstrating a tendency towards racial bias in its application.

FACTS: McCleskey (D), a black man, was convicted of killing a white police officer. The jury recommended the death penalty which the court imposed. McCleskey (D) appealed, producing statistical studies tending to prove that the penalty was imposed much more frequently on blacks than whites, particularly when the victim was white. The penalty was affirmed. The District Court refused to grant habeas corpus, and the Court of Appeals affirmed. The Supreme Court granted certiorari.

ISSUE: Is the death penalty unconstitutional because of statistics demonstrating a tendency towards racial bias in its application?

HOLDING AND DECISION: (J. Powell) No. The death penalty is not unconstitutional because of statistics demonstrating a tendency towards racial bias in its application. To prove an Equal Protection Clause violation, a person must prove he was the victim of purposeful discrimination. Evidence of statistical tendencies does not prove that the decision makers in his case were biased. In terms of Eighth Amendment analysis, the discretion that this Court has mandated in the application of the death penalty necessarily leaves room for bias. However, the only other alternative, mandatory application of the penalty, is antithetical to the fundamental role of discretion in our penal system. Finally, to hold that statistical evidence of bias in death penalty application makes it unconstitutional would open the door to a broad range of challenges to various aspects of the criminal justice system, which would impose unacceptable costs thereon. Here, as the only challenge McCleskey (D) has made is based on statistical analysis, his challenge is insufficient. Affirmed.

DISSENT: (J. Brennan) The proper analysis is not whether an arbitrary sentence has been imposed, but whether there is an unacceptable risk thereof. The studies here demonstrate this to be the case.

DISSENT: (J. Blackmun) In terms of equal protection analysis, one challenging a particular system need only show that the totality of relevant facts gives rise to an inference of a discriminatory purpose, a burden McCleskey (D) has met here.

DISSENT: (J. Stevens) The Court appears to base its conclusion on a fear that holding otherwise would ring the death knell for capital punishment in America. This is not so. Certain categories of crimes in the statistical studies show no tendency towards racial bias, and are not subject to constitutional attack.

EDITOR'S ANALYSIS: As the dissent of Justice Blackmun suggests, discrimination cases have been made based on statistical data. Examples include venue-selection cases and employment situations. However, even in instances of this nature, the variables were significantly fewer than in death penalty cases, and causation was much easier to demonstrate.

NOTES:

PEOPLE v. ARZON

Sup.Ct., N.Y.County, 92 Misc.2d 739, 401 N.Y.S.2d 156 (1978).

NOTES:

NATURE OF CASE: Motion to dismiss murder counts in an indictment.

FACT SUMMARY: A fireman died from injuries sustained when he attempted to evacuate from a building under the hazardous conditions created by the fire Arzon (D) set plus smoke from another fire.

CONCISE RULE OF LAW: A defendant's conduct can support a charge of homicide only if it was a sufficiently direct cause of the death and the ultimate harm was something which should have been foreseen as being reasonably related to his acts.

FACTS: The firemen who were called to the fifth floor fire allegedly set by Arzon (D) decided to withdraw from the building because they were making no progress in controlling it. A combination of that fire and dense smoke they encountered (which was later discovered to have been caused by another fire on the second floor with which Arzon (D) was not connected by any evidence) made evacuation from the building extremely hazardous. One fireman, in attempting to evacuate, sustained injuries from which he later died. An indictment was returned charging Arzon (D) with second degree murder for having, "Under circumstances evincing a depraved indifference to human life, recklessly engaged in conduct which created a grave risk of death to another person," thereby causing the death of the fireman, and with felony murder. He moved to dismiss these counts, maintaining that the required causal link between the underlying crime and the death was lacking.

ISSUE: To be guilty of homicide, must the defendant's conduct have been a sufficiently direct cause of the death and must the ultimate harm be something which should have been foreseen as being reasonably related to his acts?

HOLDING AND DECISION: (J. Milands) Yes. While there is remarkably little authority on precisely what sort of behavior constitutes "depraved indifference to human life," it is clear that an obscure or merely probable connection between a defendant's conduct and another person's death is not enough to support a charge of homicide. Although the defendant's conduct need not be the sole and exclusive factor in the victim's death, to be criminally liable his conduct must have been a sufficiently direct cause of the death and the ultimate harm must be something which should have been foreseen as being reasonably related to his acts. Since Arzon's (D) conduct meets these requirements, his motion to dismiss the two counts is dismissed.

[handwritten: Not totally restrictive]

EDITOR'S ANALYSIS: The standard adopted by requiring that the defendant's actions be a "sufficiently direct cause of the ensuing death" is "greater than that required to serve as a basis for tort liability." That is, it is not a but-for-causation test, and it does not sanction an "expanded application of proximate cause principles lifted from the civil law of torts." [People v. Warner-Lambert Co.], 51 N.Y.2d 295 (1980).

[handwritten: Must be much more direct than in torts]

STEPHENSON v. STATE
205 INDIANA 141, 179 N.E. 633.

NOTES:

NATURE OF CASE: Appeal from conviction for second degree murder.

FACT SUMMARY: As a result of Stephenson's (D) acts, a woman took a drug to commit suicide.

CONCISE RULE OF LAW: If an accused committed a felony such as rape or attempted rape and inflicted on the victim both mental and physical injuries as a result of which the victim was rendered mentally irresponsible and suicide followed, the accused would be guilty of murder.

FACTS: Stephenson (D) was the Grand Dragon of the Ku Klux Klan. He abducted a woman from her house and detained her on a train. He beat her and attempted to rape her on the train. Later, he forced her to get off the train, and they registered in a hotel. The woman managed to procure some drugs and took them in an attempt to commit suicide. She became extremely sick and Stephenson (D) offered to take her to a hospital, but she refused. While she was being driven back to her house, she screamed in pain for a doctor. Stephenson (D) did not stop or administer an antidote. She was left off at her house and her parents called a doctor, who gave her an antidote. Within ten days, all her wounds healed, except for one which was infected. She continued to grow worse, even after the infection had healed. Twenty-seven days after Stephenson (D) brought her back home, she died. The cause of death was a combination of shock, loss of food and rest, poison, infection, and lack of early treatment.

ISSUE: Was the victim's act in attempting suicide a foreseeable result of the defendant's acts so as to not break the causal connection between the death and the defendant's acts?

HOLDING AND DECISION: (Per Curiam) Yes. An attempted suicide was a normal and foreseeable result of the treatment inflicted upon the victim by Stephenson (D). He had complete dominion and control over the woman from the time she was abducted. She had attempted to escape several times but was thwarted on each occasion. She did not know when Stephenson (D) would again attempt to rape her as he had done on the train. The same forces were working on her when she took the drug as when the defendant attempted to rape her. The whole ordeal was a single, interrelated transaction. Stephenson (D), by his acts, rendered the victim distracted and mentally irresponsible. This mental state was a natural and probable consequence of the defendant's unlawful acts. The suicide was an intervening cause which was a foreseeable result of Stephenson's (D) acts. The fact that other causes may have also contributed to the death will not relieve Stephenson (D) from liability. His acts were working on the mental process of the victim and generated the taking of the drug.

EDITOR'S ANALYSIS: To determine causation there are two steps. First, the defendant's act must have been the actual cause of the death. That is, the act must be a substantial factor in bringing about the resulting harm. Second, the act must be direct. That is to say, it is an actual cause in itself still operative at the moment of death. This is opposed to an indirect cause, where it is some other cause which results in the death.

COMMONWEALTH v. ROOT

403 PENNSYLVANIA 571, 170 A.2d 310.

NATURE OF CASE: Appeal from conviction for involuntary manslaughter.

FACT SUMMARY: Root (D) was engaged in a drag race in which the other driver was killed when he ran into a truck.

CONCISE RULE OF LAW: For a charge of criminal homicide, it must be found that the defendant's act was the direct cause of the death and not just the proximate cause as that term is defined in tort law.

FACTS: Root (D) and the deceased engaged in a drag race. The race took place on a rural, three-lane highway. The traffic was light and the night was clear and dry. The speed limit was fifty miles per hour. The drivers were doing seventy to ninety immediately prior to the accident. When the two cars approached a bridge, the highway narrowed to two lanes. Root (D) was in front and the deceased was immediately behind him. The deceased attempted to pass Root (D). When he entered the other lane, he ran head on into an oncoming truck and was killed.

ISSUE: Does the tort law concept of proximate cause apply in determining criminal responsibility for homicide?

HOLDING AND DECISION: (C.J. Jones) No. There is no rational basis for the use of the tort law concept of proximate cause in the field of criminal homicide. Proximate cause has undergone a continuing extension in favor of broadening the scope of civil liability. Prior to that extension, the concept was equally applicable to tort and criminal law. To use the concept as it has evolved in the field of criminal law would be to extend possible criminal liability to persons charged with reckless or unlawful conduct in circumstances not generally considered to present the likelihood of a resultant death. In the present case, it was the deceased who was the direct cause of his own death. The direct cause was his acts alone. Direct causation is a criminal law concept. Even under the tort law concept of proximate cause, the defendant's acts were not the proximate cause of the death, as a matter of law. The deceased was aware of the risk created by Root (D), and thereafter the deceased caused the death by an independent act of recklessness. Root's (D) reckless conduct was not a sufficiently direct cause of the death to make him criminally liable.

DISSENT: (J. Eggan) Root (D) caused the situation by his acts. The act of the deceased was a normal response to the race and that act was foreseeable by Root (D).

EDITOR'S ANALYSIS: Proximate cause simply denotes a causative factor which the criminal law will notice as sufficient for liability. It is a label used to express, rather than to reach, results obtained by the application of the criminal law's rules of causation. A cause is direct when it is still operative at the moment of the result. A cause is indirect when, although it is in the chain of events culminating in the result, the direct cause is some intervening act. If the intervening act was generated by the indirect cause, then liability will still attach.

COMMONWEALTH v. ATENCIO AND MARSHALL
345 Mass. 627, 189 N.E. 2d 223.

NOTES:

NATURE OF CASE: Appeal from conviction for manslaughter.

FACT SUMMARY: Atencio (D) and Marshall (D) played Russian roulette with the deceased, who was killed when the gun discharged.

CONCISE RULE OF LAW: Direct causation may be established by wanton and reckless conduct found in a joint enterprise.

FACTS: The deceased and two friends, Atencio (D) and Marshall (D), were drinking wine all day in the deceased's room. Marshall (D) had gone out and returned with a gun. Early in the evening, after the deceased's brother had left, they started talking about Russian roulette. The three decided to play the game. Marshall (D) examined the gun and saw that it contained one bullet. Marshall (D) went first and there was no discharge. Atencio (D) spun the barrel and then put the gun to his head but there was no discharge. The deceased spun the barrel, put the gun to his head, pulled the trigger, and was killed.

ISSUE: Is causation established where participants engage in a reckless and wanton joint enterprise which leads to an unintended death?

HOLDING AND DECISION: (C.J. Wilkins) Yes. Atencio (D) and Marshall (D) were not under a duty to prevent the deceased from playing Russian roulette, but they were under a duty not to participate in reckless conduct which could lead to a death of one of the participants. It is not required that the defendants have forced the deceased to participate. There were not three independent acts which had no relationship to each other. This was not something only one person could do at a time. It was a joint enterprise. There is a distinction between Russian roulette and the highway drag race. In the race, it is mostly a question of skill which each driver possessed and used, independently of the other; in Russian roulette, it is solely a matter of chance and luck. All the participants were bound together by mutual encouragement, without any chance of controlling the outcome.

EDITOR'S ANALYSIS: The court is saying that the direct cause of the death was the mutual encouragement and cooperation. This joint enterprise state of mind was in existence when each person pulled the trigger. There were not three separate acts. Each pulling of the trigger was not an intervening act superseding the original agreement to play the game. The distinction from the highway drag race in [Commonwealth v. Root] was not persuasive. In the race, there was mutual encouragement and joint enterprise. The issue of luck or skill is irrelevant. Had [Root] come before this case, criminal responsibility might very well have been found to exist.

62

PEOPLE v. KRAFT
Ill.App.Ct. (1985) 133 Ill.App.3d 294, 478 N.E. 2d 1154.

NATURE OF CASE: Appeal of conviction for attempted murder.

FACT SUMMARY: Jury instructions submitted by the court in an attempted murder prosecution against Kraft (D) did not make it clear that a conviction required an intent to kill.

CONCISE RULE OF LAW: An intent to kill is an essential element of attempted murder.

FACTS: Kraft (D) engaged in a shootout with a motorist and then the police. After being arrested, he was charged with attempted murder. The court submitted instructions not specifying that an intent to kill is an element of the crime, but only that "intent to commit the offense of murder" was the required mental state. Kraft (D) was convicted, and he appealed.

ISSUE: Is an intent to kill an essential element of attempted murder?

HOLDING AND DECISION: (J. Buckley) Yes. An intent to kill is an essential element of attempted murder. Murder itself does not necessarily require an intent to kill; an intent to inflict great bodily harm may suffice. However, it is agreed that attempt crimes require not the intent to do the acts which result in the underlying crime, but to do the actual result. In terms of murder, this means that the defendant must actually intend to kill; to attempt to inflict great bodily harm will not suffice. Due to the discrepancy between the mental states required for a murder conviction and an attempted murder conviction, the instructions to the jury must make it clear that an intent to kill is required for the latter. The instructions given here did not do that, and were therefore insufficient. Reversed.

EDITOR'S ANALYSIS: Attempt has always been a "specific intent" crime. That is, the perpetrator must intend to bring about the result. Murder can be both a specific intent or general intent crime. A general intent crime only requires the intent to do the acts bringing about the result. The terms "general" and "specific" intent have fallen out of favor in some quarters, but the concepts remain.

COMMONWEALTH v. PEASLEE
117 MASSACHUSETTS 267, 59 N.E. 55.

NATURE OF CASE: Appeal from conviction for attempted arson.

FACT SUMMARY: Peaslee (D) arranged certain combustibles in order to burn down a building but never went through with his plan.

CONCISE RULE OF LAW: To determine criminal attempt, all relevant circumstances must be weighed, including the nature of the intended result.

FACTS: Peaslee (D) constructed and arranged certain combustibles in a building, in order to set it on fire. The materials were made ready to be lit, and if lit, would have set fire to the building. (Peaselee (D) wished to get the insurance proceeds.) The plan required that a candle, which was on a shelf six feet away, be placed on a piece of wood in a pan of turpentine and lit. Peaslee (D) solicited a man in his employment to go to the building and do the actual lighting. This offer was refused, however. Later, Peaslee (D) and the man drove towards the building with the intent to light the materials. When they were within a quarter of a mile from their destination, however, Peaslee (D) changed his mind and drove away. This was the nearest he ever came to accomplishing the intended arson.

ISSUE: May a wrongdoer be held criminally liable for an attempt even though he never actually went through with the last act necessary to accomplish his criminal purpose?

HOLDING AND DECISION: (C.J. Holmes) Yes. Where an act of perpetration merely comes very near to the accomplishment of an intended criminal result, the mere intent to complete it renders the crime so probable that a criminal attempt may be found to exist. Obviously, however, this is primarily a question of degree and weighing of facts. Certainly, when one commits the last act necessary to effectuate an intended criminal result, then an attempt has been committed. However, even though "attempt" suggests an act sufficient in itself to accomplish its end, mere preparations may amount to attempt in some circumstances. Of course, the degree of proximity to success necessary in such a case will vary with the circumstances (including the nature and scope of the targeted offense) but, here, there is no question but that Peaslee's (D) act of soliciting his employee to start the fire was clearly sufficient.

EDITOR'S ANALYSIS: The court indicated that attempt had been established under the facts here, but the decision was reversed on other grounds and so no decision was made. Under the rule in [Barker], this was certainly an attempt. The arranging of the combustibles on its face indicated the intent to commit arson. But the rule in [Peaslee] is closer to the reality of attempt. All the circumstances and facts must be weighed before a decision can be reached as to perpetration. As such, there is no hard and fast definition or rule to aid the student. Note, however, that this decision, written by Justice Holmes, is known as the source of the "dangerous proximity to success test" for attempt.

STATE v. YOUNG

57 NEW JERSEY 240, 271 A.2d 569.

NOTES:

NATURE OF CASE: Appeal from conviction for entering a public high school with the intent to disrupt classes and to interfere with the peace and good order of the school.

FACT SUMMARY: Young (D) went to a high school to organize a student protest.

CONCISE RULE OF LAW: The State (P) possesses the power to punish even an innocent act which falls short of attempt, if that act is done with an unlawful intent.

FACTS: Young (D) was a lay minister active in organizing student protests. After the suspension of a local high school student for refusing to stand for a flag salute, he was arrested. He had been present at the high school and had taken a leadership role in a student sit-in, when asked to leave by the superintendent of schools. From a conviction for illegal entry, he appealed.

ISSUE: Is it beyond the power of a state to punish an innocent act merely because of a forbidden purpose?

HOLDING AND DECISION: (C.J. Weintraub) No. Guilt may turn upon the intent with which something wholly innocent is done. Government cannot be limited to punishing an act only if it is undertaken in pursuit of a criminal objective. To constitute a crime, an act need not in and of itself be criminal. It may be an innocent act, but done with an unlawful intent. Indeed, conspiracy and solicitation do not require an unlawful act as long as there is an unlawful agreement or inducement. The legislature may provide a penalty even for what the common law regarded as an unpunishable act of preparation. Conviction affirmed.

EDITOR'S ANALYSIS: Even though attempt requires some act in furtherance of a crime beyond mere preparation, this does mean that the legislature cannot proscribe acts which would be classified as mere preparation, if charged as attempt. Any act may be proscribed as long as there is proof of an unlawful purpose. This is consistent with the basic rationale of attempt law, in fact. That rationale is that attempts should be punished, not to deter completed crimes but rather to subject to rehabilitation those who have manifested criminal tendencies in their conduct. Clearly, where any act is undertaken with unlawful intent, such tendencies are manifested.

McQUIRTER v. STATE
36 ALABAMA APP. 707, 63 So. 2d 388 (1953).

NATURE OF CASE: Appeal from conviction for attempt to commit an assault with intent to commit rape.

FACT SUMMARY: McQuirter (D), a black man, followed a white woman down the street and then up the street.

CONCISE RULE OF LAW: Since assault is, by definition, the attempt (i.e., intent plus some act in furtherance) to commit battery, attempted assault must be attempted battery by an act in furtherance of assault, which does not qualify as being in furtherance of battery.

FACTS: Mrs. Allen, a white woman, and her two children, walked down the street at 8 p.m. on a summer evening. McQuirter (D) was sitting in a truck as they walked by. He said something unintelligible as they walked past and then got out of the truck and followed her down the street. Allen turned into a friend's house when McQuirter (D) was two or three feet behind her. She waited ten minutes for McQuirter (D) to pass and then she proceeded on her way. She then observed McQuirter (D) walking toward her from behind a telephone pole. Allen sent the children to get another friend. When the friend appeared, McQuirter (D) went across the street and waited there thirty minutes. He then left and Allen went home. McQuirter (D) testified that he had just been walking up the street to go to another part of town and that Mrs. Allen just happened to be in front of him. When he got to the telephone pole, he waited, trying to decide whether to go on or not. After a few minutes thinking, he went on to the other part of town. He came back after thirty minutes. He denied saying anything or making any gestures toward Allen. A police chief testified that McQuirter (D) told him that he was sitting in the truck, and that he wanted a woman, and that he was going to have the first woman that came by whether he had to rape her or not. McQuirter (D) was found guilty of an attempt to commit an assault with intent to commit rape.

ISSUE: Since assault is merely the attempt to commit some battery (e.g., rape), may a person be held criminally liable for committing an attempted assault?

HOLDING AND DECISION: (J. Price) Yes. An attempt to commit an assault with intent to commit rape is merely an attempt to commit rape which has not proceeded far enough to constitute an assault. The jury need only be satisfied that the accused actually intended to rape Mrs. Allen. In determining intent, the jury may look at all the circumstances, including social conditions and customs founded upon racial differences. Here, Mrs. Allen was a white woman and McQuirter (D) was a black man, and the jury may take this into account when deciding whether McQuirter's (D) actions indicated an intent to rape. Conviction affirmed.

EDITOR'S ANALYSIS: Attempt to commit rape is a recognized offense which requires only that apparent ability to do so, and intent be proved. As such, proof of conduct, which a jury believes to manifest the intent to commit a crime, is sufficient to convict. By hornbook law, assault is the attempted battery (e.g., rape) of another with the apparent ability to succeed. Where no act in furtherance of a battery occurs, however, no assault will arise. However, acts in furtherance of the object of the contemplated assault (e.g., rape) may be sufficient to establish an attempt to accomplish that object (e.g., following Mrs. Allen). Hence, an attempted assault arises. Note, however, that since such a rule permits criminal liability merely for manifesting an intent in one's actions, this case borders on a violation of the universal criminal law requirement of actus reus.

NOTES:

UNITED STATES v. JACKSON
U.S. Ct. of Apls., 2d Cir., 1977. 560 F.2d 112.

NOTES:

NATURE OF CASE: Appeal from a conviction for conspiracy to rob and attempted robbery.

FACT SUMMARY: Jackson (D) claimed that, as a matter of law, the conduct he and his partners engaged in never crossed the line from "mere preparation" to an attempted robbery.

CONCISE RULE OF LAW: An "attempt" requires that the defendant have acted with criminal purpose and that he engaged in conduct constituting a substantial step toward commission of the target crime.

FACTS: Having been convicted of conspiracy to rob and of attempting to rob a bank, Jackson (D) contended on appeal that, as a matter of law, the line between "mere preparation" and an "attempt" had not been crossed. The evidence indicated that he and other parties got together and discussed plans to rob the bank, that they went once but arrived too late to go through with their plan; that they then changed their plans to another day, and that one of their group was arrested in the meantime. That party informed the police of the plan, so they were keeping the bank under surveillance on the day the robbery was supposed to occur. Although the arrested friend had been told that the robbery was off, the rest of the gang appeared in a car and drove around the bank, canvassing it. When they saw the police, they took off in the car. When captured, the guns to be used in the robbery were in the car, and the license plates had been altered to prevent detection.

ISSUE: To prove an "attempt," must it be shown that the defendant acted with criminal purpose and that his conduct constituted a substantial step toward commission of the target crime?

HOLDING AND DECISION: (J. Bryan) Yes. In order to find that one has perpetrated an "attempt," it must be proven that he was acting with the kind of culpability otherwise required from commission of the target crime (criminal purpose) and that he engaged in conduct constituting a substantial step toward commission of the crime. This is precisely the standard which was used in this case. The conduct must be strongly corroborative of criminal purpose in order for it to constitute a substantial step. It cannot be said that the steps taken in this case were "insubstantial" as a matter of law, so the finding that they constituted a substantial step toward commission of the target crime will not be overturned. Affirmed.

EDITOR'S ANALYSIS: Judge Learned Hand once noted that the original test for "attempts" was whether or not the person had done all that was within his power to do, but was prevented by intervention from outside. [United States v. Coplon], 185 F.2d 629 (2nd Cir. 1950). This test no longer is valid.

STATE v. DAVIS
319 MISSOURI 1222, 6 S.W. 2d 609.

NATURE OF CASE: Appeal from conviction for attempted murder in the first degree.

FACT SUMMARY: Davis (D) paid an undercover police officer to kill the husband of his lover.

CONCISE RULE OF LAW: Mere solicitation, unaccompanied by an act moving directly toward the commission of the intended crime, is not an overt act constituting an element of attempt.

FACTS: Davis (D) made a plan with a woman to kill her husband, collect the husband's life insurance, and then live together. Davis (D) approached a person to gain help in finding a hired killer. That person informed a police officer of Davis' (D) plan. The officer posed as the hired killer. Davis (D) paid the officer $600 to kill the husband, with more to be paid later. After several conferences and one aborted plan, the officer and Davis (D) decided on a course of action. The officer was to go to the husband's house, kill the husband, and cover the killing by making it look like it was done in the course of a robbery. Davis (D) gave the officer various maps and photographs of the house and its occupants. The officer went to the house, revealed his true identity, and later arrested Davis (D).

ISSUE: Did the solicitation of a planned murder, clearly indicating criminal intent, amount to a perpetration of an overt act in a criminal attempt?

HOLDING AND DECISION: (C. Davis) No. Solicitation is a separate crime, and therefore more needs to be shown than mere solicitation in order to establish an overt act. Attempt requires an act moving towards the commission of a crime and not a mere solicitation. The verbal agreement, delivery of the maps and photographs, and the payment of part of the consideration were mere acts of preparation, failing to lead directly or proximately to attempted murder. The officer never had the intent to carry out the crime, and he performed no act amounting to perpetration. He merely listened to the plans, agreed to them, and then went to the husband's house. There was no overt act. The court does not decide whether an actual assault is necessary before the crime of attempt is established.

EDITOR'S ANALYSIS: This court has come to the opposite conclusion as the court in [Berger]. Here, intent was clearly established beyond any reasonable doubt. But this court still requires that any act, to be called an overt act, must go to the very essence of a murder attempt. In [Berger], the court said that once intent is clearly established, even the slightest, most innocent act would be sufficient. The court in [Davis] requires equal emphasis on both elements of intent and act, whereas the court in [Berger] held that once intent is established, less emphasis need be put on the element of an overt act standing alone. A distinction between the two cases is that in [Davis], the crime of solicitation was clearly established, whereas in [Berger], there was no other crime to charge the defendants with other than attempt.

PEOPLE v. JAFFE
185 NEW YORK 497, 78 N.E. 169.

NATURE OF CASE: Appeal from conviction for attempt to receive stolen property knowing it to be stolen.

FACT SUMMARY: Jaffe (D) offered to buy goods that he thought were stolen; but the goods, in fact, had been previously returned to their rightful owner so that they were no longer stolen property.

CONCISE RULE OF LAW: A defendant cannot be convicted of an attempt to receive stolen property knowing it to be stolen if the goods he sought to buy were not stolen property.

FACTS: Jaffe (D) received 20 yards of cloth believing the cloth to have been stolen. However, before Jaffe (D) made the purchase, the police had arrested the thief and returned the cloth to its rightful owner, and the cloth was offered to Jaffe (D) with the true owner's consent. Therefore, the goods Jaffe (D) tried to buy were not stolen goods. Jaffe (D) was convicted of an attempt to receive stolen property knowing it to be stolen.

ISSUE: Can Jaffe (D) be convicted of an attempt to receive stolen goods knowing them to be stolen if the goods were not, in fact, stolen goods?

HOLDING AND DECISION: (J. Bartlett) No. Jaffe (D) cannot be convicted of an attempt to violate the statute because he did not have knowledge that the goods were stolen. Jaffe (D) was convicted on the authority of cases holding that a defendant may be convicted of attempt to commit a crime despite facts unknown to the defendant, which would make perpetration of the crime itself impossible. Here, Jaffe (D) made an offer to buy cloth which he believed to be stolen. But if the sale had been completed, he could not have been convicted for receiving stolen property knowing it to be stolen because he could not know a fact which did not exist. The difference between this case and the factual impossibility cases lies in the fact that the act intended by Jaffe (D) would not have been a crime if completed because the fact that the goods were, in fact, stolen is an essential element of the offense; a mere belief that goods are stolen is not sufficient because the statute requires knowledge of the stolen character. In true factual impossibility cases, the act the defendant intended would have been a crime if completed. The rule is, then, that if all the defendant intended would not have been a crime if completed, he cannot be convicted of an offense.

EDITOR'S ANALYSIS: [Jaffe], like [Osborn], turns on the elements of the offense required by statute. Since the goods were not stolen, just as in [Osborn], the substance was not noxious; any act done by the defendant was not an attempt because it was not an act in furtherance of a criminal offense. In analyzing attempt questions, look to see if all the essential elements of the offense are present in the defendant's act.

PEOPLE v. DLUGASH
Ct. of Apls. of N.Y., 1977.
41 N.Y.2d 725, 395 N.Y.S.2d 419 363 N.E.2d 1155.

NOTES:

NATURE OF CASE: Appeal from a murder conviction.

FACT SUMMARY: Dlugash (D) claimed that Michael Geller was already dead when he shot him.

CONCISE RULE OF LAW: While a defendant may not be convicted of murdering someone already dead, he can be convicted of attempted murder if he believed the person to be alive at the time.

FACTS: Two to five minutes after Bush shot Geller three times for pressing a demand for some rent money, Dlugash (D) shot Geller in the head and face five times. The expert testimony could not clearly establish precisely when Geller had died. Dlugash (D) asserted he was certain Geller was dead when he shot him and that he had only done so as he feared for his own life because Bush was holding a gun on him and telling him to shoot Geller or be killed. Dlugash (D) was convicted of murder, but the court set aside the indictment for the state's failure to prove beyond a reasonable doubt that Geller was alive when Dlugash (D) shot him. It also refused to modify the judgment to reflect a conviction for attempted murder and an appeal was taken.

ISSUE: Even though the victim may not actually have been alive at the time, can there be a conviction for attempted murder where the assailant believed the victim to be alive?

HOLDING AND DECISION: (J. Jasen) Yes. Although a murder conviction is impossible if the state does not prove beyond a reasonable doubt that the victim was alive at the time of the assault, a conviction for attempted murder is possible upon proof only that the defendant believed his victim to be alive at the time. The New York Penal Code has followed the lead of the Model Penal Code in dispensing with the traditional rule that legal impossibility is a good defense to crimes of attempt, but factual impossibility is not. Instead, the focus is on the actor's own mind, which is the best standard for determining his dangerousness to society and, hence, his liability for attempted criminal conduct. A person is guilty of an attempt when, with intent to commit a crime, he engaged in conduct tending to effect the commission of such crime. Liability exists "if such crime could have been committed had the attendant circumstances been as such person believed them to be." In this case, his contrary statements notwithstanding, Dlugash (D) believed Geller was alive when he shot him. So the judgment should have been modified to reflect a conviction for the lesser included crime of attempted murder.

EDITOR'S ANALYSIS: Under the more traditional view, factual impossibility is not a defense to an attempt crime. It exists when the criminal law prohibits what the defendant intends to do, but he is prevented from completing his plan by unanticipated outside factors. Legal impossibility, which is a defense, exists if the defendant undertook to complete an activity which, even if completed, is not prohibited by the criminal law.

HICKS v. UNITED STATES

150 U.S.442, 14 S.Ct. 144, 37 L.Ed.1137, 1893.

NOTES:

NATURE OF CASE: Action for aiding and abetting another in the commission of a murder.

FACT SUMMARY: Hicks (D) was convicted of verbally encouraging Rowe to kill the deceased.

CONCISE RULE OF LAW: Before a person can be convicted of verbally aiding and encouraging another person in the commission of a crime, it must be shown that the words were intended to encourage and aid the perpetrator of the crime.

FACTS: Hicks (D) was charged with murder because he verbally and with gestures encouraged Rowe to kill the deceased. Hicks (D) claimed that he was trying to dissuade Rowe from shooting the deceased instead of encouraging him. The jury was instructed that if they found that the effect of the words uttered by Hicks (D) was to encourage Rowe to kill the deceased, they could find Hicks (D) guilty. They were further instructed that if Hicks (D) was present in order to aid and abet Rowe, but circumstances made it unnecessary for him to do anything, he is still guilty because he was there with the intent to help if required. Hicks (D) was found guilty of murder and appealed the conviction on the ground that the requisite intent was not present.

ISSUE: When a person is convicted of encouraging another to commit a crime, must it be shown that the person actually intended the words used to help encourage the perpetrator of the crime?

HOLDING AND DECISION: (J. Shiras) Yes. The court erred in instructing the jury because it must be shown that Hicks (D) intended the words he used to encourage Rowe. It isn't enough to show that Hicks (D) intended to use the words that he did, without showing that he intended that the words encourage Rowe to murder the deceased. The court also made a mistake in telling the jury that if Hicks (D) was present in order to help Rowe that he is guilty even if no help was needed. This is improper unless it is shown that Hicks (D) and Rowe had previously conspired to kill the deceased and there was no such evidence presented at the trial. The verdict was therefore reversed and the case was remanded for a new trial.

EDITOR'S ANALYSIS: There has been an attempt in some states to hold persons present at the commission of crime responsible if it is shown that they could have done something to prevent the commission of the crime. Some statutes require that there be a duty to act and this is the majority approach, but a few states have found liability if it is shown that the person could have prevented the crime. Under that view, Hicks (D) could have been convicted if it could be shown that it was within Hicks' (D) power to prevent the crime, unless he could have shown that he really was trying to stop Rowe.

STATE v. GLADSTONE

Sup. Ct. of Wash. 78

Wash. 2d 306, 474 P.2d 274 (1980).

NATURE OF CASE: Appeal from conviction for aiding and abetting in the unlawful sale of marijuana.

FACT SUMMARY: When approached by Thompson, Gladstone (D) told him he did not have enough marijuana to sell him any but gave him the address of another who eventually did sell some to Thompson.

CONCISE RULE OF LAW: Mere communications to the effect that another might or probably would commit a criminal offense does not amount to aiding and abetting of the offense should it ultimately be committed.

FACTS: The Tacoma Police Department hired Thompson to purchase marijuana from Gladstone (D). He went to Gladstone's (D) home and asked to buy some marijuana, but Gladstone (D) said he did not have enough to sell any. He did, however, suggest that Kent might have enough to sell him and gave him Kent's address and a map he drew directing him there. Thompson did buy marijuana from Kent, and Gladstone (D) was convicted of aiding and abetting Kent in the unlawful sale of marijuana. He appealed.

ISSUE: Can one be convicted of aiding and abetting an offense for merely communicating the fact that another might or probably would commit the criminal offense that is ultimately committed?

HOLDING AND DECISION: (J. Hale) No. It would be a dangerous precedent to hold that mere communications to the effect that another might or probably would commit a criminal offense amount to an aiding and abetting of the offense should it ultimately be committed. It is true that an aider and abettor need not be physically present at the commission of the crime to be held guilty. However, it is necessary that he "in some sort associate himself with the venture, that he participate in it as in something that he wishes to bring about, that he seek by his action to make it succeed," as Learned Hand wrote. There is no evidence that Gladstone (D) did anything more than describe Kent to Thompson as an individual who might sell some marijuana. This is not enough to convict him of aiding and abetting its sale. Reversed.

DISSENT: (J. Hamilton) The jury was warranted in concluding that when Gladstone (D) affirmatively recommended Kent as a source and purveyor of marijuana, he entertained the requisite conscious design and intent that his action would instigate, induce, procure, or encourage the perpetration of Kent's subsequent crime of selling marijuana to Thompson.

EDITOR'S ANALYSIS: New York is among the few jurisdictions which have established a new statutory crime called "criminal facilitation" covering one who "believing it probable he is rendering aid to a person who intends to commit a crime...engages in conduct which provides such person with means or opportunity for the commission thereof and which, in fact, aids such person to commit a felony." [People v. Gordon], 32 N.Y.2d 62 (1973), held that a Gladstone-type defendant would not be guilty of criminal facilitation.

STATE v. MCVAY
47 R.I. 292, 131 A. 436(1926)

NATURE OF CASE: Question of law before criminal trial for manslaughter.

FACT SUMMARY: After Kelley hired McVay(D) to captain his steamer the ship's boiler exploded resulting in the loss of many lives.

CONCISE RULE OF LAW: A defendant may be indicted and convicted of being an accessory before the fact to the crime of manslaughter arising through criminal negligence.

FACTS: The steamer Mackinac's boiler exploded resulting in the loss of many lives. The steamer's captain McVay(D) was indicted for criminal manslaughter. Also indicted as an accessory to the manslaughter was Kelley, the person who hired McVay(D). Kelley's indictment stated that Kelley did "before said manslaughter was committed feloniously and maliciously aid, assist, abet, counsel, hire, command and procure....McVay". Kelley argued that he couldn't be indicted legally as an accessory before the fact since, manslaughter being inadvert and unintentional, cannot be maliciously incited before the crime is committed.

ISSUE: May a defendant be indicted and convicted of being an accessory before the fact to the crime of manslaughter arising through criminal negligence?

HOLDING AND DECISION: (J. Barrows) Yes. A defendant may be indicted and convicted of being an accessory before the fact to the crime of manslaughter arising through criminal negligence. Although there can be no accessory before the fact of a killing resulting from a sudden and unpremeditated blow, premeditation is not consistent with every manslaughter. Here, it was not contradictory to charge Kelley as an accessory before the fact. He allegedly intentionally directed and counseled the grossly negligent act, i.e. in maintaining an unsafe boiler, which the indictment charges resulted in the crime. The facts set forth in the indictment allege that Kelley with the full knowledge of the possible danger to human life, recklessly and willfully advised, counseled, and commanded McVay(D) to take the chance by negligent action or failure to act.

EDITOR'S ANALYSIS: In People v. Marshall, 362 Mich. 170, 106 N.W.2d 842(1961), the defendant gave his car keys to McCleary who the defendant knew was intoxicated. McCleary was involved in a head-on collision that killed both McCleary and the driver of the other car. The defendant was convicted of involuntary manslaughter as an accessory to McCleary's crime.

REGINA v. ANDERSON AND MORRIS

CT. OF CRIMINAL APPEAL, 1966. 2 W.L.R. 1195.

NOTES:

NATURE OF CASE: Action for manslaughter.

FACT SUMMARY: Morris (D) was with Anderson (D) when Anderson (D) killed Welch.

CONCISE RULE OF LAW: When two persons join together to commit an illegal act, and one of the parties goes beyond the contemplated acts, the other party is not liable for the consequences of the unauthorized act.

FACTS: Welch had attacked Anderson's (D) wife, and Anderson (D) and Morris (D), his friend, went after him. There was a fight in which Anderson (D) used his knife to kill Welch. There was no proof that Morris (D) knew that Anderson (D) had a knife or that he intended to use it to kill Welch. The jury was instructed that they could find Morris (D) guilty of manslaughter if he took part in the fight in which Welch was killed, even though he knew nothing about Anderson (D) having a knife or intending to use it to kill Welch. The jury found Morris (D) guilty of manslaughter and he appealed the conviction on the ground that he should not be held liable for any act committed by Anderson (D) which was beyond their joint plan.

ISSUE: Is one co-conspirator liable for the acts of the other co-conspirator when the acts go beyond the agreed scope of the conspiracy?

HOLDING AND DECISION: (C.J. Lord Parker) No. When two persons join together to commit a crime and one of the parties commits acts beyond the scope of their agreement, the other party is not liable for the consequences of the unauthorized acts. Both parties would be liable for any unusual consequences that occur from the execution of the agreed-upon actions, but when the actions of one of the parties clearly exceed their common plan, the other party is not liable for the consequences of the unauthorized acts. The jury instruction was therefore wrong, because the jury was allowed to convict Morris (D) for a crime that exceeded the common plan. Therefore, Morris (D) isn't liable as a co-conspirator of the unauthorized acts of Anderson (D). Morris' (D) conviction was therefore reversed.

EDITOR'S ANALYSIS: In finding that Anderson (D) had exceeded the scope of the conspiracy, the fact that he had used a different instrumentality than had been agreed upon was important. If Anderson (D) had beat Welch to death with his fists, it is likely that Morris (D) would have properly been found guilty of manslaughter because it is probable that he expected Anderson (D) to use his fists in beating up Welch when they found him. Generally, if the acts of one conspirator are a proximate consequence of the intended crime, all conspirators will be liable. The difficulty is in determining what acts are proximate consequences of the intended crime. The use of the knife was not a proximate consequence of their plan.

PEOPLE v. ABBOTT
N.Y. Sup. Ct. App. Div. 84 App. Div. 2d 11, 445, N.Y.S. 2d 344 (1981).

NATURE OF CASE: Appeal from negligent homicide convictions.

FACT SUMMARY: Moon (D) contended he could not be convicted for aiding criminally negligent homicide; that he could only be convicted as a principal or not at all.

CONCISE RULE OF LAW: A person is responsible for the criminal acts of another where he aids in the commission of the act with the requisite criminal mental culpability required for the commission of the crime.

FACTS: Moon (D) and Abbott (D) were engaged in an illegal drag race in their respective vehicles on a public roadway. Because of their reckless driving, they entered an intersection illegally and Abbott's (D) vehicle struck a third car, killing its occupants. Abbott (D) and Moon (D) were charged, the theory against Moon (D) being he intentionally aided the commission of criminally negligent homicide. Moon (D) appealed his conviction, contending one cannot aid an unintentional act.

ISSUE: Is a person responsible for the criminal acts of another if he aids the criminal and harbors the requisite mental state to support a conviction of the crime?

HOLDING AND DECISION: (J. Schnepp) Yes. A person is responsible for the criminal acts of another if he aids the criminal and harbors the requisite mental state for the conviction of the crime. A drag race requires two vehicles. Moon's (D) behavior was as reckless and wanton as Abbott's (D), and only by act of providence was it Abbott's (D) vehicle which actually impacted with the victim. Because Moon (D) acted with the requisite mental state to support a manslaughter conviction, he could be convicted as an aider and abettor. Affirmed.

EDITOR'S ANALYSIS: Implied in the analysis of this case is the concept of foreseeability. Participating in a joint act of unlawful conduct, such as a drag race, gives rise to foreseeable harm. Thus, when such harm does result, all actors with the requisite mens rea must be responsible, even though their specific act did not result in harm.

WILCOX v. JEFFERY

KING'S BENCH DIVISION, 1951. 1 All E.R. 464.

NOTES:

NATURE OF CASE: Action for aiding and abetting another in violating the Aliens Order of 1921.

FACT SUMMARY: Wilcox (D) bought a ticket and attended a concert by an American who was not legally permitted to perform in England.

CONCISE RULE OF LAW: If a person is present at the commission of an illegal act, the fact that he was present may be used as evidence of aiding and abetting that crime, as long as the person intended to be there and was not there accidentally.

FACTS: Mr. Hawkins, an American, and four French musicians gave a concert in London in violation of Article 18(2) of the Aliens Order, 1920. Wilcox (D) knew that the musicians were violating the law, but purchased a ticket and attended the concert anyway. It was not shown that Wilcox (D) actually applauded the performance, but neither did he get up and protest the performance of the American. After attending the performance, Wilcox (D) wrote an article for the magazine which he worked for, in which he wrote a very laudatory description of the concert. On these facts, a magistrate found that he had aided and abetted in the violation of the Aliens Order. Wilcox (D) appealed the decision, asserting that mere presence at an illegal act is not evidence of aiding and abetting that crime.

ISSUE: Is the mere presence at the commission of an illegal act evidence of aiding and abetting that crime?

HOLDING AND DECISION: (C.J. Lord Goddard) Yes. The fact that a person is present at the commission of an illegal act is evidence of the crime of aiding and abetting. However, the presence must be intended and, if it is only accidental, it cannot be used as evidence of aiding and abetting. Presence at the commission of an illegal act is only evidence to be used by the jury in determining if the person actually did aid and abet someone in committing a crime. It isn't, however, irrebuttable proof that the person actually committed the crime. It was shown that Wilcox (D) was present and his actions indicated that he supported the persons violating the law. He further took advantage of the act to write an article for his magazine. There was sufficient evidence for the magistrate to find that the crime of aiding and abetting had been committed. The judgment was therefore affirmed.

EDITOR'S ANALYSIS: This case illustrates the generally held view, but some courts have gone even further and imposed a duty on those persons present at the commission of a crime to prevent the crime if it is within their power and to hold them liable if they fail to do so. Most courts still require that there be some pre-existing duty to act before finding liability, however.

STATE v. HAYES
SUPREME CT.OF MISSOURI, 1891. 105 Mo. 76, 16 S.W. 514.

NOTES:

NATURE OF CASE: Appeal of a conviction for burglary and larceny.

SUMMARY OF FACTS: Hayes (D) was convicted of burglary even though he didn't actually enter the building.

CONCISE RULE OF LAW: When some act essential to the crime charged is done by a party who does not have the same felonious intent as the other parties, that act cannot be imputed to the other parties.

FACTS: Hayes (D) approached Hill about helping him burglarize a general store. Hill played along but was actually a relative of the store owners and advised the store owners of the plan in order to obtain the arrest of Hayes (D). In carrying out their plan, Hayes (D) raised the window to the store and helped Hill in. Hill handed out a side of bacon and then they were arrested. The jury was instructed that if Hayes (D) with a felonious intent assisted and aided Hill to enter the building, regardless of the fact that Hill had no felonious intent in entering the building, Hayes was guilty of burglary. Hayes (D) appealed his conviction asserting that the entering of the building by Hill could not be imputed to him because Hill lacked the requisite intent.

ISSUE: Can an essential act of the crime committed by one co-conspirator lacking a felonious intent be imputed to other co-conspirators who have the requisite intent?

HOLDING AND DECISION: (J. Thomas) No. In order to convict Hayes (D), it must be shown that he committed all of the elements of the crime. Since Hayes (D) did not enter the building, that act had to be imputed to him in order to find him guilty. The act of entering the building was not done with the requisite intent and therefore cannot be imputed to Hayes (D) in order to satisfy all of the elements of the crime. If Hill had entered the building with a felonious intent, that act could have been imputed to Hayes (D) and the conviction would have been proper. Hayes (D) may have been found guilty of petty larceny in taking the bacon, but the conviction for burglary is reversed.

EDITOR'S ANALYSIS: The court in this case is apparently holding that Hayes (D) cannot be convicted because Hill could not be convicted of doing the very act being imputed to Hayes (D). Other courts have been willing to convict a person for helping and encouraging another to do an act which is not a crime as to the person actually committing the act but is to the person who encourages the act. One particular case involved a person who, for a felonious reason, encouraged another to claim the privilege against self-incrimination in a grand jury investigation. It is not a crime to claim the privilege, but it is a crime to encourage the use of the privilege for a felonious purpose. It is possible that a court using this case as a precedent would have ruled differently in this case.

REGINA v. RICHARDS
COURT OF APPEALS, 1973. 3 W.L.R. 888.

NATURE OF CASE: Appeal from conviction for violation of the offenses against the Person Act of 1861.

FACT SUMMARY: Mrs. Richards (D) promised to pay five pounds to Bryant (D) and Squires (D) to attack and beat her husband, which they did, so that he would turn to her for affection.

CONCISE RULE OF LAW: Where one aids and abets the commission by another of a crime, the aider cannot be found guilty of a crime graver than the one for which the actual perpetrator is convicted.

FACTS: Bryant (D) and Squires (D) attacked Mrs. Richards' (D) husband on his way to work upon her promise to pay them five pounds. Mrs. Richards (D) had been depressed by her deteriorating marriage, had taken to drinking, and hoped that if her husband were injured he would turn to her for affection. But she had also told the attackers that she wanted Mr. Richards beaten up badly enough to put him in the hospital for a month. Mr. Richards' injuries amounted to no more than a scalp laceration requiring two stitches. Bryant (D) and Squires (D) were convicted of the misdemeanor of unlawfully and maliciously wounding another person. Mrs. Richards (D) was convicted of the more serious offense, a felony, of unlawfully wounding another, with the specific intent to inflict some grievous bodily harm.

ISSUE: Can one who aids and abets in the commission of a crime be convicted of a more serious offense than that for which the actual perpetrator is convicted?

HOLDING AND DECISION: (L.J. James) No. It cannot be said that that which was done was committed with the intention of a defendant who was not present at the time, and whose intention did not go to the offense actually committed. As Bryant (D) and Squires (D) were the persons who actually committed the crime and were convicted of a less serious offense, Mrs. Richards (D) cannot, as the one who requested the commission of the crime, be held guilty of a crime more serious than the one actually committed.

EDITOR'S ANALYSIS: Mrs. Richards (D) solicited a crime. By definition, solicitation is the urging, requesting or advising of another person to commit a felony, in some jurisdictions, also a misdemeanor. There is a conflict among jurisdictions over whether solicitation, itself a misdemeanor, is a crime where the crime urged is a misdemeanor. Some jurisdictions say the misdemeanor urged must be a serious one. At common law, where the urged crime is successfully completed, the solicitor is guilty of the same offense as is the perpetrator. That is to say, the offense of solicitation merges into the crime actually committed.

NEW YORK CENTRAL & HUDSON RIVER RAILROAD CO. v. UNITED STATES

U.S.Sup.Ct. 212 U.S. 481 (1909).

NATURE OF CASE: Appeal from a criminal conviction.

FACT SUMMARY: New York Central (D) and its assistant traffic manager were convicted for the payment of rebates to certain companies shipping sugar from New York to Detroit on its trains.

CONCISE RULE OF LAW: Although some crimes by their nature cannot be committed by a corporation, the modern authority is that a corporation can commit a crime.

FACTS: It was established that certain companies were given rebates upon shipments of sugar from New York to Detroit on New York Central's (D) trains. New York Central (D) and its assistant traffic manager were convicted for the payment of these rebates. In challenging its conviction, New York Central (D) maintained that a corporation cannot commit a crime and challenged the constitutionality of the Elkins Act. The Act provided that anything done or committed to be done by a corporation common carrier that would constitute a misdemeanor if done by one of its officers, agents, etc. would be held to be a misdemeanor committed by the corporation. It further provided that the act, omission, or failure of any officer, agent, or other person acting for or employed by the corporation would, in enforcing the aforementioned provision, be deemed to be the act, omission, or failure of the corporation common carrier.

ISSUE: Can a corporation commit a crime?

HOLDING AND DECISION: (J. Day) Yes. While the earlier writers on common law held the law to be that a corporation could not commit a crime, the modern authority, universally, is the other way. It is true that there are some crimes which, by their nature, cannot be committed by corporations. But there is a large class of offenses, of which rebating under the federal statutes is one, wherein the crime consists in purposely doing the things prohibited by statute. In that class of crimes, there is no good reason why corporations may not be held responsible for and charged with the knowledge and purposes of their agents, acting within the authority conferred upon them. Statutes against rebates could not be effectually enforced as long as individuals only were subject to punishment for violation of the law, when the giving of rebates of concessions inures to the benefit of the corporations of which the individuals were but the instruments.

EDITOR'S ANALYSIS: The Model Penal Code does not adopt so simple an approach. It actually sets up three distinct systems of corporate criminal liability. One applies to crimes of intent where no "legislative purpose to impose liability on corporations plainly appears," another to crimes of intent for which the legislature did plainly intend to impose liability on corporations, and the third to strict liability crimes.

NOTES:

UNITED STATES v. HILTON HOTELS CORP.

U.S. Ct.of Apls., 9th Cir. 467 F.2d 1000 (1972).

NOTES:

NATURE OF CASE: Appeal from a conviction for violation of the Sherman Act.

FACT SUMMARY: Hilton Hotels (D) was convicted for violating the Sherman Act after the judge charged the jury that a corporation is responsible for the acts and statements of agents, done or made within the scope of their employment, even if contrary to their actual instructions or to the corporation's stated policies.

CONCISE RULE OF LAW: As a general rule, a corporation is liable under the Sherman Act for the acts of its agents in the scope of their employment, even though contrary to general corporate policy and/or express instructions to the agent.

FACTS: Although it was against the corporate policies of Hilton Hotels (D) and constituted a violation of instructions that he take no part in the boycott, the purchasing agent for its hotel in Portland, Oregon, had threatened a supplier with loss of the hotel's business unless the supplier paid an assessment to an association which the local businesses had organized to attract convention business to Portland. The agreement among the members of the association was that those suppliers who would not pay their assessment would be "boycotted" (i.e., no purchases would be made from them). Hilton Hotels (D) was convicted for violating the Sherman Act, the judge charging the jury that a corporation is responsible for the acts and statements of its agents, done or made within the scope of their employment, even if contrary to their actual instructions or to the corporation's stated policies. On appeal, Hilton Hotels (D) cited this as error.

ISSUE: Is a corporation liable under the Sherman Act for acts its agents commit in the scope of their employment, even if against corporate policies or their express instructions?

HOLDING AND DECISION: (J. Browning) Yes. Congress may constitutionally impose criminal liability upon a business entity for acts or omissions of its agents within the scope of their employment, even without proof that the conduct was within the agent's actual authority and even though it may have been contrary to his express instructions or the policies of the corporation. While the Sherman Act does not expressly impose such liability, the construction of the act that best achieves its purpose is that a corporation is liable for acts of its agents within the scope of their authority even when done against company orders. Affirmed.

EDITOR'S ANALYSIS: In "Note, Developments in the Law - Corporate Crime: Regulating Corporate Behavior through Criminal Sanctions," 92 Harv. L. Rev. 1227, (1979), one is reminded that "Corporations have been convicted of crimes requiring knowledge on the basis of the 'collective knowledge' of the employees as a group, even though no single employee possessed sufficient information to know that the crime was being committed."

COMMONWEALTH v. BENEFICIAL FINANCE CO.

SUP.J.CT. OF MASS., 1971, Mass.275 N.E. 2d 33.

NATURE OF CASE: Appeal from a conviction for bribery and conspiracy to engage in bribery.

FACT SUMMARY: Beneficial (D), two other corporations, and several employees were convicted for bribery schemes intended to obtain favorable treatment from the Massachusetts Small Loan Regulatory Board or the Commissioner of Banks.

CONCISE RULE OF LAW: If a corporation has placed its agent in a position where he has the authority to act for and in behalf of the corporation in handling the particular corporate business, operation, or project in which he was engaged at the time he committed a criminal act, the corporation, as principal, is similarly liable.

FACTS: Beneficial (D), two other corporations, and two employees, Farrell (D) and Glynn (D), were involved in a conspiracy to bribe, and, in fact, bribed Hanley and Garfinkle, members of the Small Loans Regulatory Board. The conspiracy's purpose was to influence the Board to set a high maximum interest rate on certain loans within its jurisdiction. Glynn (D) was the direct contact with the bribed officials, while Farrell (D) supervised Glynn's (D) conspiratorial activities and chaired the intercorporate meeting at which the bribery plan was eventually adopted. Beneficial (D) alleged error in the jury instructions, claiming that it could not be held liable for the acts of Glynn (D) and Farrell (D).

ISSUE: If a corporation places its agent in a position where he has the authority to act for and in behalf of it in handling its particular business in which he was engaged at the time he committed the criminal act, is the corporation liable?

HOLDING AND DECISION: (J. Spiegel) Yes. The jury may infer a corporate policy by the corporation's placing its agent in a certain position, commissioning him to handle the particular corporate affairs in which he was engaged at the time of committing the criminal act in question. Thus, the acts and intent of natural persons (officers, directors, employees) can be treated as the acts and intent of the corporation itself. If the criminal act was committed by the agent while employing the corporate powers actually authorized for the benefit of the corporation, while acting within the scope of his employment, the act will be imputed to the corporation whether covered by the agent's instructions, whether contrary to his instructions, and whether or not lawful. Placing together the criminal standard of guilt - guilt beyond a reasonable doubt - with the rule of respondeat superior, justifies the standard applied by the trial court to a criminal prosecution of a corporation for a specific intent crime. To apply any other standard, such as a showing of approval by the Board of Directors of the agent's specific criminal conduct, would hamper law enforcement, as such approval is too easily susceptible to concealment. The size and complexity of large corporations, which necessitates the delegation of more authority to lesser corporate employees, allows lesser employees in several instances more authority and broader power in certain areas than a higher ranking corporate officer. Thus, the jury, in applying the rule, may consider the following: (1) the extent of the agent's control and authority, (2) the extent of use of corporate funds in the crime, and (3) a repeated pattern, if any, of criminal conduct which might show corporate toleration or ratification of the agent's acts.

snow corporate toleration or ratification of the agent's acts.

EDITOR'S ANALYSIS: This case contains some basic corporation law concepts. The doctrine of respondeat superior, which generally applies to employer-employee relationships, naturally arises here. Basically, the employer is liable for the conduct of his employee performed within the scope of his employment. A second concept concerned conduct of the corporation itself and its wholly-owned subsidiary, a second corporation. The two corporations being publicly represented as part of one system led the court to look through the corporate form in order to prevent the general availability of corporate insulation from protecting the corporation from punishment for wrongdoing by the other corporation with which it is basically one and the same. That is to say, where one corporation exercises management and control to such an extent over the other, the acts of the subsidiary become the acts of the parent corporation.

NOTES:

STATE v. FORD MOTOR CO.
Ind. Sup. Ct., Elkhart Cnty. No. 5324 (1979)

NATURE OF CASE: Criminal indictment by a Grand Jury.

FACT SUMMARY: The Grand Jurors of Elkhart County, Indiana, handed down a criminal indictment charging Ford Motor Co. (D) with reckless homicide and criminal recklessness for its defective design, manufacture, etc. of a Pinto automobile whose dangerous tendency to flame and burn upon rear-end impact was a proximate contributing cause of the death of the three girls when the Pinto in which they were riding was rear-ended and caught fire.

CONCISE RULE OF LAW: Not included in casebook excerpt.

FACTS: Three girls were killed when the 1973 Ford (D) Pinto they occupied was rear-ended and caught fire. Subsequently, the Grand Jurors of Elkhart County, Indiana, handed down a criminal indictment charging Ford (D) with three counts of reckless homicide and one count of criminal recklessness. The indictment charged that Ford (D) had defectively designed and manufactured the 1973 Pinto (i.e., in such a manner as was likely to cause it to flame and burn upon rear-end impact), that it had recklessly failed to repair or modify it to correct this tendency or to warn the public of it, and that Ford (D) was thus responsible for a proximate contributing cause of the deaths of the girls.

ISSUE: Not included in casebook excerpt.

HOLDING AND DECISION: Not included in casebook excerpt.

EDITOR'S ANALYSIS: This case marked the first criminal prosecution of an American corporation on the grounds that an alleged defect in its product had led to someone's death. The jury brought back a not-guilty verdict. When questioned, the jurors stated that they felt the Pinto's fuel tank was unsafe in that it was placed in such a manner that it tended to explode on rear-end impact. However, they attributed their non-guilty verdict to having heard "insufficient evidence based on the charges" in the case. N.Y. Times, March 14, 1980.

GORDON v. UNITED STATES
U.S. CT. OF APPLS., 10th Circ., 1953, 203 F.2d 248, Rev. 547 U.S.909.

NATURE OF CASE: Appeal from conviction for violation of the Defense Production Act.

FACT SUMMARY: Gordon (D) and his partners (D) in an appliance business were convicted of violating the Defense Production Act by their salesmen's making sales of sewing machines without collecting the required down payment.

CONCISE RULE OF LAW: Employers may be held liable criminally for the knowledge and acts of their agents and employees in cases involving "public welfare" offenses.

FACTS: Gordon (D) and his partners (D), also charged, run a sewing machine and appliance business. Their salesmen, in violation of the Defense Production Act, sold sewing machines without collecting the down payment required by law. The salesmen were acting in the course of their employment at the time. Gordon (D) and his partners (D) lacked knowledge of the fact that their salesmen were violating the Act.

ISSUE: May the guilty acts of the employee be imputed, in cases involving public welfare offenses, to the innocent employer where the employee was acting within the course and scope of his employment?

HOLDING AND DECISION: (J. Murrah) Yes. While it is deeply rooted in English and American criminal jurisprudence that criminal guilt is personal to the accused, and that one cannot intend an act which he did not consciously participate in, agree to, or have guilty knowledge of, in public welfare cases involving police regulation of food, drink, and drugs, the standard of proof for willful intent has been relaxed. Willfulness or guilty knowledge is not dispensed with. Rather, the employer is charged with knowledge of records which he is required to keep. Connoted is a course of conduct which may be construed by the trier of fact as deliberate and voluntary, hence, intentional.

DISSENT: (J. Huxman) A person cannot be held criminally responsible for the acts of his employee, even when committed within the scope of his employment, if he lacks personal knowledge of those criminal acts. The majority is confusing criminal law as applied to corporate employers. As a corporation is a legal fiction lacking a mind, it can only be held responsible through the knowledge of its agents. The Defense Production Act requires a willful violation which has not been shown.

ON APPEAL TO THE U.S. SUPREME COURT: (Per Curiam) Reversed for new trial. On appeal, the government admitted it was error not to require a finding of willful violation of the Act.

EDITOR'S ANALYSIS: The student is reminded to ignore the opinion of the majority above as it is erroneous. The majority mistakenly applied corporate criminal law to a case involving a partnership. While a corporation is a legal fiction, a partnership exists because of at least two real persons who lack the corporate insulation from personal responsibility. Note that the majority discusses public welfare offenses involving food, drink, and drugs. Does the sale of sewing machines appear to come under such a heading? Even if it does, note further that all cases arising in the area dealt only with laws whose violation did not require willfulness.

NOTES:

KRULEWITCH v. UNITED STATES
SUP. CT. OF U.S., 1949. 336 U.S.440, 69 Sup.Ct.716, 93 L.Ed.790.

NATURE OF CASE: Petition for certiorari after conviction for violating the Mann Act and conspiring to violate the act.

FACT SUMMARY: A statement made by Krulewitch's (D) alleged co-conspirator to the complaining witness after the three of them had been arrested plainly implied Krulewitch's (D) guilt. It was admitted as evidence.

CONCISE RULE OF LAW: A conspirator's statements against a co-conspirator are admissible as exceptions to the hearsay rule only if they were made in furtherance of the conspiracy.

FACTS: It was alleged that Krulewitch (D) and a co-defendant collaborated in inducing the complaining witness to go from New York to Florida in October 1941 for the purpose of prostitution. Testimony was admitted as to a statement made by Krulewitch's (D) alleged co-conspirator to the complaining witness which plainly implied that Krulewitch (D) was guilty. The statement was made in December 1941, after the three had been arrested.

ISSUE: Can a conspirator's statements against a co-conspirator be admitted as evidence if the statements were not made in furtherance of the crime charged?

HOLDING AND DECISION: (J. Black) No. The government argues that even after the central criminal objectives of a conspiracy have succeeded or failed, an implicit subsidiary phase of the conspiracy always survives, the object of which is to conceal the conspiracy. The government asks that the exception to the hearsay rule, which makes admissible a conspirator's declarations against a co-conspirator made in furtherance of the conspiracy, be expanded to include statements made in furtherance of this uncharged subsidiary conspiracy. We do not accept the government's arguments. In order to be admissible, a declaration must have been made in furtherance of the conspiracy charged. Since the statement in this case was not made until after the alleged conspiracy had either succeeded or failed, and the alleged conspirators had been arrested, it was inadmissible. Reversed.

CONCURRENCE: (J. Jackson) The looseness and pliability of the crime of conspiracy presents inherent difficulties. It should not be expanded.

EDITOR'S ANALYSIS: The rationale most often given for the hearsay exception is that each of the conspirators is the agent of all the others. However, the application of the exception often extends beyond that rationale. This requirement that the act or statement be in furtherance of the conspiracy is often applied broadly so that any evidence somehow relating to the conspiracy somehow comes in. Sometimes statements made prior to the formation of the conspiracy or after its termination are admitted.

BOURJAILY v. UNITED STATES
U.S.Sup.Ct. 107 Sup. Ct. 2775 (1987).

NOTES:

NATURE OF CASE: Appeal from conviction for conspiracy.

FACT SUMMARY: Bourjaily (D) contended the trial court erred in considering out-of-court statements in determining the existence of a conspiracy as a threshold to allowing the out-of-court statements into euidence.

CONCISE RULE OF LAW: A court may consider out-of-court statements to determine, by a preponderance of the evidence, that a conspiracy existed, so as to render such out-of-court statements non-hearsay.

FACTS: Bourjaily (D) was arrested for conspiracy to distribute cocaine. At trial, out-of-court statements made by Lonardo, a participant in the alleged conspiracy, were considered in determining the existence of a conspiracy. Once this was established, such statements were admitted as substantive evidence of a conspiracy under Federal Rule of Evidence 801. Bourjaily (D) appealed his conviction on the basis that the out-of-court statements could not be considered in making the preliminary finding of the existence of a conspiracy so as to render such statements non-hearsay.

ISSUE: May a court consider out-of-court statements to determine, by a preponderance of the evidence, that a conspiracy existed so as to render such out-of-court statements non-hearsay?

HOLDING AND DECISION: (C. J. Rehnquist) Yes. A court may consider out-of-court statements to determine, by a preponderance of the evidence, that a conspiracy existed, so as to render such statements non-hearsay. Once a court determines the reliability of the statements of co-conspirators, it may, consistent with the Rules, use such statements to find the existence of a conspiracy. If such is shown, the statements are considered non-hearsay and may be used as substantive evidence of the crime. As a result, the conviction here must be affirmed.

EDITOR'S ANALYSIS: The determination of reliability is a very important step in this analysis. Hearsay statements are presumptively unreliable, yet such presumption is rebuttable. The out-of-court statements of a co-conspirator, made in furtherance of the conspiracy, can then be considered non-hearsay.

PINKERTON v. UNITED STATES
U.S. SUP. CT. 1940, 328 U.S. 640, 66 S.Ct. 1180, 90 L.Ed.1489.

NATURE OF CASE: Appeal from conviction for conspiracy to violate the Internal Revenue Code.

FACT SUMMARY: Walter (D) and Daniel Pinkerton (D), brothers who live a short distance apart, were convicted of various substantive violations of the Internal Revenue Code and conspiracy to violate same.

CONCISE RULE OF LAW: As long as a conspiracy continues, the overt act of one partner may be the act of all without any new agreement specifically directed to that act.

FACTS: Walter (D) and his brother, Daniel Pinkerton (D), were convicted of various substantive violations of the Internal Revenue Code and conspiracy to violate same. They lived a short distance apart on Daniel's (D) farm and were apparently involved in unlawful dealings in whiskey. Daniel (D) contended that as only Walter (D) committed the substantive offenses, he could not be held to the conspiracy even though the substantive offenses were committed in furtherance of the conspiracy.

ISSUE: In addition to evidence that the offense was, in fact, committed in furtherance of the conspiracy, is evidence of direct participation in commission of the substantive offense or other evidence from which participation might fairly be inferred necessary?

HOLDING AND DECISION: (J. Douglas) No. Here there was a continuous conspiracy with no evidence that Daniel (D) had withdrawn from it. As long as a conspiracy continues, the conspirators act for each other in carrying it forward. An overt act of one partner may be the act of all without any new agreement specifically directed to that act. Criminal intent to do the act is found in the formation of the conspiracy. The conspiracy contemplated the very act committed. If an overt act can be supplied by the act of one conspirator, "we fail to see why the same or other acts in furtherance of the conspiracy are likewise not attributable to the others for the purpose of holding them responsible for the substantive offense."

DISSENT: (J. Rutledge) There was no evidence that Daniel (D) counseled, advised, or had knowledge of the particular acts or offenses. Simply finding them to be general partners in a crime is a dangerous precedent.

EDITOR'S ANALYSIS: It is possible that the approach taken here had in mind the development of modern organized crime. Anyone who professed his allegiance to the criminal acts of another might be held to conspiracy. Questions also arise as to punishment of one who has withdrawn from the conspiracy. The test for abandonment of a conspiracy is generally whether the abandoning conspirator has brought home to his fellow conspirators that he is quitting. Even if not a defense, a withdrawal may start the statute of limitations to run at that point, prevent his being held for crimes committed after his withdrawal, or prevent admission of evidence against him of acts or declarations his former co-conspirators did or said after his withdrawal.

UNITED STATES v. FEOLA
U.S. Sup. Ct. 420 U.S. 672 (1975).

NATURE OF CASE: Appeal from conviction for conspiracy.

FACT SUMMARY: Feola (D) contended the Government (P) had to prove he knew the identity of his victim as a federal agent before he could be convicted of conspiracy to assault a federal officer.

CONCISE RULE OF LAW: It is not necessary for a conspiracy conviction that the defendant have known the person he assaulted was a federal agent.

FACTS: Feola (D) was convicted of assaulting a federal officer and conspiracy to assault a federal officer. At trial, it was held the prosecution need not prove Feola (D) knew the victim was a federal officer before he could be guilty of conspiracy. He appealed, contending such knowledge was essential to the conviction.

ISSUE: Is it necessary for the defendant to know the governmental status of the victim to be convicted of conspiracy to assault a federal officer?

HOLDING AND DECISION: (J. Blackmun) No. It is not necessary for the defendant to know the governmental status of the victim to be convicted of conspiracy to assault a federal officer. The commission of crime occurs whether one is aware of the operative facts or not. The prearranged plan to assault carried exactly the same culpable mental state regardless of the federal standing of the victim. Affirmed.

EDITOR'S ANALYSIS: The Court rejected what has come to be known as the "corrupt motive" doctrine. Under that theory, the intent to commit a crime or an action with an evil motive must be shown to establish conspiracy where such is not necessary to establish the substantive offense.

PEOPLE v. LAURIA
CAL. DIST. CT. OF APPLS., 1967. 251 Cal.App.2d 471, 59 Cal.Rptr.628.

NOTES:

NATURE OF CASE: Action for conspiracy to further prostitution.

FACT SUMMARY: Lauria (D) knew that some of his answering service customers are prostitutes who used his service for business purposes.

CONCISE RULE OF LAW: The intent of a supplier (who knows of the criminal use to which his goods are put) to participate in the criminal activity may be inferred from circumstances showing that he has a stake in the criminal venture or by the aggravated nature of the crime itself.

FACTS: Lauria (D) and three people who used his answering service were arrested for prostitution. Lauria (D) knew that one of the people was a prostitute. He said he did not arbitrarily tell the police about prostitutes who used his service for business purposes.

ISSUE: Does a supplier necessarily become a part of a conspiracy to further an illegal venture by furnishing goods or services which he knows are to be used for criminal purposes, where the crime involved is a misdemeanor?

HOLDING AND DECISION: (J. Fleming) No. Both the knowledge of the illegal use of the goods or services and the intent to further that use are necessary to support a conviction for conspiracy. Intent may be inferred from circumstances of the sale which show that the supplier had acquired a special interest in the activity. Or a supplier may be liable on the basis of knowledge alone where he furnishes goods which he knows will be used to commit a serious crime. However, this does not apply to misdemeanors. Here, Lauria (D) was not shown to have a stake in the venture and he is charged with a misdemeanor. Hence, he could not be charged with conspiracy to further prostitution.

EDITOR'S ANALYSIS: In [U.S. v. Falcone], 311 U.S. 205, the sellers of large quantities of sugar, yeast and cans were absolved from participation in a moonlighting conspiracy. In [Direct Sales Co. v. U.S.], 319 U.S. 703, a wholesale drug company was convicted of conspiracy to violate the narcotic laws by selling large quantities of drugs to a physician who was supplying them to addicts. The Court distinguished these two leading cases on the basis of the character of the goods. The restricted character of the goods in [Direct Sales] showed that the defendant knew of their illegal use and had taken the step from knowledge to intent and agreement.

UNITED STATES v. ALVAREZ
U.S. Ct. Of Apls., 5th Cir. 610 F.2d 1250 (l980).

NATURE OF CASE: Appeal from a conspiracy conviction.

FACT SUMMARY: Alvarez (D) insisted that, at most, the evidence showed he planned to aid others in their criminal act by unloading marijuana from a plane when it landed, but that it did not show that he entered into a conspiracy with them to import marijuana.

CONCISE RULE OF LAW: For one to be guilty of conspiracy, he must have intended to enter into an agreement with others to bring about a common end, and the schemers must have had the common intent to commit an unlawful act.

FACTS: On appeal from his conviction for joining in a conspiracy to import 110,000 pounds of marijuana from Colombia, Alvarez (D) claimed that at best the evidence only showed that he had planned to unload the marijuana from the plane when it arrived in the United States. There was no proof, he insisted, that he had actually entered into an agreement with others to import marijuana. This being a necessary element to prove conspiracy on his part, he challenged his conviction.

ISSUE: In order to be convicted of conspiracy, must one have intended to enter into an agreement with others to bring about a common end, and must the schemers have had a common intent to commit an unlawful act?

HOLDING AND DECISION: (J. Rubin) Yes. Conspiracy involved two elements of intent: each party must have intended to enter into the agreement, and the schemers must have had a common intent to commit an unlawful act. For the crime to be proved, there must be evidence sufficient to warrant belief beyond a reasonable doubt that the defendant intentionally entered into an agreement to do an illegal act with the intention of consummating that act. It is not enough that a defendant may have wittingly aided a criminal act or that he may have intended to do so in the future (as seems to have happened in Alvarez's (D) case). To convict individuals of a conspiracy, the government must demonstrate that together they would accomplish the unlawful object of the conspiracy. The evidence against Alvarez (D) is insufficient to prove that he joined in an agreement to import marijuana. There is no direct proof of his consent. Nor is there any proof of his performance of an act directly in furtherance of the scheme (from which his agreement to join in the criminal conspiracy might be inferred). What Alvarez (D) intended to do is culpable, but it is not punishable as conspiracy to import marijuana. Reversed.

EDITOR'S ANALYSIS: Commentators point to the courts' unwavering insistence that the prosecution show the defendant was party to an agreement to achieve the object crime, suggesting it could well limit the reach of the conspiracy doctrine. The fact is, however, that this crucial element can be and usually is proved by inference and circumstantial evidence and thus is generally not a stumbling block to prosecutions.

KOTTEAKOS v. UNITED STATES
SUP.CT.OF U.S., 1946. 328 U.S.750, 66 Sup.Ct.1239, 90 L.Ed.1557.

NOTES:

NATURE OF CASE: Action for conspiracy to violate the National Housing Act.

FACT SUMMARY: Brown (D) made fraudulent applications for loans under the Housing Act for Kotteakos (D) and several other persons, who had no connection with each other.

CONCISE RULE OF LAW: Where one person is dealing with two or more persons who have no connection with each other, although each deals individually with the same person, they cannot all necessarily be convicted of a single conspiracy.

FACTS: Brown (D) made fraudulent application for loans under the National Housing Act for Kotteakos (D) and several other persons. No connection was shown between Kotteakos (D) and the other loan applicants, other than that Brown (D) had acted as each person's broker for obtaining the loans. Kotteakos (D) contends there was no evidence of a single conspiracy.

ISSUE: Where one person deals with two or more persons who have no connection with each other, are they all necessarily guilty of a single conspiracy?

HOLDING AND DECISION: (J. Rutledge) No. Thieves who dispose of their loot to a single fence do not, by that fact alone, become confederates. They may, but it takes more than knowledge that the fence is a fence to make them such. Here, the jury could not possibly have found that there was only one conspiracy, since many of the alleged conspirators had no connection with one another; and there was no proof that all were parties to a single common plan, scheme or design. The evidence proved the existence of not one, but of several, conspiracies. Reversed.

EDITOR'S ANALYSIS: "Wheel" conspiracies are those in which a single person or group (the hub) deals individually with two or more other persons or groups. "Chain" conspiracies are those in which there is successive communication and cooperation, analogous to the relationships between manufacturer and wholesaler, wholesaler and retailer, and retailer and consumer. A wheel arrangement is less likely to support the conclusion that the parties had a community of interest, as [Kotteakos] demonstrates. However, some wheel arrangements may be found to be conspiracies. For example, where the feasibility of an illegal horse racing service depends upon there being several customers paying high rates, subscribers aware of this situation are considered co-conspirators.

UNITED STATES v. BRUNO
U.S. CT. OF APPEALS, SECOND CIRCUIT, 1939. 105 F. 2d 921.

NATURE OF CASE: Appeal from conviction of conspiracy to import, sell, and possess narcotics.

FACT SUMMARY: Smugglers, middle people, and retailers were involved in distributing narcotics to addicts. There was no evidence of communication between the smugglers and retailers.

CONCISE RULE OF LAW: There is a single conspiracy where each member knows that the success of that part with which she was immediately concerned was dependent upon the success of the whole.

FACTS: Smugglers imported narcotics for which they were paid by middle persons who distributed them to two groups of retailers. There was no evidence of communication or cooperation between the smugglers and the retailers or between the two groups of retailers. 88 people from all four groups were indicted for a single conspiracy to import, sell and possess narcotics.

ISSUE: Can a single conspiracy exist among people who neither cooperate nor communicate with each other?

HOLDING AND DECISION: (Per Curiam) Yes. There is a single conspiracy where each member knows that the success of that part with which she was immediately concerned was dependent upon the success of the whole. Here, the smugglers knew that the middle people must sell to retailers and the retailers knew that the middle people must buy from importers. Thus, the conspirator at one end knew that the unlawful business would not stop with their buyers, and those at the other end knew that it had not begun with their sellers. Likewise, the retailers were as much a part of a single undertaking as sales people in the same shop. There was, therefore, only one conspiracy.

EDITOR'S ANALYSIS: [Bruno] is an example of the chain conspiracy. [U.S. v. Peoni], 100 F.2d 401, also involved a chain. There, Peoni sold counterfeit money to Regno, who sold it to Dorsey, who passed it onto innocent persons. Peoni was held not to be a co-conspirator with Dorsey since there was no evidence that Peoni planned sales beyond Regno or that it made any difference to him whether Regno passed the bills himself or sold them to a second passer. [Peoni] is, thus different from the usual chain conspiracy involving an ongoing scheme from which it may be concluded that the defendants had knowledge of and were dependent upon each other whether they ever actually communicated or not.

BRAVERMAN v. UNITED STATES
SUP. CT. OF U.S., 1942. 317 U.S.49, 63 Sup.Ct.99, 87 L.Ed.23.

NATURE OF CASE: Appeal after conviction for conspiracy.

FACT SUMMARY: Although it was proved that Braverman (D) and others had made a single agreement to violate several laws, they were each charged with several conspiracies.

CONCISE RULE OF LAW: Where co-conspirators make one agreement, even to violate several laws, they can be convicted of only one conspiracy.

FACTS: Braverman (D) and others collaborated in the illicit manufacture, transportation and distribution of liquor in violation of several Internal Revenue laws. They were charged and convicted on several counts. Each count charged a conspiracy to violate a different law.

ISSUE: Can co-conspirators who conspire to violate several laws be convicted of a conspiracy as to each law violated?

HOLDING AND DECISION: (C.J. Stone) No. Whether the object of a single agreement is to commit one or many crimes, it is the agreement which constitutes the conspiracy. The one agreement cannot be taken to be several agreements and, hence, several conspiracies because its object is the violation of several statutes rather than one. The single agreement is the prohibited conspiracy, and however diverse its objects, it violates only one section of the criminal code. Hence, only one penalty can be imposed. The convictions in this case must be reversed because more than one penalty was imposed for the single agreement.

EDITOR'S ANALYSIS: [Braverman] has been criticized on the ground that an agreement to commit several crimes should be treated in the same way as an attempt to commit several crimes. La Fave says that this objection is not convincing for two reasons. The first is that conspiracy, unlike attempt, is defined in terms of agreement. The second is that conspiracy, in contrast to attempt, reaches farther back into preparatory conduct. [Braverman] has also been criticized as tending to place a premium on foresight in crime.

UNITED STATES v. ELLIOTT
U.S. Ct. of Appls., 5th Cir., 1978. 571 F.2d 880.

NATURE OF CASE: Appeal from convictions for criminal conspiracy.

FACT SUMMARY: Elliott (D) and others were involved in a criminal organization which engaged in various criminal activities, the details and specifics of which were not known to every member thereof.

CONCISE RULE OF LAW: When the charge is not conspiracy to engage in a crime but conspiracy to engage in criminal enterprise, it is proper to try jointly defendants accused of specific crimes committed in furtherance of the conspiracy but not within the knowledge of all the defendants and to introduce evidence of those crimes.

FACTS: Several defendants, including Elliott (D), were tried and convicted of violating the Racketeer-Influenced and Corrupt Organizations Act of 1970 (RICO) by being involved in a conspiracy to engage in criminal enterprise. Some of the defendants allegedly furthered this enterprise by committing specific crimes of which the other defendants were unaware. On this basis, Elliott (D) and the others appealed their convictions, arguing that proof of multiple conspiracies was improper when the charge was that a single conspiracy existed. In essence, the argument was that defendants could not be tried en masse for the conglomeration of distinct and separate offenses committed by others.

ISSUE: If defendants are charged with conspiracy to engage in criminal enterprise rather than conspiracy to commit a crime, is it proper to try them jointly and introduce evidence of the specific crimes each participated in to further the conspiracy despite the fact that some of the defendants might not have had knowledge of or participated in those particular crimes?

HOLDING AND DECISION: (J. Simpson) Yes. When the charge is not conspiracy to engage in a crime but conspiracy to engage in criminal enterprise, it is proper to try the defendants jointly and introduce evidence of the specific crimes each participated in to further the conspiratorial enterprise despite the fact that some of the defendants might not have had knowledge of or participated in those particular crimes. Elliott (D) and the others agreed to engage in organized criminal enterprise to produce profit, and where this type of "enterprise conspiracy" is alleged, there is no impropriety in introducing proof of the individual crimes committed by various defendants in furtherance of their collective goal. It is of no consequence that the particular crimes were not known to or participated in by all the defendants. The congressional intent in creating this new type of conspiracy law was to reach those bastions of organized crime unreachable under general conspiracy principles by redefining the nature of certain conspiracies so as to authorize effective new remedies, such as this type of joint trial.

EDITOR'S ANALYSIS: The first concept of conspiracy envisioned a spoke-like organization where each defendant radiated outward from a central "hub," necessitating at least one common illegal object. Then came recognition of chain conspiracies, each defendant being bound to the conspiracy by the realization that he was a cog in a chain which resulted in illegal activity. With the sophistication of organized crime, these former theories of conspiracy proved outdated and ineffective in coping with large-scale crime, so Congress passed the Act addressed in this case.

NOTES:

GEBARDI v. UNITED STATES

U.S.SUP.CT., 1932. 287 U.S. 112, 53 S.Ct.35, 77 L.Ed. 206.

NATURE OF CASE: Appeal of conviction for conspiracy to violate the Mann Act.

FACT SUMMARY: Gebardi (D), not then married, transported a woman across state lines and engaged in illicit sexual relations with her.

CONCISE RULE OF LAW: When a woman acquiesces to being transported across state lines for the purpose of engaging in illicit sexual relations, thus not being herself in violation of the Mann Act, she and the man involved may not be convicted of a conspiracy to violate the Mann Act.

FACTS: Gebardi (D) purchased railway tickets, and a woman (D), not then his wife, consented to travel with him across state lines for the purpose of engaging in illicit sexual relations. No other person conspired and no evidence showed that the woman took an active role in conceiving or carrying out the transportation. The two were found guilty of conspiring to violate the Mann Act.

ISSUE: Where a woman has not violated the Mann Act, may she be convicted of a conspiracy with the man to violate it?

HOLDING AND DECISION: (J. Stone) No. Under the Mann Act, mere acquiescence by the woman transported in violation of the Mann Act is not, in itself, a violation by the woman of the Mann Act. However, incapacity of one to commit the substantive offense does not necessarily imply that he may, without fear of punishment, conspire with others who are able to commit it. Here, the criminal object of the conspiracy involved the agreement of the woman to her transportation by the man, the very conspiracy charged. The failure of the Mann Act to condemn the woman's consent is evidence of an affirmative legislative policy to leave unpunished her acquiescence. If she cannot commit the substantive offense, and only one other person, the man, is involved, she cannot conspire to commit the offense. And as a conspiracy necessarily requires at least two persons, there could be no conspiracy here.

EDITOR'S ANALYSIS: It is proper to convict a person of conspiracy only if he will be guilty of participation in the crime that was committed. In a comment to the Model Penal Code, Tent. Draft No. 10 (1960), it was said, "The doctrine is clear upon principle, for an agreement to aid another to commit a crime is not rendered less dangerous than any other conspiracy by virtue of the fact that one party cannot commit it so long as the other party can." But here the woman could not be punished for conspiring to commit a legal act, and the man alone could not be a conspiracy of one.

GARCIA v. STATE
Sup.Ct. of Ind. 71 Ind. 366, 394 N.E.2d 106 (1979).

NATURE OF CASE: Appeal from a conviction of conspiracy to commit murder.

FACT SUMMARY: The only party with whom Garcia (D) conspired in her effort to have her husband murdered was a police informant who only feigned his acquiescence in the scheme.

CONCISE RULE OF LAW: Under a penal code which adopts a "unilateral" concept of conspiracy, as opposed to the common law's traditional "bilateral" concept, a person can be convicted of conspiracy even if the only party with whom he "conspired" feigned acquiescence in the plan.

FACTS: Garcia (D) contacted Young to solicit the murder of her husband, whom she claimed constantly beat her and her children. The subsequent interactions culminated in her arrest and conviction of conspiracy to commit murder. Young, the only one with whom she allegedly "conspired," was a police informant who claimed he had only feigned his acquiescence in the scheme. Garcia (D) appealed her conviction on the ground that no conspiracy existed because there was thus no "conspiratorial agreement."

ISSUE: Does a penal code which adopts a "unilateral" concept of conspiracy permit one to be convicted of conspiracy even though the only party with whom one "conspired" feigned acquiescence in the plan?

HOLDING AND DECISION: (J. Prentice) Yes. Where, as in this case, a penal code has abandoned the traditional common law "bilateral" concept of conspiracy in favor of a "unilateral" concept, it is entirely possible for a person to be convicted of conspiracy even though the only party with whom he "conspired" feigned acquiescence in the scheme. The Model Penal Code, which takes the "unilateral" approach, explains rather well that "the major basis of conspiratorial liability - the unequivocal evidence of a firm purpose to commit a crime - remains the same" despite the fact that the person with whom the defendant conspired secretly intended not to go through with the plan. Thus, the traditional viewpoint that conspiracy necessitates actual mutual agreement on the part of two or more parties is not valid under the concept of conspiracy that Indiana's penal code now embraces, as do at least 26 states. Affirmed.

EDITOR'S ANALYSIS: The "unilateral" concept of conspiracy "creates" liability in a number of other situations where it would not traditionally exist. As the Model Penal Code states (in its comments after Section 5.03), liability is intended to attach even in those cases where "the person with whom the defendant conspired has not been apprehended or tried, or his case as been disposed of in a manner that would raise questions of consistency about a conviction of the defendant."

UNITED STATES v. PETERSON
U.S. Ct. of Apls., Dist. of Col. Cir. 483 F.2d 1222 (1973).

NOTES:

NATURE OF CASE: Appeal from a manslaughter conviction.

FACT SUMMARY: Peterson (D) appealed a manslaughter conviction after a trial in which he advanced the theory that he had acted in self-defense.

CONCISE RULE OF LAW: In order for one to have the legal right to maim or kill in self-defense, there must have been an unlawful and immediate threat, either actual or apparent, of the use of deadly force against the defender; he must have believed he was in imminent peril of death or serious bodily injury, and that the force he used was necessary to save himself therefrom.

FACTS: The issue of self-defense was at hand in Peterson's (D) appeal of his conviction for manslaughter.

ISSUE: Does one's right to maim or kill in self-defense depend on there having been an unlawful and immediate threat (either actual or apparent) of the use of deadly force against him so that he believed he was in imminent peril of death or serious bodily injury, and that the force he used was necessary to save himself therefrom?

HOLDING AND DECISION: (J. Robinson) Yes. The doctrine of homicidal self-defense emerges from the body of the criminal law as a limited exception to legal outlawry of the arena of self-help in the settlement of potentially fatal personal conflicts. It remains as viable now as it was in Blackstone's time; it also remains a law of necessity. The right of self-defense arises only when the necessity begins, and equally ends with the necessity. Thus, to have the legal right to maim or kill in self-defense, there must have been an unlawful and immediate threat (actual or apparent) of the use of deadly force against the defender. The defender must have believed he was in imminent peril of death or serious bodily harm, and that his response was necessary to save himself therefrom. These beliefs must not only have been honestly entertained, but also objectively reasonable in light of the surrounding circumstances. Nothing less than a concurrence of these elements will suffice.

EDITOR'S ANALYSIS: Most modern statutes maintain the traditional requirement that the defender's honest belief that the defensive force he used was necessary to save himself from death or serious bodily harm be objectively reasonable. English commentators, the Criminal Law Revision Committee, and Professor Glanville Williams have supported the notion that a wholly subjective test should be used instead, i.e., one which concerns itself only with whether the defender honestly believed he needed to use the force he did to save himself from death or serious bodily injury.

PEOPLE v. GOETZ
N.Y.C. App. 68 N.Y.2d 96, 497 N.E.2d 41 (1986).

NATURE OF CASE: Appeal from dismissal of attempted murder charges.

FACT SUMMARY: Goetz (D) contended that he was justified in shooting his assailants if he alone reasonably believed he was in danger, and not if a reasonable man believed so.

CONCISE RULE OF LAW: A person is justified in the use of deadly force if, objectively, a reasonable man would, in his position, believe he was in danger of life or physical being.

FACTS: Goetz (D) was approached on a subway by several youths who asked him for money. Goetz (D), who had been attacked years before, subjectively believed he was being robbed and pulled a gun. He shot at the youths several times, even though they ran away. In one case, Goetz (D) approached an unarmed youth and shot him. Goetz (D) admitted he wanted to kill the youths. The prosecution instructed the Grand Jury that self-defense could be found only if Goetz (D) objectively, as a reasonable man, could have concluded his life was in danger. Indictments were handed down, yet the trial court dismissed them because it held the prosecution erroneously instructed that an objective rather than a subjective standard applied. The State (P) appealed.

ISSUE: Does an objective test apply to the determination of the availability of self-defense?

HOLDING AND DECISION: (J. Wachtler) Yes. A person is justified in the use of self-defense by deadly force if, objectively, a reasonable man would believe he was in danger of life. Subjective basis for the use of such force cannot be the standard a civilized society uses. It is too easy to fabricate a justification for the use of force. The situation must objectively require the use of such force, and the factors must be identifiable by the trier of fact.

EDITOR'S ANALYSIS: A common thread that runs through the defense of self-defense and the defense of insanity is the objective test. As seen above in [Goetz], an objective reasonable person test was applied to determine whether the defendant was justified in taking the action he did to protect his own life. In insanity defense cases, the preferred approach is similar. If objectively viewed, the defendant cannot appreciate the illegality of his conduct, then the insanity defense can be asserted.

STATE v. WANROW
Sup. Ct. of Wash. 88 Wash. 2d 221, 559 P.2d 548 (1977).

NATURE OF CASE: Appeal from reversal of a second-degree murder conviction.

FACT SUMMARY: A reversal of Wanrow's (D) second-degree murder conviction had been obtained on the grounds that the jury instructions regarding the law of self-defense was improper.

CONCISE RULE OF LAW: In determining if a defendant engaged in what is legally permissible self-defense, his or her actions are to be judged against his or her own subjective impressions, and not those which a detached jury might determine to be objectively reasonable.

FACTS: Yvonne Wanrow (D) was convicted of second-degree murder, although she claimed to have acted in self-defense when she killed the man she suspected had molested her daughter and other neighborhood children. The evidence indicated that her friend, Chuck Michel, had gone to talk to the victim and that they went to the house in which Mrs. Wanrow (D) was staying to supposedly try to straighten out the situation; that he entered the house alone, and that he declined to leave when Mrs. Wanrow (D) asked him to upon seeing him. At the time, Mrs. Wanrow (D), who was 5'4" tall and used a crutch because of a broken leg, testified that she went to the door and shouted for Chuck Michel's aid. She then turned around to find the suspected molester directly behind her. Whereupon, Mrs. Wanrow (D) testified, she became gravely startled and shot him in a reflex action. In reversing her conviction for second-degree murder, the Court of Appeals held that the jury instructions regarding self-defense had been improper. First of all, they instructed the jury to consider only those acts and circumstances occurring at or immediately before the killing in deciding whether Mrs. Wanrow (D) had been under the apprehension of death or serious bodily harm when she fired the fatal shot. This meant the jury could not consider Mrs. Wanrow's (D) knowledge of the victim's reputation for aggressive acts based upon events that had occurred over a period of years. The jury instructions also continuously used the masculine gender in setting up an objective standard for determining if the defendant had acted in self-defense.

ISSUE: When the issue of self-defense is raised, are a defendant's actions to be judged against his or her own subjective impressions?

HOLDING AND DECISION: (J. Utter) Yes. When, as in this case, self-defense is raised as an issue, the defendant's actions are to be judged against his or her own subjective impressions and not those which a detached jury might determine to be objectively reasonable. The vital question is the reasonableness of the defendant's apprehension of danger, but only in the sense that the jury must stand, as nearly as practicable, in the shoes of the defendant; and from this point of view, determine if the act was the result of the defendant's reasonable apprehension of death or serious bodily harm. It is thus apparent that the jury should have considered Mrs. Wanrow's (D) knowledge of the victim's prior reputation for aggressive acts and not just those circumstances "at or immediately before the killing." Under the law of this state, the jury should have been allowed to consider this information in making the critical determination of the "degree of force which... a reasonable person in the same situation... seeing what (s)he sees and knowing what

[handwritten: Test]

(s)he knows then would believe to be necessary." Another fatal flaw in the instructions is that they did not make clear that the defendant's actions are to be judged against her own subjective impressions and not those which a detached jury might determine to be objectively reasonable. A defendant's conduct is to be judged by the condition appearing to her at the time, not by the condition as it might appear to the jury in light of testimony before it. The instructions clearly misstated our law in creating an objective standard of "reasonableness." They then compounded that error by utilizing the masculine gender and thus suggesting that the defendant's conduct should be measured against that of a reasonable male individual finding himself in the same circumstances. Furthermore, the impression created - that a 5'4" woman with a cast on her leg and using a crutch must, under the law, somehow repel an assault by a 6'2" intoxicated man without employing weapons in her defense, unless the jury finds her determination of the degree of danger to be objectively reasonable - constituted a separate and distinct misstatement of the law. The defendant was entitled to have the jury consider her actions in the light of her own perceptions of the situation, including those perceptions which were the product of our nation's "long and unfortunate history of sex discrimination." Until such time as the effects of that history are eradicated, care must be taken to assure that our self-defense instructions afford women the right to have their conduct judged in the light of the individual physical handicaps which are the product of sex discrimination. *[handwritten: Policy consider women's view]*

EDITOR'S ANALYSIS: In many states where the objective reasonableness of the defendant's apprehension and response must still be shown when self-defense is claimed, the ultimate question becomes what to do with those people whose apprehension and response was honest but not objectively reasonable. Many jurisdictions have solved this dilemma by making such parties guilty of the crime of "voluntary manslaughter" instead of murder.

NOTES: *[handwritten: Opposite to Goetz]*
[handwritten: Problem created by "subjective standard"]

STATE v. KELLY
97 N.J. 178, 478 A.2d 364 (1984).

NATURE OF CASE: Appeal from conviction for reckless manslaughter.

FACT SUMMARY: Kelly (D) appealed from a decision affirming her conviction of reckless manslaughter, contending that the trial court erred in ruling that expert testimony concerning the "battered-woman's syndrome" was inadmissible on the issue of self-defense.

CONCISE RULE OF LAW: The battered-woman's syndrome is an appropriate subject for expert testimony, and such testimony is admissible on the issue of self-defense.

FACTS: On May 24, 1980, Kelly (D) stabbed her husband to death with a pair of scissors. The facts surrounding the actual stabbing were in dispute. Kelly (D) claimed that she stabbed him in self-defense, while the State (P) contended that she was the aggressor in the attack. Evidence presented during the trial indicated that the marriage between Kelly (D) and her husband was a rocky one, with Kelly (D) being subjected to frequent, periodic beatings at the hand of her husband. Evidence was also presented that Kelly (D) had been threatened with death by Mr. Kelly on more than one occasion. Kelly (D) attempted to introduce expert testimony on the battered-woman's syndrome to help establish her claim of self-defense. The trial court, apparently believing that the purpose of the testimony was to explain and justify Kelly's (D) perception of being in fear of her life, ruled the testimony inadmissible, and Kelly (D) was convicted of reckless manslaughter. The Appellate Court affirmed the conviction, and from this decision, Kelly (D) appealed.

ISSUE: Is the battered-woman's syndrome an appropriate subject for expert testimony, and is such testimony admissible on the issue of self-defense?

HOLDING AND DECISION: (G.J. Wilentz) Yes. The battered-woman's syndrome is an appropriate subject for expert testimony, and such testimony is admissible on the issue of self-defense. The battered-woman's syndrome is what some sociologists and psychologists call the effects of a sustained pattern of physical and psychological abuse that undeniably a substantial number of women suffer from. Among the effects of such abuse, and which the battered-woman's syndrome attempts to explain, is the demoralizing and degrading situation in which these women often exist and are often trapped by their own fear, Kelly's (D) credibility is a key issue in this case, since in order to find for her, the jury must believe that she acted in self-defense. The expert testimony excluded was clearly relevant to her state of mind, namely that it was admissible to show she honestly believed that she was in imminent danger of death, by showing that Kelly's experience was common with other women in similar abusive relationships. The testimony would be relevant solely for this purpose, but not as to the objective reasonableness of Kelly's (D) belief. The battered-woman's syndrome is an area where the trier of fact's common perceptions may be mistaken. (After determining the testimony admissible, the court went on to rule that the testimony satisfied state Evidence Rule requirements for admissibility, in that the area was not one within lay knowledge, and that the testimony was sufficiently reliable.) Reversed; remanded for new trial.

EDITOR'S ANALYSIS: The battered-woman's syndrome creates problems for prosecutors, because the syndrome can help explain the actions of a battered woman who may act not in the fact of an immediate threat, but in the fact of an imminent threat, since the actions manifest over a period of time as a result of frequent and persistent abuse. Courts, in evaluating this type of case on appeal, are often called to rule based on perceptions of the battered woman situation which do not comport with the opinions of sociologists and psychologists who have studied this situation extensively.

NOTES:

STATE v. ABBOTT
SUP. CT. OF N.J., 1961. 36 N.J. 63, 174 A.2d 881.

NOTES:

NATURE OF CASE: Appeal from conviction of assault and battery.

FACT SUMMARY: Abbott (D) and Michael, Mary and Nicholas Scarano were in a fight during which Abbott (D) hurt Nicholas with a hatchet.

CONCISE RULE OF LAW: A person has a duty to retreat before using deadly force to defend himself, but he need only retreat where he knows that he can do so with complete safety.

FACTS: There was a fight between Nicholas Scarano and Abbott (D). A jury could find Nicholas was the aggressor. Michael Scarano joined the fight armed with a hatchet, and Mary Scarano joined, armed with a knife. All of the Scaranos were hit with the hatchet. Abbott (D) claimed that they were hit while struggling for the hatchet. A jury could find, however, that Abbott (D) intentionally inflicted the blows.

ISSUE: Does a person have a duty to retreat before using deadly force to defend himself?

HOLDING AND DECISION: (C.J. Weintraub) Yes. Deadly force may not be used in self-defense when there is an opportunity to retreat. However, the actor must know of the opportunity and must be able to escape with complete safety. The burden is on the defendant to produce evidence to support the defense. But the state has the burden of proving, beyond a reasonable doubt, that the defense is not true. In a case involving the issue of retreat, the state must prove beyond a reasonable doubt that the defendant knew that he could retreat in complete safety. While the retreat issue only arises when deadly force was used, it is relevant where deadly force results in injury, rather than death. In this case, if Abbott's (D) version of the story, which is that all of the Scaranos came after him, is believed, it may be that the retreat issue should be resolved in his favor. His conviction is reversed.

EDITOR'S ANALYSIS: It is agreed that one need not retreat before using nondeadly force. The majority of U.S. jurisdictions hold that the defender need not retreat, even though he knows he can do so safely, before using deadly force upon an assailant whom he reasonably believes will kill him. While there is a strong policy against the unnecessary taking of human life, there seems to be a stronger policy against making one act in a "cowardly" and "humiliating" manner. Advocates of 'no retreat' say that "The manly thing is to hold one's ground and society should not demand what smacks of cowardice." A strong minority of jurisdictions, in which "courageous" men have not prevailed, do not reward such male foolishness, and hold that one must retreat before using deadly force, if the defendant knows he can retreat in safety.

UNITED STATES v. PETERSON
U.S. Ct. of Apls., Dist. of Col. Cir. 483 F.2d 1222 (1973).

NATURE OF CASE: Appeal from conviction for manslaughter.

FACT SUMMARY: Peterson (D) challenged an instruction that the jury might consider whether he was the aggressor in the altercation that led to the homicide he claimed to have committed in self-defense.

CONCISE RULE OF LAW: An affirmative unlawful act reasonably calculated to produce an affray foreboding injurious or fatal consequences is an aggression which, unless renounced, nullifies the right of homicidal self-defense.

FACTS: Peterson (D) was convicted of manslaughter in a trial at which the evidence showed that he had killed one Keitt in an incident that started when Peterson (D) came out of his house to find Keitt in the process of removing the windshield wipers from Peterson's (D) wrecked car. After a verbal exchange, Peterson (D) went back into the house, got his pistol, returned to his yard, loaded his pistol, and then shouted to Keitt (who had since joined his companions in his car and was about to leave), "If you move, I will shoot." Walking to his gate, Peterson (D) then said, "If you come in here I will kill you." Keitt alighted from his car, took a few steps toward Peterson (D), exclaimed "What the hell do you think you are going to do with that?" (meaning the pistol), went to his car and got a lug wrench, raised it while he advanced toward Peterson (D), and continued to advance after Peterson (D) warned him not to "take another step." Peterson (D) shot him when he was about 10 feet away. He claimed self-defense and, on appeal, challenged the jury instruction that allowed the jury to consider whether he had been the aggressor in the altercation that immediately preceded the homicide.

ISSUE: Does an affirmative unlawful act reasonably calculated to produce an affray foreboding injurious or fatal consequences constitute an aggression which, unless renounced, nullifies the right of homicidal self-defense?

HOLDING AND DECISION: (J. Robinson) Yes. While there appears to be no fixed rule on the subject, the cases hold, and this court agrees, that an affirmative unlawful act reasonably calculated to produce an affray foreboding injurious or fatal consequences is an aggression which, unless renounced, nullifies the right of homicidal self-defense. This court cannot escape the abiding conviction that the jury could readily find Peterson's (D) "challenge" to be a transgression of that nature. Affirmed.

EDITOR'S ANALYSIS: Consider in this vein the case in which a court held that a defendant had lost his right of self-defense when he became the "aggressor" by way of engaging in intimate contact with the victim's wife and thus provoking the victim, who caught them in the act. [Barger v. State], 235 Md. 556, 202 A.2d 344 (1964).

PEOPLE v. CEBALLOS
SUP.CT. OF CALIF., 1974. 12 Cal.3d 470, 526 P.2d 241.

NOTES:

NATURE OF CASE: Appeal from conviction for assault with a deadly weapon.

FACT SUMMARY: Ceballos (D) was convicted of assault with a deadly weapon when a trap gun he set up in his garage fired into the face of a teenage boy who broke open the garage door.

CONCISE RULE OF LAW: A person may be held criminally or civilly liable if he sets upon his premises a deadly mechanical device and that device kills or injures another.

FACTS: Ceballos (D) lived in his apartment over his garage. One month, some tools were stolen from his garage. Later, he noticed the lock had been bent and that there were pry marks on the door. Ceballos (D) then set up a trap gun which would fire when someone opened the garage. Two boys, Robert, 15, and Stephen, 16, both unarmed, pried off the lock. When Stephen opened the door, he was shot in the face by the trap gun.

ISSUE: Could Ceballos (D), who contends the shooting would have been justified had he been present, do indirectly - use deadly force - what he could have done directly?

HOLDING AND DECISION: No. A person may be held criminally or civilly liable under statutes prescribing homicides with intent to injure if he sets upon his premises a deadly mechanical device and that device kills or injures another. An exception has been recognized where the intrusion is, in fact, such that the person, were he present, would be justified in taking life or inflicting the bodily harm with his own hands. But if the actor is present, there is the possibility that he will realize that deadly force is not necessary, while a device lacks that discretion. Deadly devices should be discouraged because, even though the law of torts recognizes an exception as stated above, that exception is not appropriate to criminal law, for it does not prescribe a workable standard of conduct; liability depends on fortuitous results. While burglary is a dangerous crime at common law, by statute that crime has a much wider scope, so where the character and manner of a burglary would not create a fear of great bodily harm, there is no cause for the use of deadly force.

EDITOR'S ANALYSIS: Defense of property relies on the theory that a man's home is his castle. Deadly force may be used where it appears reasonable and necessary to prevent an unlawful trespass apparently committed to harm the occupants or for the purpose of committing a felony therein. A mere trespass without felonious intent or not creating a serious threat of danger to the occupants will not justify the use of deadly force. Notice that the exception being argued on appeal is a rule of tort law, and that the court noted that its decision was against the position of the Restatement Second of Torts. The tort rule simply did not state a clear enough standard to be applicable to criminal situations.

DURHAM v. STATE
SUP.CT. OF IND., 1927, 199 Ind. 567, 159 N.E. 145.

NATURE OF CASE: Appeal from conviction of assault and battery.

FACT SUMMARY: Durham (D), a game warden, arrested Long for illegal fishing. While Long was beating him with an oar, Durham (D) shot him.

CONCISE RULE OF LAW: While a police officer is not justified in killing or inflicting great bodily harm in attempting to arrest one accused of a misdemeanor, where the accused resists arrest, the officer may repel such resistance with such force as is necessary, short of taking life, and may seriously wound or kill the accused if necessary to prevent the accused from seriously wounding or killing him.

FACTS: Durham (D), a game warden, arrested Long for illegal fishing. Long attempted to escape in his boat. Durham (D) pursued him, and while Long was beating him with an oar, Durham (D) shot him in the arm.

ISSUE: Is an arresting officer ever justified in seriously wounding one whom he is attempting to arrest for a misdemeanor?

HOLDING AND DECISION: Yes. An officer may use all the force reasonably necessary to arrest one accused of a misdemeanor. However, he may not, merely for the purpose of effecting the arrest, kill or inflict great bodily harm. Hence, he may not kill a fleeing misdemeanant. If the accused resists, however, the officer may repel the resistance with such force, short of taking life, as is necessary to effect the arrest. Further, in repelling the resistance, the officer is justified in seriously wounding or killing the accused if that is necessary to prevent the accused from seriously wounding or killing the officer. Durham's (D) conviction is reversed.

EDITOR'S ANALYSIS: Generally, an officer may use deadly force, if he reasonably believes it necessary to prevent the escape of a person fleeing from an arrest for a felony, although as stated in [Durham], he may not use such force against one fleeing from an arrest for a misdemeanor. Thus, an officer is not justified in shooting at a speeding auto which does not heed his signal to stop. If he aims at and kills the driver, he is guilty of murder. If he aims at the tire, he is guilty of manslaughter if the driver's death results. La Fave feels that while the felony portion of this rule may have made some sense when all felonies were punishable by death, it is too harsh in present times when many felonies do not carry such a penalty. He advocates that an officer's right to use deadly force to arrest an accused felon be limited to dangerous felonies generally involving a substantial risk of death or great bodily harm.

TENNESSEE v. GARNER
U.S.Sup.Ct. (1985) lO5 S.Ct. 1964.

NATURE OF CASE: Appeal from reversal of dismissal of civil rights action.

FACT SUMMARY: Garner's (P) decedent, an unarmed suspect, was shot and killed while fleeing from arrest.

CONCISE RULE OF LAW: A police officer may not use deadly force to prevent the escape of an unarmed suspect unless it is necessary to prevent the escape and the officer has probable cause to believe the suspect poses a significant threat to others.

FACTS: Memphis police officers responded to a dispatch sent out regarding a prowler. When they arrived at the scene, Garner's (P) decedent was seen to run across the back yard. One officer was able to see that he was unarmed. The decedent failed to stop when ordered to, and one of the officers fired at him, killing him. Tennessee law permitted the use of deadly force to stop a fleeing suspect in all circumstances. Garner (P) brought a civil rights action.

ISSUE: May a police officer use deadly force to prevent the escape of an unarmed suspect unless it is necessary to prevent the escape and the officer has probable cause to believe the suspect poses a significant threat to others?

HOLDING AND DECISION: (J. White) No. A police officer may not use deadly force to prevent the escape of an unarmed suspect unless it is necessary to prevent the escape and the officer has probable cause to believe the suspect poses a significant threat to others. The rights of the individual must be balanced against the governmental interest. The suspect's interest in not being killed is obvious. The use of deadly force is a highly suspect procedure in effecting arrest, as a dead suspect cannot be arrested. Further, it dates from a time when almost all felonies were punishable by death so the suspect would merely receive his punishment a bit sooner. This is not so today. The fact that using deadly force against nondangerous suspects is disfavored is demonstrated by the fact that less than 15% of all police departments allow it. For these reasons, such force is unconstitutional when applied to nondangerous suspects, and the individual's interest outweighs those of the government. Here, the police had no cause to believe the decedent was dangerous, so the force was excessive. Affirmed.

DISSENT: (J. O'Connor) To allow a suspect to escape is often to lose all hope of ever catching him. Society has an interest in being protected against suspects at large. Further, an officer in the field cannot be expected to analyze the situation to the extent the Court's rule requires.

EDITOR'S ANALYSIS: The Court analyzed this case in terms of the Fourth Amendment. The use of deadly force was seen as a seizure of the person. The private interest-governmental interest balancing test the Court used has become the established method of determining the constitutional validity of a seizure.

UNITED STATES v. HILLSMAN
U.S. Ct. of Apls., 7th Cir. 522 F.2d 454 (1975).

NATURE OF CASE: Appeal from convictions for assaulting a federal officer.

FACT SUMMARY: Hillsman (D) and Bush (D) insisted that the trial judge had erred in refusing to instruct the jury that if they reasonably believed the federal officer they "assaulted" to be a fleeing felon, they must be acquitted of the charges of assaulting a federal officer.

CONCISE RULE OF LAW: A private citizen has the right to arrest one who has committed a felony in his presence, and may even arrest one he reasonably believes to have committed a felony - so long as the felony was in fact committed.

FACTS: As a defense to the charge that they had assaulted a federal officer while attending a funeral, Hillsman (D) and Bush (D) maintained that they had reasonably believed the federal officer (a Drug Enforcement Administration agent conducting undercover surveillance in street clothes and an unmarked car) was a fleeing felon. Basically, they saw the officer running from the scene at which a shot had been fired. Someone in the crowd had pointed to the agent saying, "He is the one; there he goes." As the agent drove away, shots were fired at his car, but he was not injured. Hillsman (D) and Bush (D), who were members of the group that chased his car and were observed shooting at it, challenged their conviction on the grounds that the court had erred in refusing to instruct the jury that they should be acquitted if they reasonably believed the federal officer to be a fleeing felon.

ISSUE: Does a private citizen have the right to arrest one he reasonably believes to have committed a felony only if it turns out that the felony was in fact committed?

HOLDING AND DECISION: (J. Pell) Yes. The ultimate question in this case is whether because of the agent's actions, the defendants would have been justified in using force against him had he, in fact, been a "civilian." Indiana follows the common law rule that "a private citizen has the right to arrest one who has committed a felony in his presence, and may even arrest one he reasonably believed to have committed a felony, so long as the felony was in fact committed." The jury was expressly told that if they found a felony had occurred, then they could apply the law of citizen's arrest. That was sufficient.

CONCURRENCE: (J. Tone) I am uncomfortable in holding a defendant criminally accountable for conduct which he may have reasonably thought was not only lawful but socially desirable.

EDITOR'S ANALYSIS: A private citizen acts at his own peril in attempting an arrest, but if in fact the felony has been committed, the citizen has the right to use deadly force to effect such an arrest in an appropriate case. Typically, statutes permit such use of deadly force to effect the arrest of one who is in immediate flight from the commission of serious crimes like murder, manslaughter, forcible rape, sodomy, etc.

PEOPLE v. UNGER
66 Illinois 2d 333 (1977).

NOTES:

NATURE OF CASE: Prosecution for escape from prison.

FACT SUMMARY: Unger (D) escaped from a minimum security honor farm allegedly to avoid homosexual assaults and threats of death.

CONCISE RULE OF LAW: The defenses of necessity and compulsion are available in escape cases, and the jury should be so instructed where evidence adduced at trial is sufficient to raise the defense.

FACTS: Unger (D) was repeatedly sexually assaulted and threatened with death and physical injury at a minimum security honor farm. Unger (D) left the farm and was apprehended several days later. Unger (D) alleged that his escape was not voluntary and had been caused by compulsion (the acts of others) and necessity (outside forces, e.g., natural conditions). The court refused to instruct the jury that these facts were a defense to the charge. Rather, the court instructed the jury that Unger's (D) reasons for escaping were immaterial.

ISSUE: Are compulsion or necessity defenses to an escape charge?

HOLDING AND DECISION: (J. Ryan) Yes. While escape situations do not fit within the traditional ambit of either compulsion or necessity defenses, they have been recognized by several jurisdictions in similar situations. Since compulsion requires an imminent threat of great bodily harm, many commentators suggest that the situation fits within the necessity defense. The prisoner is forced to choose between the lesser of two evils. We likewise find that compulsion and necessity are a defense to a charge of escape. Where the defendant raises sufficient evidence at trial, the jury should be instructed as to the availability of the defense. It is a limited defense and the jury may consider factors such as whether the defendant's fears were justified; whether the threat was imminent and sufficiently severe; whether there was time to resort to either the courts or prison officials and if this would be effective; and whether the prisoner immediately reported his escape to the police. These factors go to the weight of the defense. A jury might find the defense valid even if one or more of these factors are missing. Reversed.

DISSENT: (J. Underwood) An unconditional recognition of these defenses could lead to future problems. I would allow the defenses only where the prisoner exactly complies with the requirements stated by the majority. Failure to immediately report the escape should prevent their being pleaded as a defense.

EDITOR'S ANALYSIS: Duress was recognized as a defense to escape in a situation similar to [Unger. People v. Harmon], 53 Mich. App. 482 (1974). The traditional response by most jurisdictions is that the defense should not be available on public policy grounds. Other jurisdictions would allow the defense on a limited basis, only if certain conditions existed which were similar to those stated by the majority in [Unger. People v. Lovercamp], 43 Cal. App. 3rd 823 (1974).

UNITED STATES v. KRONCKE
451 F.2d 697 (8th Circuit, 1972).

NATURE OF CASE: Appeal from conviction for hindering and interfering with the administration of the Military Selective Service Act by force, violence, and otherwise.

FACT SUMMARY: Kroncke (D) and Therriault (D) forcibly entered the Selective Service office, intending to destroy the county's draft files. They claim that their actions were justified as protest to the Vietnam war.

CONCISE RULE OF LAW: The defense of necessity is not available to defendants whose purpose is to effect a change in governmental policies which, according to the defendant, may result in a future saving of lives.

FACTS: Kroncke (D) and Therriault (D) forcibly entered the Selective Service office intending to destroy the county's draft files. They were motivated by religious and moral convictions and their beliefs that the Vietnam war is illegal and immoral and in violation of international law. They also believe that the political leadership is not responsive to the will of the people and that there is no legal recourse to bring the war to an end. The trial court refused to submit the defense of justification to the jury.

ISSUE: Is the defense of justification available to defendants who act illegally for the purpose of bringing about the end of the Vietnam war?

HOLDING AND DECISION: (J. Heaney) No. For the defense of necessity to be available, the defendant must have had a reasonable belief that it was necessary for him to act to protect his or others' lives from direct and immediate peril. The defense is not permitted where, as here, the defendant's purpose is to effect a change in governmental policies which, according to the defendant, may result in a future saving of lives. Furthermore, the Vietnam war was not illegal because it was undeclared, and the Selective Service system is not unconstitutional insofar as it functions to draft men for that war. Lastly, while in restricted circumstances, a morally motivated act contrary to the law may be ethically justified, the action must be nonviolent and the actor must accept the penalty for his action. The exercise of a moral judgment based on individual standards does not carry with it legal immunity from punishment for breach of the law. The trial court did not err in refusing to submit the defense of justification to the jury.

EDITOR'S ANALYSIS: The court ends its decision with a reference to the great "power of the vote." However, looking back, it is difficult not to agree with these defendants that they had "no legal recourse to bring about an end to the war." The defense of necessity is available only in situations wherein the legislature has not itself, in its criminal statutes, made a determination of values. The Model Penal Code specifically limits the defense to those situations in which a legislative purpose to exclude the justification does not plainly appear (i.e., old abortion statutes which provided that a crime is committed even when the abortion is performed to save the mother's life, thereby foreclosing the defense that the abortion was necessary to save life).

NOTES:

STATE v. TOSCANO
Sup.Ct. of N.J. 74 N.J. 421, 378 A.2d 755 (1977).

NATURE OF CASE: Appeal from conviction for conspiracy to obtain money by false pretenses.

FACT SUMMARY: The trial judge decided that Toscano's (D) claims that he engaged in certain illegal acts because of fear that another party would harm himself or his wife in the future were, even if true, insufficient to constitute a defense of duress - and he so instructed the jury.

CONCISE RULE OF LAW: Duress is a defense to a crime (other than murder) if the defendant engaged in conduct because he was coerced to do so by the use of, or threat to use, unlawful force against his person or the person of another, which a person of reasonable firmness in his situation would have been unable to resist.

FACTS: At his trial for conspiracy to obtain money by false pretenses, Toscano (D), a chiropractor, admitted that he had aided in the preparation of a fraudulent insurance claim by making out a false medical report. He maintained that he did so, however, because the architect of the conspiracy had implied that the future safety of himself and his wife depended on it. Because he found there was no evidence that Toscano (D) acted under a present, imminent, and impending threat of serious bodily injury to himself or another, the trial judge instructed the jury that "the circumstances described by Dr. Toscano (D) leading to his implication in whatever criminal activities in which you may find he participated are not sufficient to constitute the defense of duress." The Appellate Division affirmed his conviction.

ISSUE: Is the defense of duress available to one who was coerced into illegal conduct by the use of or threat to use unlawful force against his person or the person of another?

HOLDING AND DECISION: (J Pashman) Yes. At common law, the defense of duress applied only if the alleged coercion involved a use or threat of harm which is "present, imminent and pending" and "of such a nature as to induce a well-grounded apprehension of death or serious bodily harm if the act is not done." Not satisfied with this common law standard, some commentators have advocated a flexible rule which would allow a jury to consider whether the accused actually lost his capacity to act in accordance with "his own desire, or motivation, or will," under the pressure of real or imagined forces. The focus, then, would be on the weaknesses and strengths of a particular defendant, and his subjective reaction to unlawful demands. In essence, this approach does away with the common law's "standard of heroism" (where one is expected to lay down his own life rather than be coerced by threats into taking another innocent life) in favor of a set of expectations based on the defendant's character and situation. The drafters of the Model Penal Code and this state's penal code sought to steer a middle course between these two extremes by focusing on whether the standard imposed upon the accused was one with which "normal members of the community will be able to comply..." Thus, they proposed that a court limit its consideration of an accused's "situation" to stark, tangible factors which differentiate the actor from another, like his size or strength or age or health," excluding matters of temperament. They substantially departed from the existing statutory and common law limitations requiring that

the result threatened be death or serious bodily harm, that the threat be immediate and aimed at the accused, or that the crime be a non-capital offense. While these factors would be given evidentiary weight, the failure to satisfy one or more of these conditions would not justify the trial judge's withholding the defense from the jury. In this particular case, the jury may well have found that threats were made to Toscano (D) that induced a reasonable fear in him. It would then have been solely for the jury to determine whether a "person of reasonable firmness in his situation" would have failed to seek police assistance or refused to cooperate, or whether as a person Toscano (D) should reasonably have been expected to resist. Exercising our authority to revise the common law, this court has decided to adopt this approach as the law of New Jersey. Henceforth, duress shall be a defense to a crime other than murder if the defendant engaged in conduct because he was coerced to do so by the use of, or threat to use, unlawful force against his person or the person of another, which a person of reasonable firmness in his situation would have been unable to resist. Reversed and remanded.

EDITOR'S ANALYSIS: As the holding in this case implies, the New Jersey Penal Code does not permit duress as a defense to murder, although it can reduce murder to manslaughter. In contrast, the Model Penal Code treats duress as an affirmative defense to a murder charge. At common law, of course, duress served as a defense for an entire range of serious offenses, yet it would not excuse the killing of an innocent person.

NOTES:

ROBERTS v. PEOPLE
19 Mich. 401 (1870).

NATURE OF CASE: Appeal from conviction for assault with intent to murder.

FACT SUMMARY: Roberts (D) was convicted for assault with intent to murder and argues that at the time of the act he was too drunk to have had the required intent to murder.

CONCISE RULE OF LAW: If a crime requires a specific intent, voluntary intoxication which makes the defendant incapable of entertaining that specific intent is a valid defense.

FACTS: Roberts (D) was charged and convicted of assault with intent to murder by shooting at another person with a gun. At the time of the shooting, he was voluntarily intoxicated.

ISSUE: Will voluntary intoxication be a defense to a crime which requires a specific intent?

HOLDING AND DECISION: (J. Christiancy) Yes. If the statute makes an offense out of an act combined with a particular intent, here the intent to murder, then the intent, as well as the act, must be proved for conviction, particularly if the offense is an attempt to commit some other offense. If, at the time of the act the defendant is voluntarily drunk and incapable of having the necessary intent, then he is not guilty of the crime. If he had the required intent before he became drunk, however, then his subsequent drunkenness would not be a defense. The question in the case, then, is whether the defendant was so intoxicated as to be incapable of the required intent, and that is a question of fact for the jury to determine by examining the circumstances of the act, defendant's conduct and statements, and the mental capacity that the required intent demands. The jury should be instructed that the defendant is guilty only if he knew what he was doing, why he was doing it, and that his actions were likely to kill; otherwise, he is not guilty. It is no defense that even though he had the intent to kill, he was so drunk that he didn't realize that the act was wrong because, by voluntarily becoming drunk, he blinded his moral principles. Also, it would be no defense if he had the required intent but wouldn't have had that intent if he weren't drunk.

EDITOR'S ANALYSIS: It is a universal rule that voluntary intoxication at the time of an act is not by itself a defense; the defendant is still held responsible for his intent regarding the consequences of the act. The basis of this rule is that it should be no excuse that the defendant would have not committed the act but for his drunkenness. In [Roberts], even though Roberts (D) was too drunk to form the required intent to kill, he still will be guilty of simple assault. Involuntary drunkenness, however, is a defense to the act, as well as the intent, only if the defendant is so drunk as to be legally insane. [Roberts] states the generally accepted rule that drunkenness will be a defense to the extent that it negates a specific intent or knowledge of a fact required for the crime charged.

PEOPLE v. HOOD
SUP. CT. OF CALIF., 1969. 1 Cal.3d 444, 462 P.2d 370.

NATURE OF CASE: Appeal from conviction for assault with a deadly weapon upon a peace officer and assault with intent to commit murder.

FACT SUMMARY: While intoxicated, Hood (D) resisted the efforts of a policeman to arrest and subdue him by grabbing the officer's gun and shooting him in the legs.

CONCISE RULE OF LAW: In crimes of general intent, evidence of the accused's intoxication shall not be considered in determining guilt or innocence.

FACTS: While a policeman attempted to subdue and arrest Hood (D) who was drunk, Hood (D), in the struggle, grabbed the officer's gun and shot him in the legs. Hood (D) was convicted on a count of assault with a deadly weapon upon a peace officer and on a count of assault with intent to commit murder. The conviction on the first count was reversed for failure to instruct on the lesser offense of simple assault, with the other count reversed because of the conflicting instructions given on the effect of intoxication.

ISSUE: In crimes of general intent, should evidence of the accused's intoxication be admitted?

HOLDING AND DECISION: (J. Traynor) No. The difficulty in making this determination rests upon the confusion in defining the terms "general intent" and "specific intent." Usually, when the definition of a crime consists of only a description of the particular act without reference to intent to do a further act or achieve a future consequence, an intention to do a proscribed act is deemed to be general criminal intent. When the definition refers to doing some further act or some additional consequence, the crime is deemed to be specific intent. Under the California Criminal Code, there is ambiguity as to whether assault is to be defined as general or specific. In the context of assault with a deadly weapon and simple assault, the distinction between general and specific intent is minor. Whether or not to hear evidence of intoxication rests on different considerations, such as the effect of alcohol on human behavior. Alcohol distorts judgment and relaxes control on aggressive and anti-social behavior. While a drunk man may be able to form a simple intent, he is not as capable of exercising judgment on the social consequences of his act. A drunk man is more apt to act rashly and impulsively or in the heat of passion. Evidence of intoxication should not relieve one of blame for simple assault or assault with a deadly weapon, crimes which are frequently committed rashly or in anger. (A retrial was ordered.)

EDITOR'S ANALYSIS: In most jurisdictions, intoxication is a defense at least to negate specific intent. But note that intoxication of the accused itself at the time of commission of the crime does not constitute a defense apart from evidencing legal insanity or rebutting [mens rea]. A criminal act is no less criminal for having been committed in a state of voluntary intoxication.

STATE v. HALL
SUP. COURT OF IOWA, 1974. 214 N.W. 2d 205.

NATURE OF CASE: Appeal from a conviction for first degree murder.

FACT SUMMARY: Hall (D) killed the person from whom he had hitched a ride during a drug-induced (apparently LSD) hallucination.

CONCISE RULE OF LAW: A temporary mental condition caused by the voluntary ingestion of a known mind-affecting drug does not constitute a complete defense.

FACTS: Hall (D) was given a pill, apparently LSD, which he was told was a "little sunshine" and "groovy." He swallowed the pill and, while riding with a person from whom he had hitched a ride, he hallucinated that the deceased (who was asleep) was a rabid dog. Hall (D) grabbed the deceased's gun and in panic shot him. He was found sane and convicted of first degree murder.

ISSUE: Should a temporary mental condition, caused by the voluntary ingestion of a mind-affecting drug, constitute a complete defense?

HOLDING AND DECISION: (J. Uhlenhuff) No. As a temporary mental condition caused by voluntary intoxication from alcohol does not constitute a complete defense, and there is no legal distinction between the voluntary use of drugs and the voluntary use of alcohol in determining criminal responsibility. Hall (D) knew the pill was hallucinogenic; he did not take it by mistake, thinking it to be candy, or not knowing it was mind-affecting.

DISSENT: (J. LeGrand) The rules applied to alcohol intoxication should not apply to drug intoxication because modern hallucinatory drugs result in effects very different from alcohol and are not yet well enough researched scientifically. While insanity from alcohol use requires use over a long period of time, drugs can create flashes of insanity at different times. And while Hall (D) knew the pill was supposed to make him feel good, it is not clear he knew it would cause hallucinations.

EDITOR'S ANALYSIS: The majority view here is widely accepted. Note than an exception arises where insanity is caused by extended use of alcohol. In such cases, alcohol insanity is treated as any other insanity, but otherwise a temporary condition caused by voluntary intoxication does not excuse a person from responsibility for his conduct.

M'NAGHTEN'S CASE
10 Cl. & F. 200, 8 Eng. Rep. 718.

NATURE OF CASE: Debate in House of Lords following finding of not guilty of murder by reason of insanity.

FACT SUMMARY: M'Naghten (D) was found not guilty of murder by reason of insanity.

CONCISE RULE OF LAW: A defendant will be found not guilty by reason of insanity if, as a result of mental disease, he did not know the nature or quality of the criminal act he committed or did not know that what he was doing was wrong.

FACTS: M'Naghten (D) was indicted for murder. His defense was that at the time of the killing he was insane and obsessed with morbid delusions. The judge instructed the jury that M'Naghten (D) should be found not guilty if, at the time the act was committed, he did not know that the act he was doing was wrong and did not know that he was violating the laws of God and man. The jury found M'Naghten (D) not guilty by reason of insanity. The holding resulted in a debate on the defense of legal insanity in the House of Lords. The House invited Lord Chief Justice Tindal to answer certain questions as to legal insanity, and his answers resulted in the [M'Naghten] rule.

ISSUE: Should the defense of legal insanity be based on the defendant's ability to know if his act was right or wrong?

HOLDING AND DECISION: (J. Tindal) Yes. Every defendant will be presumed sane until the contrary is proved in defense. To establish the defense of legal insanity, it must be clearly proved that at the time of the commission of the act, the defendant had a mental disease so as not to know the nature and quality of the act he was doing or, if he did know the nature and quality of his act, he did not know that what he was doing was wrong. The basic question is whether, at the time of the act, he knew the difference between right and wrong. If the defendant did not know that his act was illegal but did realize that it was wrong, he will be held guilty. The question of legal insanity is a question of fact to be decided by the jury.

EDITOR'S ANALYSIS: The [M'Naghten] rule, also known as the "right-from-wrong" test, is the test for legal insanity in the majority of jurisdictions. This rule focuses solely on the cognitive ability of the defendant. Some courts supplement this test with the "irresistible impulse" test, which states that the defendant will also be found legally insane if, as a result of mental disease, he is unable to control his conduct. The third standard for legal insanity is the "substantial capacity" test which finds a defendant legally insane if, as a result of mental disease, he lacks the substantial capacity to apprehend the nature, quality or wrongfulness of his conduct or to conform his conduct to the requirements of law. The final standard is the "product" test, which is discussed in the case of [Durham v. United States].

112

STATE v. CRENSHAW
Wash. Sup. Ct. (1983) 98 Wash. 2d 789, 659 P.2d 488.

NATURE OF CASE: Appeal of murder conviction.

FACT SUMMARY: Crenshaw (D), contending he killed his wife out of religious duty, argued that the insanity defense may apply to one not aware that his conduct is morally wrong.

CONCISE RULE OF LAW: The insanity defense requires that a defendant be unable to differentiate right from wrong legally as opposed to morally.

FACTS: Crenshaw (D) suspected that his new wife had been unfaithful. He beat her unconscious, stabbed her to death, and dismembered her body, hiding the parts. The murder was discovered, and Crenshaw (D) was tried for murder. He argued in his defense that his religion compelled him to kill an unfaithful wife, and that therefore he had been unable to perceive, morally speaking, the wrongness of the act. He was convicted, and appealed.

ISSUE: Does the insanity defense require that a defendant be unable to differentiate right from wrong legally as opposed to morally?

HOLDING AND DECISION: (J. Brachtenbach) Yes. The insanity defense requires that a defendant be unable to differentiate right from wrong legally as opposed to morally. It is society's morals, not the individual's morals, that are the standard for judging whether one can appreciate the wrongness of one's acts, for purposes of the insanity defense. If individual moral beliefs were the standard, the criminal law would be seriously undermined. This being so, only if a defendant was unable to appreciate the illegality of his conduct may the insanity defense be applied. Here, there was ample evidence that Crenshaw (D) understood the illegality of his conduct. Affirmed.

EDITOR'S ANALYSIS: The test used here was the classic [M'Naghten] rule, which relied strictly on cognitive ability. At one point, this test began to be replaced by a test that permitted the insanity defense if the defendant suffered from an "irresistible impulse." In the last decade, however, this test has fallen out of favor.

STATE v. GREEN
Tenn. Ct. of App. 643 S.W.2d 902 (1982).

NOTES:

NATURE OF CASE: Appeal from conviction for murder.

FACT SUMMARY: Green (D) contended his conviction should be set aside because of the overwhelming evidence of his insanity at the time of the crime.

CONCISE RULE OF LAW: The prosecution must prove beyond a reasonable doubt that the defendant was legally sane at the time of the act.

FACTS: Green (D) was arrested for the shooting of a police officer. He had been in and out of mental health facilities most of his life and often acted out of touch with reality. He pleaded insanity at trial and several experts testified unequivocally that he was a paranoid schizophrenic and insane at the time of the shooting. The State (P) presented no expert testimony and relied upon testimony of police officers having contact with Green (D) before and after the shooting. They testified that Green (D) acted odd but not insane. Green (D) was convicted of murder and appealed, contending the State (P) had not met its burden of proving his sanity at the time of the shooting.

ISSUE: Must the prosecution prove beyond a reasonable doubt that the defendant was legally sane at the time of the act?

HOLDING AND DECISION: (J. Daughtrey) Yes. The prosecution must prove beyond a reasonable doubt that the defendant was legally sane at the time of the act. The prosecution failed to present any evidence, other than lay percipient testimony, that disputed the defense experts' opinion that Green (D) had a mental illness which prevented him from distinguishing between right and wrong. Thus, the verdict was not supported by substantial evidence and must be overturned.

EDITOR'S ANALYSIS: Once the defendant raises the insanity defense, the prosecution must refute the evidence of insanity and prove sanity beyond a reasonable doubt. The focal point is the defendant's state at the time of the crime, not his state before or after. Such a determination is very difficult to make.

UNITED STATES v. FREEMAN
U.S.Ct. of App., 2nd Cir. (1966) 357 F.2d 606.

NOTES:

NATURE OF CASE: Appeal of conviction for selling heroin.

FACT SUMMARY: Freeman (D), charged with selling heroin, contended that due to mental disease, he lacked the capacity to appreciate the criminality of his actions.

CONCISE RULE OF LAW: It is a defense to criminal charges that, as a result of a mental disease, one lacks the capacity to appreciate the criminality of his actions.

FACTS: Freeman (D) was charged with selling heroin. He contended that, due to severe addiction to heroin and alcohol, as well as trauma incurred while a prizefighter, he suffered from a mental defect making it impossible for him to appreciate the criminality of his act. The court, sitting without a jury, applied the [M'Naghten] test, and found that his impairment was not so severe that he could not tell right from wrong. The court convicted him. Freeman (D) appealed.

ISSUE: Is it a defense to criminal charges that, as a result of mental disease, one lacks the capacity to appreciate the criminality of his acts?

HOLDING AND DECISION: (J. Kaufman) Yes. It is a defense to criminal charges that, as a result of mental disease, one lacks the capacity to appreciate the criminality of his acts. The classic [M'Naghten] test, which focuses on a defendant's ability to differentiate right from wrong, is lacking in several respects. It does not take into account those who can distinguish right from wrong but nonetheless, due to mental defect, cannot control their behavior. Furthermore, it unduly withholds pertinent information from the trier of facts by forcing an expert witness to concentrate on what may be a largely irrelevant area. To this court, it appears proper to adopt the Model Penal Code approach, which permits the defendant to plead insanity when he can show that, as a result of a mental disease, he cannot appreciate the criminality of his acts or conform his behavior properly. This permits both the trier of fact and the expert witness to explore the totality of the factors influencing the defendant's behavior. Since the [M'Naghten] test was used here, the issue of insanity must be retried. Reversed.

EDITOR'S ANALYSIS: The Model Penal Code was one test that was formulated to replace the [M'Naghten] test. Another was the "irresistible impulse" test which this court rejected as too limited in terms of potential application. Another test was developed by the D.C. Circuit in 1954, which made insanity a defense if the unlawful act was "the product of mental disease or mental defect." This test was seen as too conclusory in its terms and was later abandoned.

UNITED STATES v. LYONS
U.S.Ct. of Apls., 5th Cir. (1984) 731 F.2d 243, 739 F.2d 994.

NATURE OF CASE: Appeal from conviction for possession of narcotics.

FACT SUMMARY: Lyons (D) was convicted of narcotics possession, over his defense that his addiction prevented him from conforming his conduct to law.

CONCISE RULE OF LAW: The insanity defense only applies where a defendant is unable to understand the wrongfulness of his conduct.

FACTS: Lyons (D) was arrested and charged with possession of narcotics. His defense was that he was an addict, and that the drugs had affected his brain so that he had lost the capacity to conform his conduct according to the law. The District Court did not allow Lyons (D) to introduce this defense, and he was convicted. Lyons (D) then appealed.

ISSUE: Does the insanity defense only apply where a defendant is unable to understand the wrongfulness of his conduct?

HOLDING AND DECISION: (C.J. Gee) Yes. The insanity defense only applies where a defendant is unable to understand the wrongfulness of his conduct. The advances in psychology earlier this century led to the "irresistible impulse" definition of insanity, which could exculpate a defendant if he lacked the ability to conform his conduct with the law. The adoption of this standard now appears premature. It simply is not within the state of the art in psychology to discern between an irresistible impulse and a choice to behave criminally. To use this standard is to base the defense on speculation, something this court does not see as present. Here, Lyons (D) could not show he lacked the ability to understand the wrongfulness of his act, so his conviction was proper. Affirmed.

DISSENT: (J. Rubin) An adjudication of guilt requires moral blameworthiness, something that cannot exist when a defendant cannot conform with the law. Mere difficulty in applying a test in an area as crucial as this should not justify scuttling it.

EDITOR'S ANALYSIS: The insanity defense has come under sharp disfavor in the last several years. Deserved or not, there is a public perception that it allows the guilty to go scot-free. Since the highly-publicized acquittal of John Hinckley, the process of retreating from the "irresistible impulse" test to the one adopted by the court here has accelerated.

STATE v. GUIDO
N.J.Sup.Ct. 40 N.J. 191, 191 A.2d 45 (1963).

NOTES:

NATURE OF CASE: Appeal from conviction for murder.

FACT SUMMARY: Guido (D) contended the prosecution unjustifiably told the jury she and her defense team had defrauded the court by changing a psychiatric report to include a more expansive legal test of insanity.

CONCISE RULE OF LAW: A person with a disease of the mind severe enough to preclude distinction between right end wrong is incapable of guilt.

FACTS: Guido (D) shot her husband who had physically abused her in the past. She claimed temporary insanity and was examined by doctors to determine her mental state. Believing the legal standard for insanity required a diagnosed psychosis, the doctors concluded she was legally sane. Guido's (D) defense attorney pointed out the correct standard based upon the ability to show a distinction between right and wrong, and the doctors changed their legal conclusion. The prosecutor pointed out this change to the jury and claimed it represented a fraud on the court. The jury convicted her, and she appealed.

ISSUE: Is a person with a diseased mind, who is unable to make a distinction between right and wrong, legally insane?

HOLDING AND DECISION: (J. Weintraub) Yes. A person with a disease of the mind severe enough to preclude distinction between right and wrong is incapable of guilt. The change in the doctor's report was a change in the legal standard applied. The medical conclusions did not change. Thus, it was improper of the prosecution to charge such change was a fraud. The jury was thus misled, and the conviction must be overturned.

EDITOR'S ANALYSIS: An ongoing problem exists concerning the classification of the issue of sanity as a legal or a medical concept. Medical experts can testify concerning their findings based upon examinations and tests. These results must then be used by the trier of fact in applying them to the legal standard of sanity.

JONES v. UNITED STATES

U.S.Sup.Ct. (1983) 463 U.S. 354.

NATURE OF CASE: Petition for release from a mental facility.

FACT SUMMARY: Jones (D) contended he had to be released from commitment to a mental hospital because his period of commitment exceeded the maximum prison sentence for the crime charged.

CONCISE RULE OF LAW: Commitment may be as long as necessary to treat a defendant's illness which rendered him incapable of guilt.

FACTS: Jones (D) was arrested for petit larceny and pled innocent by reason of insanity. He was committed to a mental hospital. He had been hospitalized for over one year, the maximum time he could have been sentenced had he been convicted. He appealed the denial of his release petition on the basis that he could not be committed for a period longer than he could have been sentenced.

ISSUE: May commitment based on an acquittal for insanity exceed the maximum sentence for guilt?

HOLDING AND DECISION: (J. Powell) Yes. Commitment may be for as long as necessary to treat the illness which rendered the defendant unable to be convicted. The finding of innocence is based upon the defendant's diseased mind rendering him incapable of formulating the requisite [mens rea] to commit the crime. His commitment is thus aimed at treating this disease. He is not being punished but treated, and such treatment must continue until he is no longer acting with a diseased mind. Thus, the rejection of his petition was proper.

DISSENT: (J. Brennan) A finding of innocence by reason of insanity does not give the State (P) the right to impose indefinite commitment on a defendant.

DISSENT: (J. Stevens) Indefinite commitment does not follow from a minor offense such as this.

EDITOR'S ANALYSIS: An important aspect of this case is the so-called presumption of continued insanity. Once a mental state is found, it is presumed to continue until the challenger proves it has changed. Thus, once committed, the defendant has the burden of proving his mental state has changed.

NOTES:

REGINA v. QUICK
CT. OF APPEALS, Crim. Div., 1973, 3 W.L.R. 26.

NATURE OF CASE: Appeal from a conviction for assault occasioning actual bodily harm.

FACT SUMMARY: Quick (D), a nurse in a mental hospital and himself a diabetic, inflicted bodily injury upon a patient when he lapsed into a hypoglycaemic coma-like state.

CONCISE RULE OF LAW: A person who suffers a defect of reason from a disease of the mind may show that such defect was caused by an external factor and not by a bodily disorder in the nature of a disease which disturbed the workings of his mind.

FACTS: Green, a paraplegic spastic patient at Farleigh Mental Hospital, was found with two black eyes, a broken nose, a cut lip, and other bruises. Quick (D), the nurse in charge, witnesses said, was found sitting astride the struggling Green and later collapsed on the floor. During the attack, Quick (D) had a glassy-eyed look, and he later testified that he could not remember the incident, but admitted that he had been drinking whiskey and rum. Quick (D), a diabetic, had taken prescribed insulin that morning and had eaten a small breakfast but no lunch. On twelve occasions, he had been admitted to the hospital unconscious or semi-conscious due to hypoglycaemia, which can result in violent and aggressive conduct without the sufferer recalling such episodes. The trial judge ruled that under these circumstances, any defense must be based upon insanity. Quick (D) decided to plead guilty and appeal the ruling instead.

ISSUE: May a person who suffers from a defect of reason attempt to show that it was caused by an external factor rather than a bodily disturbance?

HOLDING AND DECISION: (L.J. Lawton) Yes. The problem in this case results from whether Quick's (D) "disease of the mind" can rightly be said to be an insanity for which he should be detained in a mental hospital. "Disease of the mind" is fundamentally a malfunctioning of the mind caused by disease. But such a malfunctioning caused by an external factor, such as violence, drugs, alcohol, or hypnosis cannot be said to be a disease. While a disease of the mind will relieve criminal responsibility (though not from hospital detention), a defect caused by external factors will not always relieve one from criminal responsibility, e.g., where the external factor could be reasonably foreseen as a result of either doing or omitting to do something. Quick (D) should have been permitted a defense of unforeseen external factors with the jury determining the issue.

EDITOR'S ANALYSIS: A defense of insanity must be pleaded where the defect in reason from disease of the mind is caused by some internal malady. Quick's (D) defect did not result from the internal factor, diabetes, but from an external factor, perhaps insulin or misuse of alcohol. By allowing a defense based upon unconscious automatic conduct, questions regarding what caused his mental condition, including whether it was due to hypoglycaemia or alcohol and if he knew the episode was coming on, could have been answered. The jury could then have determined whether criminal responsibility should or should not arise.

UNITED STATES v. BRAWNER
U.S. Ct. of Apls., D.C. Cir., 471 F.2d 969 (1972).

NOTES:

NATURE OF CASE: Appeal from conviction for second-degree murder and carrying a dangerous weapon.

FACT SUMMARY: In considering Brawner's (D) appeal from his convictions for carrying a dangerous weapon and second-degree murder, the court reconsidered the rule of [Fisher v. United States], which limited the use of a diminished capacity defense on issues of premeditation and deliberation.

CONCISE RULE OF LAW: Evidence of the condition of the mind of the accused at the time of the crime, together with the surrounding circumstances may be introduced, not for the purpose of establishing insanity, but to prove that the situation was such that a specific intent was not entertained, i.e., to show absence of any deliberate or premeditated design.

FACTS: Brawner (D) was convicted of second-degree murder and carrying a dangerous weapon. In this portion of its opinion adjudicating Brawner's (D) appeal, the Court of Appeals reconsidered the rule of [Fisher v. United States] 149 F.2d 28 (1946), in which the court upheld the trial court's refusal to instruct the jury that on issues of premeditation and deliberation "it should consider the entire personality of the defendant, his mental, nervous, emotional and physical characteristics as developed by the evidence in the case."

ISSUE: May evidence of the condition of the mind of the accused at the time of the crime, together with the surrounding circumstances, be introduced to show absence of any deliberate or premeditated design?

HOLDING AND DECISION: (J. Leventhal) Yes. Evidence of the condition of the mind of the accused at the time of the crime, together with the surrounding circumstances may be introduced, not for the purpose of establishing insanity, but to prove that the situation was such that a specific intent was not entertained, i.e., to show absence of any premeditated or deliberate design. On the other hand, a claim of insanity cannot be used for the purpose of reducing the degree of the crime of murder or reducing murder to manslaughter. If the defendant is responsible at all, he is responsible in the same degree as a sane man; if he is not responsible at all, he is entitled to acquittal no matter what the degree. In overruling the rule of [Fisher], the court permitted the introduction of expert testimony as to abnormal condition, if it is relevant to negate, or to establish the specific mental condition that is an element of the crime.

EDITOR'S ANALYSIS: The rule of [Brawner] must be distinguished from what is generally termed "diminished" or "partial responsibility." Under the "partial responsibility" doctrine, a defendant who is mentally disturbed, although not to the degree necessary to prove the defense of insanity, is entitled to a reduction in severity of his sentence. [Brawner], instead, goes to the question of intent. The court stated, " Neither logic nor justice can tolerate a jurisprudence that defines the elements of an offense as requiring a mental state such that one defendant who properly argues that his voluntary drunkenness removed his capacity to form the specific intent - but another defendant is inhibited from a submission of his contention that an abnormal mental condition for which he was in no way responsible - negated his capacity to form a particular specific intent, even though the condition did not exonerate him from all criminal responsibility."

STATE v. WILCOX
Oh. Sup.Ct. (1982) 70 Ohio St.2d 182, 436 N.E.2d 523.

NATURE OF CASE: Appeal of conviction for murder.

FACT SUMMARY: Wilcox (D), charged with murder, argued diminished capacity as a defense.

CONCISE RULE OF LAW: Diminished capacity is not a defense to a criminal charge.

FACTS: Wilcox (D) was charged with murder and burglary. At trial, Wilcox (D) attempted to introduce medical testimony that, although the insanity defense was not available to him, he suffered from certain mental afflictions resulting in diminished capacity. The trial court refused to allow the introduction of this evidence, and Wilcox (D) was convicted. He appealed.

ISSUE: Is diminished capacity a defense to a criminal charge?

HOLDING AND DECISION: (J. Sweeney) No. Diminished capacity is not a defense to a criminal charge. The concept of diminished capacity grew out of perceived deficiencies in the old [M'Naughten] rule, regarding culpability and mental state. The doctrine applies to a situation where a defendant was legally sane at the time he committed a crime but under such a psychological handicap that he could not form the specific intent for the charged crime. It is this court's opinion that the doctrine is unsound and should not be adopted. First, the narrow [M'Naughten] rule has been expanded, and therefore a major justification for diminished capacity no longer exists. Also, another major reason for the doctrine's formulation, the unjust application of capital punishment, has been undercut by the drastic narrowing of the scope of capital punishment in recent years. Finally, the doctrine asks a factfinder to make distinctions so subtle as to approach arbitrariness. For these reasons, diminished capacity will not be accepted as a legal doctrine. Affirmed.

EDITOR'S ANALYSIS: The defense of diminished capacity, never a majority rule, has fallen out of favor. The state to have embraced it most fully was California. The doctrine was statutorily abrogated in the early 1980's in that state, following the famous and successful Dan White "Twinkie defense" in his trial for assassinating San Francisco Mayor George Mosconi and Supervisor Harvey Milk.

STATE v. SIKORA
SUP. CT. OF NEW JERSEY, 1965. 44 N.J.453, 210 A.2d 193.

NATURE OF CASE: Appeal from a conviction for first degree murder.

FACT SUMMARY: Sikora (D) killed Hooey after Hooey and others joked about his girlfriend having left him and after Hooey and the others beat him up and threw him out of the tavern they were at.

CONCISE RULE OF LAW: While psychiatric evidence is admissible upon the question of whether the accused premeditated a first degree murder, such evidence is not admissible where it is unreliable, too speculative, or incompetent when tested by concepts established in law for the determination of criminal responsibility.

FACTS: Sikora (D), who was orphaned and had "an unfortunate childhood," had broken up with the woman with whom he had been living, and she had recently refused to take him back. Sikora (D) went drinking at a tavern, where an acquaintance, Hooey, made rude remarks regarding his break-up, and with some friends beat up Sikora (D) and threw him out of the tavern. Sikora (D) got his gun, test-fired it, and returned to the tavern intending to kill Hooey and later, the woman. He met Hooey outside the tavern where he shot and killed him. He could not find the woman and was arrested. The trial court refused to hear novel psychiatric testimony expressing a theory of psychodynamic human behavior which suggests that no matter how quickly executed, actions are never fully the result of the apparent immediate cause, and must be judged according to the probable unconscious motivations of an individual in consideration of his life history.

ISSUE: Did the trial court err in excluding expert psychiatric testimony on the theory of psychodynamic behavior?

HOLDING AND DECISION: (J. Francis) No. While the jury should be excused and counsel be permitted to make a proffer of proof, there was no error. The evidence was unreliable, too speculative or incompetent when tested by concepts established in law for the determination of criminal responsibility. Guilt cannot be judged on a theory that negates free will and excuses the offense in whole or part on opinion evidence admitting that while the accused knew right from wrong, he was predetermined to act by unconscious influences set in motion by emotional distress. "In a world of reality, such persons must be held responsible for their behavior." The [M'Naghten] rule not only determines who is suffering from a mental disorder, but also selects those of the mentally ill whose punishment will aid and protect society because they can rationally choose between right and wrong. If a person plans and executes a crime at a conscious level, the criminality of his act cannot be denied on the grounds that his conscious plan was influenced by unconscious reasons which were the product of his genes and lifelong environment. To accept such an argument would be to wipe out the legal doctrine of [mens rea].

CONCURRENCE: (C. J. Weintraub) While the psychiatric view presented is scientific and is not really disputed, the law being based on criminal blameworthiness requires the concept of [mens rea], an evil mind, to be determined at the level of conscious behavior.

EDITOR'S ANALYSIS: Criminal blameworthiness is usually so cloudy an area that judges tend to let as much evidence in on the subject as possible. However, the expert testimony presented here could not be admitted if the court would be unable to be instructed on the legal effect it might have. In this case, the effect would be to charge a man with his unconscious motivations. As this goes against all doctrine concerning [mens rea], it could not be admissible.

NOTES:

ROBINSON v. CALIFORNIA
SUP.CT.OF U.S.,1962. 370 U.S.660, 82 Sup.Ct.1417, 8 L.Ed.2d 758.

NATURE OF CASE: Appeal from conviction for narcotic addiction.

FACT SUMMARY: A California (P) statute makes it a criminal offense for a person to be addicted to the use of narcotics.

CONCISE RULE OF LAW: A state law which imprisons a person addicted to narcotics, even though he has never touched any drug within the state or been guilty of any irregular behavior there, inflicts a cruel and unusual punishment in violation of the Eighth and Fourteenth Amendments.

FACTS: A California (P) statute makes it a criminal offense for a person to be addicted to the use of narcotics. The evidence against Robinson (D) was a police officer's testimony that Robinson (D) had scar tissue, discoloration, and needle marks which indicated his frequent use of narcotics.

ISSUE: Is a law which makes narcotics addiction a criminal offense constitutional?

HOLDING AND DECISION: (J. Stewart) No. Narcotic addiction is an illness which may be contracted innocently or involuntarily. Like mental illness, leprosy, or venereal disease, a state could establish a program of compulsory treatment, involving quarantine or confinement for narcotic addicts. However, a law which makes a criminal offense of narcotic addiction inflicts a cruel and unusual punishment in violation of the Eighth and Fourteenth Amendments. The California (P) statute imprisoning a person addicted to narcotics, even though he has never used any drug within the state, or been guilty of any irregular behavior there, is unconstitutional.

CONCURRENCE: (J. Douglas, J. Harlan) Confinement for the purposes of punishing, rather than curing, drug addiction cannot be upheld.

DISSENT: (J. White) The court has removed the state's power to deal with the recurring case where there is ample evidence of use but no evidence of the precise location of use.

EDITOR'S ANALYSIS: Following the [Robinson] case, the California Supreme Court upheld an involuntary five-year commitment of a person on a finding that he was a narcotic addict. After examining both the "civil" and "criminal" features of his commitment, the court decided that the "civil" overtones predominated and that it was, therefore, not unconstitutional under [Robinson]. In Re De La O, 59 Cal. 2d 128 (1963). [Robinson] may have established the Eighth Amendment as a basis for invalidating legislation that is thought to inappropriately invoke criminal sanction, despite an entire lack of precedent for the idea that punishment may be cruel not because of its mode but because the conduct for which it is imposed should not be subjected to the criminal sanction." Packer, 77 Harv. L.Rev. 1071 (1964).

POWELL v. TEXAS

U.S.SUP.CT., 1968, 392 U.S.514, 88 S.Ct.2145, 20 L.Ed.2d 1254.

NATURE OF CASE: Appeal from conviction for public drunkenness.

FACT SUMMARY: Powell (D), a chronic alcoholic, was found to have a condition beyond his control which resulted in his being intoxicated in public, an act for which he was arrested.

CONCISE RULE OF LAW: In light of current medical knowledge, it appears that chronic alcoholics in general do not suffer from such an irresistible compulsion to drink and to get drunk in public, that they are utterly unable to control their performance of either or both of these acts, and thus cannot be deterred at all from public intoxication.

FACTS: Powell (D), a chronic alcoholic, was found guilty of being drunk in public. It was argued that his appearance in public was not of his own volition, and that to punish him for his illness would be cruel and unusual in violation of the Eighth Amendment as applied to the states by the Fourteenth Amendment. The medical profession has not firmly determined whether alcoholism is an illness, is physically addicting, or merely psychologically habituating.

ISSUE: Is alcoholism a condition of such an involuntary nature that to punish an appearance in public while intoxicated would be cruel and unusual?

HOLDING AND DECISION: (J. Marshall joined by C.J. Warren, J. Black and J. Harlan) No. There is widespread argument in the medical profession over whether alcoholism is a disease. A disease is anything the medical profession determines it to be. Facilities for treating indigent alcoholics are woefully lacking. At least a short time in jail permits the alcoholic to sober up. Generally, commission to an institution is for the time it takes to cure, while time in jail for drunkenness is usually limited. Powell (D) was not convicted for being a chronic alcoholic, but for being drunk in public. He is not within the ambit of [Robinson], which holds that a conviction for being of the status of a drug addict alone is cruel and unusual. Here, the conviction protects public safety and health. [Robinson] says a person may be punished only for committing some act which society has an interest in preventing.

CONCURRENCE: (J. Black with whom J. Harlan joins) "... The States should (not) be held constitutionally required to make the inquiry as to what part of a defendant's personality is responsible for his actions and to excuse anyone whose action was, in some complex, psychological sense, the result of a 'compulsion.'"

CONCURRENCE: (J. White) If it cannot be a crime to have an irresistible urge to use narcotics, it should not be a crime to yield to that compulsion. But here, there is nothing in the record to show that the chronic alcoholic has a compulsion to drink in public.

DISSENT: (J. Fortas with whom J. Douglas, J. Brennan and J. Stewart join) "... Alcoholism is caused and maintained by something other than the moral fault of the alcoholic, something that, to a greater or lesser extent...cannot be controlled by him..." Thus, to punish the alcoholic would be cruel and unusual punishment.

EDITOR'S ANALYSIS: It would appear, at least according to Mr. J. White, that once one proves his compulsion, he cannot be protected from conviction for failing to take precautions against it. For example, an epileptic may not be punished for his illness, unless he drives a vehicle. Yet the dissent, while stipulating that the statute did not punish the mere status of alcoholism, feels that the accused was punished for a condition he was helpless to avoid. Is the majority then taking the pragmatic way out? Recognizing the lack of adequate care facilities for indigent chronic alcoholics, it would seem that the Court would rather have the public drunk spend a night in jail to dry out than be committed for an unspecified term to an inadequate institution until deemed "cured."

NOTES:

UNITED STATES v. MOORE

U.S. CT. OF APPLS., D.C. Circ., 1973. 486 F.2d 1139.

NATURE OF CASE: Appeal from conviction for possession of heroin.

FACT SUMMARY: Moore (D) was convicted on two counts of possession of heroin.

CONCISE RULE OF LAW: Evidence of long and intensive dependence on drugs resulting in substantial impairment of behavioral controls and self-control over the use of the drug in question is not admissible on the issue of criminal responsibility.

FACTS: Moore (D), a heroin addict and apparently a trafficker in the drug, was convicted on two counts of possession of heroin. He contends his conviction was improper because as an addict having an overpowering need for heroin, he should not be held responsible for its possession.

ISSUE: Is evidence of a drug user's long and intensive use and dependence on a drug resulting in substantial impairment of his behavioral controls and a loss of self-control over the use of the drug relevant to his criminal responsibility, in this case for unlawful possession?

HOLDING AND DECISION: (J. Wilkey) No. Moore's (D) claim that he has lost the power of self-control with regard to his addiction cannot be a defense to the capacity to control behavior which is a prerequisite to criminal responsibility. To hold otherwise would carry over to all other illegal acts of any type having a purpose to obtain narcotics for personal use.

CONCURRENCE: (J. Leventhal) It is illogical to claim that because there are different kinds of addicts, such as those who can limit their use of drugs to acquiring what they need for their habit and those who commit crimes other than possession to support their habit, punishment should be based upon the compulsion under which various addicts act. While Moore (D) claims he has lost self-control, he contends he does not commit crimes other than possession and acquisition. But it would appear that the addict who must commit crimes against others to support his habit has even less self-control. If lack of self-control could negate [mens rea], it would have to be a defense to all actions taken under compulsion of need to obtain the drug. Just because one condition, such as insanity, excuses a crime if it results in impaired behavioral control, it does not follow that any other condition resulting in similar impairment should be a defense. Rather than a broad principle of exculpation on grounds of lack of control, there is a series of particular defenses made clear in manageable areas calling for justice to the individual in ascertainable and verifiable conditions within the limitations of society's interests.

DISSENT: (J. Wright) Two dominant value judgments have shaped the concept of criminal responsibility in Western society. First, punishment must be morally legitimate. Second, it must not unduly threaten the individual's liberties and dignity in his relationship to society. Thus, to be criminally responsible, a man's actions must result from his free will. While at some time in the past each addict voluntarily decided to use drugs, it is the present that must be considered in seeing that the addict lacks self-control. "The law looks to the immediate, and not to the remote cause."

CONCURRENCE IN PART/DISSENT IN PART: (C.J. Bazelon) Loss of self-control as a result of drug addiction should be a defense to armed robbery or trafficking in drugs in determining whether the defendant was acting under duress or compulsion because of which he could not conform his conduct to the law's requirements.

EDITOR'S ANALYSIS: This is another case raising the problem of what defenses are acceptable within established legal doctrine, in this case, [mens rea]. Criminal responsibility is a cloudy area. Courts generally attempt to allow in as much evidence as possible on that issue. But where a defense could wipe out a legal doctrine so basic, here to the criminal law, chances are it will be excluded.

NOTES:

STATE v. STRASBURG
60 WASHINGTON 106, 110 P. 1020.

NATURE OF CASE: Appeal from conviction for assault.

FACT SUMMARY: A State (P) statute prohibited the use of the defense of insanity in criminal trials, and Strasburg (D) asserts that this statute is unconstitutional.

CONCISE RULE OF LAW: The constitutional guarantee of a trial by jury forbids a legislature from enacting a statute denying a defendant the opportunity to prove the defense of insanity.

FACTS: Strasburg (D) was charged with assault in the first degree. A new State (P) statute stated that it would be no defense to a criminal charge that at the time of the criminal act the defendant was, by reason of insanity, unable to comprehend the nature and quality of his act or to understand that it was wrong. The statute further provided that after conviction a trial judge could order an insane defendant committed to a hospital for the insane. Strasburg (D) was convicted and argues that the statute's refusal to allow his defense of insanity was a denial of due process and a deprivation of his constitutional right to a jury trial.

ISSUE: Is the State (P) statute's denial of the right to assert a defense of insanity to a criminal charge a deprivation of the defendant's constitutional rights?

HOLDING AND DECISION: Yes. Such a statute violates a defendant's constitutional right to a trial by jury. Sanity at the time of the act is as much an element of the crime as the act itself. If Strasburg (D) was insane to the point that he was unable to comprehend the nature and quality of his act, then he had no will tn control the act he performed. An act done while insane is not the act of the defendant. The prosecution argues that the current humane treatment of imprisoned criminals makes imprisonment the equivalent to commitment for insanity. But there is a difference in status between the convicted criminal and the insane, and imprisonment is essentially punishment. If Strasburg (D) was insane at the time of his act, then he cannot be convicted for that act.

EDITOR'S ANALYSIS: This case illustrates the basic function of the plea of insanity in our criminal system - insanity goes to adjudication of guilt and not to the disposition of the defendant after conviction. There is, then, a clear demarcation between the insane and the criminal. The basis of the statute in this case was that insanity is irrelevant to the concept of guilt since all should be held accountable for their acts, but that the question of insanity would be considered in determining what kind of treatment the criminal would have after conviction.

COMMONWEALTH v. TLUCHAK
166 PENNSYLVANIA SUPER. 16, 70 A. 2d 657.

NOTES:

NATURE OF CASE: Appeal from conviction for larceny.

FACT SUMMARY: The Tluchaks (D) sold their house and certain personal property, but failed or refused to deliver the personal property to the buyer.

CONCISE RULE OF LAW: Larceny is a crime against the lawful possession of personal property, and one who is in lawful possession, even though not the owner, is incapable of trespassing on his own lawful possession.

FACTS: The Tluchaks (D) agreed in a written instrument to sell their farm to the buyer. The agreement did not recite any personal property, but did include items such as lighting fixtures, shrubbery, and plants. When the purchasers took possession, they found certain items missing which had been on the premises when the sale was executed. These items included an unattached commode and washstand, some peach trees, a hay carriage, and an electric cord. The State (P) argued that these items, which were not covered by the written agreement, had been sold by an oral agreement between the parties. This court assumes for the decision that the Tluchaks (D) sold but failed or refused to deliver the goods to the purchasers under the terms of the oral contract.

ISSUE: Are sellers, in lawful possession of goods, who refuse or fail to deliver goods sold to their purchasers, capable of a trespassory taking of these goods, considered as the personal property of the purchasers?

HOLDING AND DECISION: (J. Reno) No. Larceny is a crime against lawful possession. One who is in lawful possession of goods or money of another cannot commit larceny by feloniously converting them to his own use. The defendants had possession of the goods, and not mere custody. Even though lawful title passes to the purchasers upon payment of the purchase price, possession remained rightfully in the sellers. When the sellers converted those goods to their own use, it was not a trespass on the purchaser's lawful possession. The defendants were incapable of committing larceny. They had retained possession after the sale without trick or fraud and without any fraudulent intent to convert the goods to their own use. Because they were incapable of trespassing on their own lawful possession, the crime of larceny cannot be charged to them.

EDITOR'S ANALYSIS: The court suggested that the defendants could have been charged and found guilty of fraudulent conversion of goods rightfully in possession but later converted to one's own use. Perhaps larceny by bailee would have been possible if the vendor retaining the goods sold can be charged as a constructive bailee until delivery. Larceny is solely a crime against lawful possession of personal property, regardless of who may have lawful title. Larceny is the trespassory taking and carrying away of the personal property of another with the specific intent to deprive the possessor of it permanently. In this case, there simply was no trespass against another's possession.

TOPOLEWSKI v. STATE
130 WISCONSIN 244, 109 M.W. 1037.

NATURE OF CASE: Appeal from conviction for larceny.

FACT SUMMARY: Topolewski (D) stole meat with the aid of a bogus accomplice who provided Topolewski (D) with the meat in order for the police to capture him.

CONCISE RULE OF LAW: Where the owner of property aids in the commission of the offense of larceny of such property, then the accused is not guilty of that crime.

FACTS: Dolan, an employee of a meat packing company, owed Topolewski (D) some money. As payment, Topolewski (D) arranged for Dolan to place some meat on a company loading platform so that Topolewski (D) could put it on his wagon and drive away. Dolan informed the company of the plan. He was told to feign cooperation. The company instructed its loading platform manager, Klotz, not only to put the meat on the platform but also that a man would come and take it away. Klotz was not told about the impending theft. Klotz inferred that Topolewski (D) was that man and that it was proper to deliver the meat to him. Klotz did not assist Topolewski (D) in the loading of the meat, but he did allow the meat to be taken and did help arrange the wagon. Klotz also took an order from Topolewski (D) for the dispensation of a separate barrel of meat. From a conviction for larceny, Topolewski (D) appeals.

ISSUE: Does consent to a taking of property negate the element of trespassory taking in the crime of larceny?

HOLDING AND DECISION: (J. Marshal) Yes. There can be no larceny without a trespass. Trespass is lacking where one allows his property to be taken or delivered to a person intending to commit larceny, regardless of the guilty purpose of the accused. Where the setting of a trap to catch a suspected thief goes no further than to afford an opportunity to carry out a criminal purpose, the deception so practiced is not sufficient in and of itself to excuse the would-be criminal. But the deception must not amount to a consent in the taking. Here, Klotz, the agent of the company, actually permitted the accused to take the meat as per his instructions from the company. In effect, meat was given to the accused by the company. A mere guilty purpose is not sufficient for conviction when one of the essential elements of the crime of larceny is missing. Since taking of the meat here was not a trespassory taking, conviction is reversed.

EDITOR'S ANALYSIS: It would seem that under these facts there would be no way for the company to set a trap to catch the accused. Once the company was informed of the plan by Dolan, they could not allow anyone to place the meat on the platform for the accused to take it away. Any placing of the meat on the platform, knowing that the accused would steal it, would amount to a consent to the taking. Trespass means that the accused's action at the time he takes possession must be wrongful as against some other person's lawful possession. The company here consented to the accused taking possession and, therefore, the taking was not trespassory.

NOLAN v. STATE
213 MARYLAND 298, 131 A. 2d 851.

NATURE OF CASE: Appeal from conviction for embezzlement.

FACT SUMMARY: Nolan (D) appropriated money from his employer's cash drawer at the end of the work day.

CONCISE RULE OF LAW: Once property of the employer has passed from the rightful possession of the employee into the constructive possession of the employer, the employee is incapable of committing the crime of embezzling those funds.

FACTS: Nolan (D) was the office manager of the Federal Discount Corporation, a finance company which made loans and collections. As payments were received, they would be placed in the cash drawer. At the end of the day, an accomplice would prepare a report showing the daily cash receipts. Nolan (D) would then appropriate some of the cash from the drawer. The accomplice would then recompute the adding tapes to equal the remaining sum of cash.

ISSUE: Is property in the constructive possession of its owner where the employee has placed the property where the owner has directed with the intent to steal the property at a later time?

HOLDING AND DECISION: (J. Collins) Yes. Where the property is taken from the owner's possession, the crime is larceny and not embezzlement. Embezzlement only covers the situation where the accused is in rightful possession of his employer's or master's property and wrongfully appropriates it to his own use before the owner has gained possession. Larceny is the crime against possession. This money had reached its destination, the cash drawer. Once there, the money is in the constructive possession of the owner, though not the actual possession. The cash drawer is the exact place where the employer had instructed his employees to put any cash belonging to the employer. Once in the cash drawer, the employee is incapable of embezzling it. Because of these technical differences between larceny and embezzlement, it is always prudent to join a count of larceny with that of embezzlement. The accused has committed larceny, but because he was charged with the wrong crime, the conviction is reversed.

CONCURRENCE: (J. Prescott) The majority has made an overly fine distinction between larceny and embezzlement. Such refinements aid only the criminal. The legislature should pass a law allowing conviction for either crime under an indictment which charges only one of those crimes to the accused.

EDITOR'S ANALYSIS: One who fraudulently converts property of another rightfully entrusted to his possession is guilty of embezzlement. The issue in this case revolved around whether the accused converted the money already in his employer's constructive possession - larceny - or whether the conversion took place before the owner had possession - embezzlement. Such a refinement is a result of the fact that embezzlement was not a common-law crime and was therefore, strictly construed to be different from larceny in its essentials.

STATE v. TAYLOR
14 UTAH 2d 107, 378 P.2d 352.

NOTES:

NATURE OF CASE: Appeal from conviction for embezzlement.

FACT SUMMARY: Taylor (D) issued shorted weight slips to customers in order to accumulate scraps of meat which he converted to money.

CONCISE RULE OF LAW: Where the intent to take the property of another is formed prior to the taking, and is coupled with some deception or trick to acquire possession of the property, the crime is not embezzlement because one cannot embezzle what he has already stolen.

FACTS: Taylor (D) drove a truck for the Utah By-Products Company. He would pick up scraps of meat from various places. He gave each customer a receipt which showed the weight of the items. The company would then issue a check to those customers. One of the customers, Hill Field Air Force Base, required payment in cash rather than check. So the company would issue a check payable to Taylor (D), who would cash it and pay Hill Field. Taylor (D) issued shorted weight slips to the customers other than Hill Field and he was therefore able to accumulate $84.25 worth of scraps. He then made out a slip for that amount showing a pickup at Hill Field. The scraps were delivered to the company, and he was given a check payable to himself for that amount. He cashed the check and kept the money for himself. Neither Hill Field nor the company had been cheated, but only the other customers who had been shortweighted.

ISSUE: Can one embezzle what he has already stolen?

HOLDING AND DECISION: (J. Crockett) No. Taylor (D) is not liable for embezzlement where the company which he was accused of embezzling from has not lost anything as a result of the transaction. Whether the accused could be charged with embezzlement or larceny as regards the other customers who were shortweighted is not before the court. Taylor (D) committed the wrong in gaining possession. Embezzlement requires that the accused have gained possession honestly and rightfully, and only after gaining possession, converting the property to his own use. Where the intent to take the property of another is formed before the taking, and is coupled with some deception or trick to acquire possession of the property, the crime is perhaps larceny, but it is certainly not embezzlement. One is incapable of embezzling what one has already stolen. The crime was in the shortweighting of the other customers, and not in receiving the cash from the company.

EDITOR'S ANALYSIS: Taylor (D) should have been charged with larceny by trick from the other customers or perhaps with obtaining property by false pretenses from his employer. The court is simply stating that because the company was not cheated at all, Taylor (D) could not have embezzled from it. The property had already been stolen before there was any entrustment of the money to the accused.

BURNS v. STATE

SUPREME COURT OF WISCONSIN, 1911. 145 Wis.373, 128 N.W.987.

NOTES:

NATURE OF CASE: Appeal of larceny conviction.

FACT SUMMARY: Burns (D), a constable, misappropriated funds taken off a person he arrested.

CONCISE RULE OF LAW: Where a person who comes into possession of the property of another is under any duty to preserve or restore it, he is bailee of that property and, as such, any later conversion of it is a constructive trespass sufficient to establish larceny.

FACTS: Burns (D), a constable, and others pursued a certain insane man, Adamsky. Upon catching him, Burns (D) was given money, which Adamsky had dropped, by a fellow pursuer. Burns (D) later misappropriated this money and was charged with larceny for doing so. At his trial, the trial court judge instructed the jury that Burns (D) was the bailee of the money he received - qualifying him as such as a "bailee breaking bulk" for larceny purposes (i.e., constituting a constructive trespass). This appeal followed.

ISSUE: May a bailment relationship for larceny purposes arise absent evidence of some contractual relationship between the parties involved?

HOLDING AND DECISION: (J. Marshall) Yes. Where a person who comes into possession of the property of another is under any duty to preserve or restore it, he is a bailee of that property and, as such, any conversion of it later is a constructive trespass (i.e., bailee breaking bulk) for larceny purposes. It makes no difference who entrusts the property to the bailee - the owner, his agent, or even a finder may do so. Where a bailee converts property so entrusted to him, he is guilty of larceny (the old distinction between simple larceny and larceny by bailee was abolished long ago). Here, Burns (D) accepted the money of another as a constable. In such a capacity, he surely was to hold it for the owner. Conviction affirmed.

EDITOR'S ANALYSIS: This case points up the "bailee breaking rule" of constructive trespass for larceny. By Hornbook law, larceny is the trespassory taking and carrying away of the personal property of another with the intent to permanently deprive. The element of trespass often causes problems, however. At common law, for example, it was held that a common carrier was deemed to have possession only of the container of any goods shipped. The contents remained in the constructive possession of the owner of the goods. If the carrier opened the container before converting it in its entirety, he was trespassorily taking the contents out of the "constructive possession" of the owner, which was larceny. This was called the "breaking bulk doctrine" and was used to get around the fact that the carrier ostensibly had lawful possession and was immune to larceny. As this case illustrates, this rationale was later applied to bailees who originally had a lawful possession but later appropriated the goods to their own use.

STATE v. RIGGINS
ILL. SUP. CT. 1956, 8 Ill.2d 78, 132 N.E. 2d 519.

NATURE OF CASE: Appeal from a conviction for embezzlement.

FACT SUMMARY: Riggins (D), operator of a collection agency, commingled funds and did not report collection of accounts to the client whom he represented.

CONCISE RULE OF LAW: A collection agent who acts in the fiduciary capacity of agent to his principal is within the purview of embezzlement statutes.

FACTS: Riggins (D), operator of a collection service, called on Tarrant and asked to collect her business' delinquent accounts. They reached an oral agreement whereby he need not account until the bill was paid in full, at which time he was to remit by check. It was not clear whether the amount remitted should be in full with commission to be deducted or to be in net amount with commission already deducted. Riggins (D) admittedly commingled funds collected for all clients in a personal bank account from which he drew for personal, business, and family expenses. Tarrant brought embezzlement charges when she found that Riggins (D) had collected accounts in full but had not remitted to her. Riggins (D) claimed he was not her agent but, rather, an independent business not within the ambit of embezzlement statutes.

ISSUE: Is a collection agent acting in such a fiduciary capacity within the purview of embezzlement statutes?

HOLDING AND DECISION: (C.J. Hershey) Yes. While early decisions had held that a collection agent operating as an independent businessman and who had a right to commingle funds could not be convicted as an "agent" under general embezzlement statutes, a change in statutory language then held that embezzlement occurred irrespective of whether the agent claims any commission or interest in the collected debt. In accordance with the statute, Riggins (D) was an agent who received money in a fiduciary capacity. The relationship of principal and agent is a fiduciary one.

DISSENT: (J. Schaefer) Riggins' (D) clients knew of the commingled account and could not be held vicariously liable for Riggins' (D) actions in collecting their accounts. The statute should be strictly construed with the word "agent" not being given a popular meaning.

EDITOR'S ANALYSIS: The dissent contends that the meaning of "agent" was improperly construed as meaning a person who transacts business for another by the latter's authority and renders an account of such business in a popular sense. The majority felt that a fiduciary relationship arose whereby special confidence was reposed in Riggins (D), who was thereby bound in good conscience and in equity to act in good faith with due regard to the interest of the person reposing the confidence. The court appears to be plugging a loophole in the law of embezzlement, which was designed to plug a loophole in the law of larceny. Embezzlement filled a gap left when larceny laws did not cover personalty entrusted to one which was then misappropriated by the one to whom it was entrusted.

NOTES:

COMMONWEALTH v. STAHL
183 PENNSYLVANIA SUPER. 49, 127 A. 2d 786.

NATURE OF CASE: Appeal from conviction for fraudulent conversion (embezzlement).

FACT SUMMARY: Stahl (D) financed the purchase and sale of used cars by transferring title to the cars to a finance company in return for cash. He failed to pay back the cash or return the cars.

CONCISE RULE OF LAW: Embezzlement statutes do not apply to a failure by a borrower to fulfill a contract to repay money loaned.

FACTS: Stahl (D), a used car dealer, made a contract with a finance company whereby the company gave him cash in return for Stahl's (D) personal judgment note secured by bailment leases on certain cars. The company never had ownership or possession of the cars and was aware that Stahl (D) used this arrangement to buy and sell used cars. The parties operated under this arrangement for two years. Then the used car market declined, and Stahl (D) was unable to meet the obligations, either by paying off the notes or returning the cars (since they had evidently been sold). He was convicted of embezzlement for having "converted" four cars, title to which was held by the finance company.

ISSUE: May the failure of a borrower to pay off his debts give rise to a conviction for embezzlement?

HOLDING AND DECISION: (J. Gunther) No. Embezzlement statutes do not apply to the mere failure of a borrower to fulfill a contract to repay money. Rather, embezzlement requires a "conversion" of the property of another by someone already in lawful possession of it. Here, the court may not assume that merely because title to certain vehicles was given to a finance company in return for cash, the finance company became the owner of the cars. Rather, the courts must look to the real nature of the transaction, disregarding the pretenses and screens of paper titles, in order to determine the true relationship of the parties. Here, the notes, titles, and bailments were obviously merely evidence of indebtedness. The finance company never had ownership or possession of the cars. The financial arrangement was understood by both parties - its foundation credit, and its relationship debtor to creditor. There was no obligation for Stahl (D) to account for the proceeds from any specific sale or transaction. Stahl (D) was only obligated to pay off the loans when they were due. As such, there was no fraudulent conversion here because the property was the defendant's own, even though purchased by borrowed money and secured by a note on the property. Conviction reversed.

EDITOR'S ANALYSIS: Embezzlement is normally limited, explicitly or implicitly, to situations in which property has been entrusted to an agent or servant. In this case, the titles to the cars were transferred to the finance company not to give the company ownership of the cars, but only to give the company security for its loan. While the cars would belong to the company if the loan were not paid off, Stahl (D) remained the true owner. Stahl (D) was not entrusted with the cars or the money, but owned them, and he was therefore incapable of converting what he already owned. His intent, criminal or not, at the time the loans are to be repaid is irrelevant to a charge of embezzlement.

HUFSTETLER v. STATE
37 ALABAMA APP., 71, 63 So. 2d 730.

NATURE OF CASE: Appeal from conviction for petit larceny.

FACT SUMMARY: Hufstetler (D) had gasoline put in his car but failed to pay for it.

CONCISE RULE OF LAW: If the possession of property is obtained by fraud or trick with the intent at that time to convert the property to one's own use, then larceny has been established as long as the owner intends merely to part with possession and not with title to the property.

FACTS: Hufstetler (D) drove his car into Wharton's gas station. There were two or three other men in the car. One man got out and went to look for a phone. Wharton informed him that there was not a phone on the premises. Wharton was then told to fill up the tank. Six and a half gallons were put into the car. Wharton was then told to get a quart of oil to put in the car. As Wharton went for the oil, Hufstetler (D) drove off without paying the $1.94 for the gasoline.

ISSUE: Can the element of trespass in the crime of larceny be established even though the owner of the goods voluntarily gave up possession of those goods?

HOLDING AND DECISION: (J. Carr) Yes. If the possession is obtained by fraud or trick with the intent, at the time the goods are received, to convert them to one's own use, then larceny has been established so long as the owner intended merely to part with possession and not with title to the goods. The trick or fraud will vitiate the consent of the owner to part with possession. The owner will still be considered in constructive possession of his property. Larceny, a crime against lawful possession, can be proven without an actual trespass, where fraud or trick is present. In this case, the fraud is inferable from the factual background.

EDITOR'S ANALYSIS: This crime is more specifically known as a larceny by trick. The defendant's fraud or trick is deemed to vitiate the owner's consent to the defendant taking possession. The owner is still deemed to be in constructive possession and therefore the taking is a trespass. It can only be committed when the owner intends to part simply with possession, not with title to the goods. It is the owner's belief that controls, not the thief's intent. If the owner intended to give up both possession and title, then the crime of false pretenses would be the correct charge. In the above case, the court stated that Wharton only intended to give up possession of the gas. There was no intent to give up title until the gasoline had been paid for.

GRAHAM v. UNITED STATES
U.S. CT. OF APPEALS, D.C. Circuit, 1910. 187 F.2d 87.

NATURE OF CASE: Appeal from conviction for grand larceny.

FACT SUMMARY: Graham (D), an attorney, told his client, Gal, that he could prevent Gal's arrest from damaging his application for U.S. citizenship for $2,000 to be used to bribe police, which was never done.

CONCISE RULE OF LAW: One who obtains money from another upon the representation that he will perform certain service therewith for the latter, intending at the time to convert the money and actually converting it to his own use is guilty of larceny.

FACTS: Francisco Gal, an immigrant, had been arrested for disorderly conduct. He went to Graham (D) in Graham's (D) professional capacity as a lawyer, fearing his arrest would impede his obtaining U.S. citizenship. Gal testified that Graham (D) said he required $200 for his fee and $2,000 to "talk" with the police. The police officer talked with Graham (D), said Gal was in no trouble, and testified that Graham (D) offered him no money for his help. Graham (D) kept the money, claiming Gal gave him full title to it.

ISSUE: Did Graham (D) commit larceny by trick?

HOLDING AND DECISION: (J. Washington) Yes. There is a distinction between one who gives up possession of a chattel for a special purpose to another who, by converting it to his own use, is held to have committed a trespass and one, although induced by fraud or trick, who still actually intends that title shall pass to the wrongdoer. Here, Gal intended to give the money to Graham (D) for a special purpose. It was not intended to be a fee. Thus, a trespass was committed against Gal, for which Graham (D) is criminally liable.

EDITOR'S ANALYSIS: In larceny by trick, the use of fraud to procure possession of an item or money vitiates the consent with which it was given. If the recipient forms the fraudulent intent later on, there still is larceny but by a doctrine of continuing trespass. Do not confuse this with embezzlement, which concerns the fraudulent conversion of rightfully-possessed property.

STATE v. GRIFFEN
239 NORTH CAROLINA 41, 79 S.E. 2d 230.

NOTES:

NATURE OF CASE: Larceny by trick and embezzlement.

FACT SUMMARY: Griffen (D) fraudulently represented himself as a fund raiser in order to enrich himself.

CONCISE RULE OF LAW: A person cannot be found to be guilty of both larceny and embezzlement as to the same transaction because larceny requires that possession be gained through a trespass, whereas in embezzlement possession must be gained lawfully.

FACTS: On four occasions, Griffen (D) represented himself as a fund raiser for a hospital. On each occasion, he procured funds by claiming that the money would be used to buy a car to be raffled off for the benefit of the hospital. He assured each victim that if they contributed, they would receive their money back with six percent interest as well as the winning raffle ticket. He was indicted for both larceny by trick and embezzlement for each transaction. Both crimes were charged using the same persons, property, and acts as the factual basis. The prosecutor was not required to make an election between the two crimes either before or during the trial. For each of the four different transactions, Griffen (D) was convicted of both larceny by trick and embezzlement.

ISSUE: Can a defendant be guilty of the crimes of larceny by trick and embezzlement on the same factual situation?

HOLDING AND DECISION: (C.J. Devin) No. A defendant cannot be guilty of both obtaining certain property by trespass (larceny), and (simultaneously) converting that property after obtaining it lawfully (embezzlement). Larceny (by trick) requires that an accused defraud or trick an owner into giving up his property (a "constructive trespass"). Embezzlement requires an accused, as agent, servant or employee of the owner, be entrusted with the owner's property and later convert it to his own use. In larceny, the accused's gaining illegal possession and conversion happen simultaneously, whereas in embezzlement the possession is lawful and the fraudulent intent and conversion come later. The evidence in the present case is susceptible to conviction on either crime, but both crimes cannot exist at the same time. As such, the prosecutor here should have been forced to elect which crime the defendant was to be charged with. Fortunately, however, the judge only imposed sentences where the jury convicted the defendant of larceny by trick. All sentences for embezzlement were then made to run concurrently with those for larceny. As such, the error was not prejudicial. The conviction stands.

DISSENT: (J. Barnhill) The verdicts are irreconcilable. In each instance, the jury found that the accused came into possession lawfully and unlawfully. There should be a new trial.

EDITOR'S ANALYSIS: Griffen (D) was unable to defend an assertion that he received the money unlawfully (larceny) by claiming he received it lawfully (embezzlement). However, it is possible that in jurisdictions which have grouped these two offenses under the general crime of "theft" would have affirmed as long as it was found that the defendant accomplished the elements of one of the theft offenses.

PEOPLE v. ASHLEY
SUP.CT. OF CALIF., 1954. 42 Cal.2d 246, 267 P.2d 277.

NOTES:

NATURE OF CASE: Appeal from conviction for theft.

FACT SUMMARY: Ashley (D) procured "loans" from two elderly ladies upon false promises to repay.

CONCISE RULE OF LAW: A promise made in exchange for something of value with no present intention to perform that promise is the obtaining of property by false pretenses where the fraudulent and deceitful acquisition includes both title and possession.

FACTS: Ashley (D) was convicted of grand theft. He obtained $7,200 from an elderly lady by promising that the loan would be secured by a first mortgage on certain improved property owned by his corporation. Ashley (D) gave her no more than a note for that amount and threatened to kill himself so she could collect on his life insurance. The corporation only leased the property in question. Ashley (D) obtained another loan of $13,590 from a second woman and did not provide her the promised security. He obtained another $4,470 from her after taking out a gun in front of her. Ashley (D) contends the evidence was insufficient to find guilt either for larceny by trick or obtaining property by false pretenses.

ISSUE: Is a false promise a false pretense for the purpose of satisfying the elements of obtaining property by false pretenses?

HOLDING AND DECISION: (J. Traynor) Yes. Larceny by trick and device is the appropriation of property, possession of which is fraudulently obtained. Obtaining property by false pretenses differs in that it has the additional element of acquisition of possession and title. It must be shown that there was a false pretense or misrepresentation with intent to defraud the owner of his property, and that the owner was in fact defrauded. The majority rule has not held accountable future promises made without intention to perform because a promise of future conduct from which any injury might arise could be averted by common prudence and caution. This view was based on two erroneous English cases and a third case from Massachusetts. It has been supported by the argument that it protects debtors who might be found to have acted criminally in default on their obligations. But the problem of proving intent when the false pretense is a false promise is no more difficult than when the false pretense is a misrepresentation of existing fact. Thus, the intent not to perform a promise is regularly proved in civil actions for deceit. "If false promises were not false pretenses, the legally sophisticated, without fear of punishment, could perpetrate on the unwary fraudulent schemes like that divulged by the record in this case."

CONCURRENCE: (J. Schauer) The evidence establishes obtaining property by false pretenses as to existing facts, making it unnecessary for this case to go against the majority rule.

EDITOR'S ANALYSIS: In many modern jurisdictions, larcenous crimes are consolidated into the single crime of theft, but their elements have not changed as a result.

NELSON v. UNITED STATES
227 F.2d 21, 53 A.L.R. 2d 1206.

NATURE OF CASE: Appeal from conviction for obtaining goods by false pretenses.

FACT SUMMARY: Nelson (D) purchased property on credit, giving as security a car which already had an outstanding lien on it.

CONCISE RULE OF LAW: A person may be convicted of false pretenses despite no direct evidence of any intent to defraud at the time property passed.

FACTS: Nelson (D) purchased merchandise from a wholesaler, Potomac Distributors, for the purpose of resale. His account with the company was in arrears more than thirty days for in excess of $1,800. On September 18, 1952, Nelson (D) sought more merchandise from Potomac, asserting that he had already sold the merchandise (and even produced the sales contracts). He promised payment that night, offering as security for the merchandise a car worth $4,260 - asserting total ownership of the car except for one $55 payment not yet due. In reliance on these representations, Potomac gave Nelson (D) merchandise worth $349 secured by a mortgage on the car and the merchandise. Nelson (D) was supposed to make payment on the total amount he owed Potomac within a few days. Nelson (D) left town without paying. The car was involved in an accident which caused $1,000 worth of damage to it and was thereupon repossessed by the bank which had the prior chattel mortgage on it for the amount of $3,028. From a conviction for false pretenses, Nelson (D) appeals.

ISSUE: In a prosecution for false pretenses, may intent to defraud be presumed from unlawful acts?

HOLDING AND DECISION: (J. Danaher) Yes. The intent to injure or defraud in false pretenses is presumed when an unlawful act, which results in loss or injury, is proved to have been knowingly committed. Intent is presumed from commission of the unlawful act. An accused's assertion of innocent intent cannot justify misrepresentations known and intended to be false and to be relied upon. Here, the fact that $349 worth of merchandise was exchanged for a security interest in a car which Nelson (D) had over $1,000 worth of equity in is irrelevant. Potomac would not have exchanged the property if Nelson (D) had not misrepresented facts which he knew Potomac would rely upon. Conviction affirmed.

EDITOR'S ANALYSIS: It is not sufficient that an accused merely make an untrue representation; he must know it to be false before the crime of false pretenses occurs. An accused "knows something to be false" when he has personal knowledge of its falsity, or when he believes it to be false and it is in fact false, or when he knows that he does not know whether it is false or not and it is in fact false. The perpetrator of false pretenses also must possess the intent to defraud when he makes the misrepresentation (a specific intent). As this case illustrates, however, the prosecution does not have to come up with specific and direct proof of the accused's specific intent to defraud. Indeed, for most cases, that would be an impossible task; instead, the intent may be inferred.

IN RE CLEMONS
168 OHIO ST. 83, 151 N.E. 2d 553.

NATURE OF CASE: Appeal from conviction for forgery.

FACT SUMMARY: Clemons (D) made out a check in his own name on a bank in which he did not have an account.

CONCISE RULE OF LAW: Forgery includes the false making of any document having apparent legal significance and is not limited to the situation where an accused forger has signed or affixed the name of another person to a document.

FACTS: Clemons (D) made and issued, with intent to defraud, a check signed by himself with his own name, but drawn on a bank in which Clemons (D) did not have a checking account.

ISSUE: Is the crime of forgery limited to the situation where the accused has signed the name of another person or altered the signature of another person?

HOLDING AND DECISION: (J. Matthias) No. A person is guilty of forgery where a check is drawn upon a bank in which the maker has no funds, and is made with the intent to induce another person to give credit to the check as genuine and authentic. It makes no difference that the maker signs his own name to the instrument and not that of another person. This is the false making of a check within the purview of the Ohio statutes. The majority American position is that forgery is the making or altering of a writing so as to make the writing or alteration purport to be the act of some other person. Under that rule, the making of a check upon a bank in which the maker has no funds would not be forgery as long as the person signed his own name. The Ohio statutes and the common-law rule allow for a broader definition in that forgery merely requires the making of a false writing having apparent legal significance. The signing of another's name is not an essential element to the crime.

DISSENT: (J. Taft) The check was exactly what it was purported to be. It was a check drawn on a bank, signed by the maker. Even though there were no funds to back up the check, the check itself was genuine. As long as the instrument is genuine, the intent to defraud is irrelevant in a prosecution for forgery.

EDITOR'S ANALYSIS: Forgery is the making of a false writing having apparent legal significance, with the intent to defraud. The majority opinion states that the signing of one's own name is irrelevant where the check itself had apparent legal significance and was made with the specific intent to defraud. The essential focus of forgery is the fact that the victim is relying upon the integrity of the document and not the integrity of the person who made the statements in the document. The minority opinion feels that the check was genuine in all it purported to be and therefore there could be no forgery. The minority would perhaps rely on a prosecution for false pretenses.

STATE v. MILLER
SUP.CT. OF OREGON, 1951. 192 Ore. 188, 233 P.2d 786.

NOTES:

NATURE OF CASE: Appeal from conviction of obtaining property by false pretenses.

FACT SUMMARY: Miller (D) induced one company to guarantee his indebtedness to another upon the misrepresentation that he owned a tractor free and clear while it was actually purchased under a conditional sales contract.

CONCISE RULE OF LAW: Property capable of being the subject of larceny must be something capable of being possessed and the title to which can be transferred.

FACTS: Miller (D) induced the Hub Lumber Company to agree to guarantee his indebtedness to another upon his false representation that he owned a tractor free and clear and upon his executing a chattel mortgage thereto as security. Actually, Miller (D) was buying the tractor under a conditional sales contract. He was charged with obtaining property by false pretense.

ISSUE: Can intangible property be the subject of larceny?

HOLDING AND DECISION: (J. Lusk) No. The history of the crime of false pretenses generally holds that the thing obtained must be the subject of common-law larceny. By statute, the obtaining of a signature with intent to defraud or the making of a bill of sale has been added so as to be criminal and indicates that intangibles could not previously be the subject of larceny; that they were not to be regarded as property. Here, the conduct was only oral and not the subject of any statute. No crime could thus have been committed.

EDITOR'S ANALYSIS: Originally, property for the purposes of larceny had to be tangible and personal. Modern statutes are now more expansive in most jurisdictions and cover virtually all property, tangible or intangible, real or personal.

NOTES:

UNITED STATES v. GIRARD
U.S.Ct. of Appls., 2nd Cir.,1979. 601 F.2d 69.

NATURE OF CASE: Appeal from convictions for sale of government information.

FACT SUMMARY: Girard (D), who was convicted of selling government information, argued that the applicable federal statute covered only tangible property or documents.

CONCISE RULE OF LAW: A statute which makes it a crime to sell any "thing of value" without authority to do so is not limited to covering the sale of tangible property and encompasses the sale of information.

FACTS: 18 U.S.C. Section 641 makes it a crime to sell or knowingly receive any "record... or thing of value" of the United States without authority. Girard (D) was convicted under the statute for using an inside source at the Drug Enforcement Administration to get information on whether or not certain parties were government informants. He used this information pursuant to his promise to one Bond that he could, for $500 per name, secure DEA reports that would show whether any participant in a proposed illegal drug venture was a government informant. Girard (D) appealed his conviction on the ground that the aforementioned statute covered only the sale of tangible property and did not encompass the sale of information.

ISSUE: If a statute makes the unauthorized sale of any "thing of value" a crime, does it cover the sale of information?

HOLDING AND DECISION: (J. VanGraafeiland) The reach of a statute making it a crime to sell any "thing of value" without authority is not limited to the sale of tangible property, but extends its coverage to the sale of information. The phrase "thing of value" is found in many criminal statutes. These words have become, in a sense, words of art and the word "thing" is generally construed to cover intangibles as well as tangibles. The Government (P) has a property interest in certain of its private records which it may protect by statute as things of value. It has done so by enacting Section 641, which is not simply a statutory codification of the common law of larceny. Indeed, theft is not a requisite element of the statutory offense, which is based upon unauthorized sale or conversion. Inasmuch as all the challenges to this conviction fail of their own accord, it must stand. Affirmed.

EDITOR'S ANALYSIS: That a "thing of value" includes intangibles is well-documented in case law. For example, amusement was held a "thing of value" under gambling statutes and sexual intercourse or the promise thereof a thing of value under bribery statutes. A promise to reinstate an employee, an agreement not to run in a primary election, and testimony of a witness have also been held to be "things of value."

OXFORD v. MOSS
Div. Ct. 68 Crim. App. 183 (1978).

NOTES:

NATURE OF CASE: Appeal from dismissal of prosecution for theft.

FACT SUMMARY: The stipendiary magistrate of Liverpool was of the opinion that Moss (D) could not be guilty of theft for taking the proof of an examination paper belonging to Liverpool University with the intent of returning it without detection and thus doing well on the exam.

CONCISE RULE OF LAW: Confidential information itself is not "property" of the type which is capable of being the subject of a charge of theft.

FACTS: Moss (D), a student at Liverpool University, managed to get hold of the proof of an examination paper for an examination in Civil Engineering he was due to take the following month. He took it with the intention of returning it undetected so as to make good his plan to use his knowledge of the contents of the test to perform well on it. He never intended to steal any tangible element belonging to the University (e.g., the paper itself or the ink), only the confidential information thereon. He was charged with theft, but the stipendiary magistrate of Liverpool dismissed the charge on the grounds that confidential information is not property of the type which is capable of being the subject of a charge of theft. The prosecutor appealed.

ISSUE: Is confidential information "property" of the type which is capable of being the subject of a charge of theft?

HOLDING AND DECISION: (J. Smith) No. Confidential information itself is not "property" of the type which is capable of being the subject of a charge of theft. The Theft Act of 1968 provides that "property" includes "money and all other property real or personal, including things in action and other intangible property. Confidential information is simply not a form of intangible property. The cases emanating from the area of trade secrets and matrimonial secrets have been cited as an aid in deciding this case. Those are, however, cases concerned with what is described as the duty to be of good faith. They are clear illustrations of the proposition that, if a person obtains information which is given to him in confidence and then sets out to take unfair advantage of it, the courts will restrain him by way of an order of injunction or will condemn him in damages if an injunction is found to be inappropriate. They do not suggest that the confidential information itself is "property" that can be the subject of a theft.

EDITOR'S ANALYSIS: One comment on this case advanced an argument as to why it should constitute a case of theft. It noted that Moss' (D) borrowing of the exam paper was essentially equivalent to an outright taking or disposal of it since his act rendered it useless - much as would the "borrowing" of a season ticket that is returned after the season. Crim.L.Rev. 120 (1979).

UNITED STATES v. SIEGEL
U.S.Ct. of App., 2d Cir. 717 F.2d 9 (1983).

NATURE OF CASE: Appeal from wire fraud convictions.

FACT SUMMARY: Siegel (D) contended his conviction for wire fraud could not be supported merely by evidence of a breach of fiduciary duty.

CONCISE RULE OF LAW: A breach of fiduciary duty, standing alone, will not support a wire fraud conviction.

FACTS: Siegel (D) and another corporate officer of Mego, Inc., were charged with wire fraud in conjunction with the personal use of corporate funds. They appealed their convictions on the basis that the only evidence presented was that they had breached a fiduciary duty to the corporation and such was insufficient to support a wire fraud conviction.

ISSUE: Will a breach of fiduciary duty alone be sufficient to support a wire fraud conviction?

HOLDING AND DECISION: (J. Pratt) No. A breach of fiduciary duty alone is not sufficient to support a wire fraud conviction. The evidence presented, however, gave rise to a reasonable inference that the breach involved the personal unauthorized use of corporate funds. Thus, this involved not just a technical breach of fiduciary duty, but an actual fraudulent use of funds. Thus, the use of the telephones and mails in furtherance of these acts were sufficient to support the conviction. Affirmed.

DISSENT: (J. Winter) This decision expands the reach of the wire fraud statute in an unwarranted area.

EDITOR'S ANALYSIS: This crime would have been simple common-law theft or embezzlement without the wire fraud statute. The use of the mails or the telephone, instruments of interstate commerce, makes the same behavior a federal crime.

NOTES:

McNALLY v. UNITED STATES
U.S.Sup.Ct. 107 Sup.Ct. 2875 (1987).

NATURE OF CASE: Appeal from mail fraud convictions.

FACT SUMMARY: The federal Government (P) contended that McNally (D) violated the citizen's right to fair government and that such a violation supported a mail fraud conviction.

CONCISE RULE OF LAW: Actual violation of property rights is essential to a wire or mail fraud conviction.

FACTS: McNally (D) was involved in a scheme whereby state insurance commissions were funnelled through various agencies. His actions were not specifically illegal, yet the federal Government (P) charged him with violating the citizens' right to honest government and based thereon convicted him of mail fraud. He appealed, contending such intangible rights could not support a mail fraud conviction.

ISSUE: Are actual violations of property rights essential to mail fraud convictions?

HOLDING AND DECISION: (J. White) Yes. Actual invasions of property rights are essential to mail fraud convictions. The statute is expansive in scope, yet not so much as to include such intangible rights as those to good government. Reversed.

DISSENT: (J. Stevens) The language of the statute clearly reaches this type of conduct.

EDITOR'S ANALYSIS: The case prompted Congress to amend the mail fraud statute in 1988. The amendment specifically included the right to honest services, the breach of which can be the basis for a conviction.

NOTES:

PEOPLE v. BROWN
Sup.Ct. of Calif., 1894, 105 Cal. 66, 38 P.518.

NATURE OF CASE: Prosecution for larceny.

FACT SUMMARY: Brown (D) took a boy's bicycle to "get even" with him for the boy's throwing oranges at him. Brown (D) intended to return the bicycle but was apprehended before he could do so.

CONCISE RULE OF LAW: For there to be felonious intent for a larceny, the one who takes another's property must intend to permanently deprive the owner of it.

FACTS: Brown (D) took a boy's bicycle to "get even" with the boy who had been throwing oranges at him previously and did not stop when told to do so by Brown (D). Brown (D) tried to hide the bicycle but was apprehended before he was able to return it. He did not intend to keep it.

ISSUE: Can there be a larceny if the taker does not intend to deprive the owner of his property permanently?

HOLDING AND DECISION: (J. Garovie) No. There must be felonious intent to deprive the owner of the property permanently. If there is no such intent, the taking is merely a trespass. The intent need not be to convert the property to the taker's own use, only to permanently deprive the owner of it.

EDITOR'S ANALYSIS: Intent to steal, commonly appearing in the Latin, animus furandi, requires an intent to deprive the owner of his property permanently. It takes more than the unlawful and antisocial conduct of intentionally borrowing another's property temporarily for there to be a larceny. Intentional use for a short period of time usually will not imperil the owner's substantial rights in the property. If a person is caught before he can return the property, he runs the risk of conviction for larceny, as the jury might not believe the taker's intent as testified, but the instruction to the jury must clearly describe the intention requisite for conviction.

NOTES:

REGINA v. FEELY
CT. OF APPLS., 1972. (1973) 2 W.L.R. 201.

NATURE OF CASE: Appeal from a conviction for theft.

FACT SUMMARY: Feely (D), branch manager for a firm of bookmakers, was convicted of theft of 30 pounds which he had taken from the till, intending to repay it.

CONCISE RULE OF LAW: A taking committed without evil intent is not within the concept of stealing at common law or under modern theft statutes.

FACTS: Feely (D) was the branch manager for a bookmaking firm. Circulars were sent to all branch manager instructing them that the practice of borrowing from the till must stop. Even so, Feely (D) took 30 pounds from the branch safe and a few days later happened to be transferred to another branch. When his successor found a 40 pound shortage, Feely (D) gave him an IOU for that amount. Feely (D) explained to the security staff that 10 pounds accounted for bets paid out, but that he took 30 pounds because he was short of cash; that he was owed 70 pounds by his employer, and intended to deduct the amount he took from that owed him. The trial judge said it was no defense to say he intended to repay the money. Feely (D) was convicted of theft.

ISSUE: May the accused defend himself by showing that he did not intend to keep the amount he took and intended to repay it?

HOLDING AND DECISION: (L.J. Lawton) Yes. Theft is defined as a dishonest appropriation of property belonging to another with the intention of permanently depriving the other of it. Whether the taking is dishonest relates to the person's state of mind, and whether an accused has a particular state of mind is a question to be determined by the jury. A taking made without evil intent does not appear to be within the concept of theft.

EDITOR'S ANALYSIS: Note that an intent to repay is not a defense to embezzlement or false pretense charges. It is not clear whether this case changes that view or whether the court simply thought the trial judge invaded the province of the jury. It is also not clear if the decision was primarily a result of England's Theft Act of 1968, which redefined offenses in everyday language. It is possible that the concept of dishonesty is being given a more "everyday" meaning.

NOTES:

PEOPLE v. REID
N.Y. Ct. App. 69 N.Y.2d 469, 508 N.E.2d 661 (1987).

NATURE OF CASE: Appeal from robbery convictions.

FACT SUMMARY: Reid (D) contended his claim of right, forced through violence, negated larcenous intent.

CONCISE RULE OF LAW: A good faith claim of right does negate the intent to commit robbery through the use of force.

FACTS: Reid (D) used force to retrieve money owed to him. He was convicted of armed robbery and appealed, contending his good faith claim of right to the money negated any criminal intent.

ISSUE: Does a good faith claim of right negate the intent to commit robbery through the use of force?

HOLDING AND DECISION: (J. Simmons) No. The good faith claim of right does not negate the intent to commit robbery through force. The legislature has implied that the claim of right defense is available only in enumerated situations and not in cases involving the use of force. Thus, the use of force renders defense unavailable. Affirmed.

EDITOR'S ANALYSIS: The court also indicated that policy considerations required this result. It was unwilling to expand permissible methods of self-help. Such unwarranted violence subverts the role of the judicial system in dispute resolution.

NOTES:

PEOPLE v. FICHTNER
N.Y.SUP.CT., App. Div., Second Dept., 1952. 281 App. Div. 159, 118 N.Y.S.2d 392, aff'd without opin., 305 N.Y.864, 114 N.E.2d 212.

NATURE OF CASE: Appeal from conviction for extortion.

FACT SUMMARY: Smith stole some items from Hill Market. Fichtner (D) and McGuinness (D), Hill employees, induced Smith to pay $25 to the market by threatening to accuse him of larceny.

CONCISE RULE OF LAW: One who uses threats to induce another to repay money is guilty of extortion even where the victim actually did steal some goods and the defendant honestly believed the victim was guilty of theft.

FACTS: Smith stole some items from Hill Market. Fichtner (D) and McGuinness (D) testified that they believed that over several months Smith had stolen $75 worth of merchandise from the market. They told Smith they would accuse him of larceny if he did not pay them $75. He agreed to pay and gave them $25. They did not keep any of the money, but it went into the Hill Market company funds.

ISSUE: Is a defendant who uses threats to induce another to repay money guilty of extortion where the victim actually did steal some goods and the defendant honestly believed the victim was guilty of theft?

HOLDING AND DECISION: (J. Johnston) Yes. The extortion statutes are intended to prevent the collection of money by the means of threats to accuse the debtor of a crime, even where the victim is in fact guilty of the crime the defendant actually believes him to be. Here, Fichtner (D) and McGuinness (D) are guilty of extortion since they induced Smith to pay Hill Market $25 by threatening to accuse him of larceny. It is also irrelevant that they did not keep the money themselves. The convictions are affirmed.

DISSENT: (J. Wenzel) If Fichtner (D) and McGuinness (D) were not acting on their own behalf and if they acted with good faith and without malice, they could not be guilty of extortion as there would be no criminal intent.

EDITOR'S ANALYSIS: It is, of course, no defense to extortion that the victim is guilty of the crime or poses the defect which the defendant threatens to expose. There is a dispute concerning how far one who has been injured by another's crime can go in threatening to expose the wrongdoer's guilt unless the latter makes restitution. Some courts find that in these circumstances there is no intent to extort or to gain. Other courts dealing with statutes which do not specifically require an intent to gain have found the threatened guilty under these circumstances. The statute involved in [Fichtner] was of the latter type. It defined extortion as obtaining another's property through "a wrongful use of fear."

NOTES: